International Relations Theory

SAGE COURSE COMPANIONS

KNOWLEDGE AND SKILLS *for* SUCCESS

International Relations Theory

Oliver Daddow

Los Angeles | London | New Delhi
Singapore | Washington DC

First published 2009

Apart from any fair dealing for the purposes of research
or private study, or criticism or review, as permitted
under the Copyright, Designs and Patents Act, 1988, this
publication may be reproduced, stored or transmitted in
any form, or by any means, only with the prior
permission in writing of the publishers, or in the case of
reprographic reproduction, in accordance with the terms
of licences issued by the Copyright Licensing Agency.
Enquiries concerning reproduction outside those terms
should be sent to the publishers.

SAGE Publications Ltd
1 Oliver's Yard
55 City Road
London EC1Y 1SP

SAGE Publications Inc.
2455 Teller Road
Thousand Oaks, California 91320

SAGE Publications India Pvt Ltd
B 1/I 1 Mohan Cooperative Industrial Area
Mathura Road
New Delhi 110 044

SAGE Publications Asia-Pacific Pte Ltd
33 Pekin Street #02-01
Far East Square
Singapore 048763

Library of Congress Control Number: 2008930216

British Library Cataloguing in Publication data

A catalogue record for this book is available from
the British Library

ISBN 978-1-4129-4742-8
ISBN 978-1-4129-4743-5 (pbk)

Typeset by C&M Digitals (P) Ltd., Chennai, India
Printed by CPI Antony Rowe, Chippenham, Wiltshire
Printed on paper from sustainable resources

Mixed Sources
Product group from well-managed
forests and other controlled sources
www.fsc.org Cert no. SGS-COC-2953
FSC © 1996 Forest Stewardship Council

contents

For Kerry

acknowledgements

I first got the idea for this book at the BISA conference at St Andrews in December 2005. It was during a chat with David Mainwaring in the publisher's exhibition that we spotted a potential gap in the market for a pedagogically inclined book aimed at students new not just to the study of IR in general but the increasingly diverse field of IR theory in particular. David is now my editor at Sage and I can safely say that had that conversation not taken place, this book would certainly not have been written – such are the fortuitous vagaries of academic life. I can further say that, without his constant support for the project and his judicious advice on all manner of things relating to it, the book would not have seen the light of day anywhere near as smoothly as, fortunately, it has. Thanks also to Ian Antcliff and everyone at Sage who helped get the book ship-shape through its various drafts, especially my excellent copyeditor Susan Dunsmore.

Thanks to Moya Lloyd for lending me her books and reading through drafts of earlier chapters. I am similarly grateful to Alex Prichard, Ruth Kinna and Saku Pinta for Anarchist readings and pointers and to Alex for reading through an early version of that chapter. Any errors or omissions in this book are of course my responsibility alone. Thanks finally, but not least, to all the students in the Department of Politics, International Relations and European Studies at Loughborough University who have commented and critiqued extracts from the book I used as hand-outs on my 2007-8 IR Theory module. Magnus Evjebraten, Matthew Breeds and Chris Hills have been particularly helpful.

- Scattered throughout the book are **Taking it further** boxes (see p. 8) where issues of particular significance within the discipline are developed in a little more detail than in the body text. I hope these will be useful in stimulating you to read more widely around the issues they raise.
- For each of the chapters on the substance of IR theories I have provided a list of **Key terms** associated with those theories. Making a list of these key terms with all the different definitions and interpretations placed upon them by IR academics will help you in two ways. First, it will help you understand the particular 'language' of IR. Second, you will generate a stock of critical reference material for use in your coursework and exam essays.
- I have provided a series of **Questions to ponder** at the end of each of the chapters, together with a brief overview of how you might wish to set about tackling each one. These questions are likely to appear in some form as coursework assignment questions or exam questions.
- At the end of each chapter there are **References to more information** where you will find a list of sources you could read to deepen your understanding of the issues raised in the chapter. Your tutor will doubtless provide you with an extensive reading list for each theory so the two together should give you ample to go on. I have tried to include less well known sources along with the 'canonical' texts. It is usually obvious from the title what the book or article is about but for many of the entries I have included a few lines by way of explanation.

Part Three is all about study skills. It offers advice and practical guidance in study, writing and revision skills so that you can present your knowledge in the most effective possible way in essays, coursework assignments and exams. Chapters 3.1 and 3.2 explain how you can get the most out of university lectures and seminars by developing techniques and strategies for critically engaging with the relevant material before, during and after them. Chapter 3.3 considers the difficult process of planning and writing academic essays. It encourages you to appreciate the importance of essay structure and demonstrates practical steps you can take to help deliver well-balanced, well-argued and clearly structured answers. Chapters 3.4 and 3.5 consider the two things you need to do to succeed at exams: revise effectively and clearly communicate your thoughts in writing. Chapter 3.6 summarizes the key points from Part Three by showcasing examples of best practice in exam writing from past IR theory students. By the end of Part Three you should be in a position to prepare well-argued, well-balanced and structurally sound coursework submissions, know how to make the most of your revision time and how to do the very best you can in an exam on IR theory.

Developing good essay technique is vital for succeeding at courses in International Relations theory. The ingredients of a good coursework essay are the same that go into cooking up a good exam answer.

In *Part Four,* you will find the Glossary and the References.

Thinking like an IR theorist

What do IR theorists *do*?

- IR theorists are interested in explaining the interactions between states in the international system.
- IR theorists have become increasingly interested in the behaviour of actors in the international system which operate across, or transcend, state borders. They include supranational organizations such as the United Nations (UN) and the European Union (EU), multinational corporations such as Shell or Nike, transnational networks such as Al Qaeda and transnational pressure groups such as Greenpeace or Amnesty International.
- IR theorists have developed an array of theories to explain the particular inter-action or set of interactions that interest them the most.
- IR theorists use logic and argument to build support for their respective theories
- IR theorists use case studies from the 'real world' of politics, economics, history and law to support these arguments with evidence.
- Different IR theories explain or interpret the same event or process in very different ways.
- IR theory is eclectic in that it draws upon evidence, ideas and arguments from across several disciplines in the humanities and social sciences: philosophy, law, politics, economics and history all feature in various theories to differing degrees.

It is vital that you try and learn to think like an IR theorist. Courses in IR theory are likely to test a lot more than simply your knowledge about the individual theories them-selves. They will also look to see you engaging with debates about the role and value of 'theorizing' international relations. The experts whose works you read on this course have to grapple with these difficult questions every day and if you can show that you comprehend their predicament, you are likely to succeed at your course.

Seeing what it is that IR theorists *do* helps us understand a bit more about the academic enterprise itself. Every academic discipline has its own terminology, shared language, practices and expectations about what counts as knowledge and progress in the field. It is a bit like taking part in a sport you have not played before: what you do is useless unless you understand the basics about the aim of the game, who is supposed to do what and the shared meanings behind the actions of the various participants in the game. In football, for example, it is only by knowing how the offside rule works that you can appreciate why the players stop when the linesman raises his/her flag, and learning tactics and techniques for keeping onside is a key part of being a successful footballer. So it is in the academic world that the best students tend to be the ones who most quickly understand the 'rules of the game' and make the most effort to get into the mindset of the experts they read and for whom they write essays and exam answers. This book will give you advice on just how to achieve this goal and how to express your thoughts in the language of the IR theorist. In short, it will help you better understand the 'rules of the game' in IR theory – what it is that IR theorists *do* when they go to work every morning.

On your course you are likely to be assessed on two main grounds: (1) your understanding of each of the theories you cover on the curriculum; and (2) your ability to critique each of those theories.

Running themes

There is a wide assortment of IR theories, all of which claim to make sense of the subject. It is safe to say that throughout your course you will be exposed to, and expected to engage with, aspects of all these debates about the role, nature and value of theorizing international relations. Here are five of the most common themes you are likely to encounter:

1 **The nature of theory** – there is no firm agreement among scholars of IR on what theory *is*. The word 'theory' is often used interchangeably with words like 'approaches' or 'perspectives', highlighting ongoing disputes over what 'makes' a theory and when a particular body of writing is sufficiently well developed to constitute a distinct theory of IR.

2 **Ontology** – or the object of study. The problem, issue or set of events different writers or groups of writer are trying to explain will necessarily affect both how they study IR and the nature of the evidence they deploy to test their theory. The question of ontology is therefore vital: do you think different theorists are viewing the same

world or are they 'seeing' different worlds – do they have the same ontological assumptions or different ones?

3 Epistemology – or the theory of knowledge. The stuff of international relations is not as tangible and easy to put under a microscope in the same way that, for example, atoms are for physicists, as molecules are for chemists, or as DNA profiles are for forensic scientists. In IR theory there are ongoing disputes about epistemology: what counts as reliable evidence about a particular problem area.

4 Argument – IR theorists use arguments to try and persuade readers of the strength of their case. This use of argumentation usually has two dimensions to it. The theorist has to construct a theory that flows logically from the evidence gathered and the ontological assumptions s/he has made about the object of study, meaning the theory must have *internal* logic. The theorist will often also question the assumptions, interpretations and evidential base of other theorists; this is the *external* dimension where rival theories are critiqued and knocked down.

5 Positivist/normative divide – takes us back to disputes about the nature of theory. For positivists, the study of the social sciences can proceed using the same methods as in the natural sciences and result in generalizations, predictions and laws about IR. Normative theorists question the applicability of methods drawn from the natural sciences and tend to be more open about the agendas to which they write and the uses to which their theories might be put in the 'real world' of politics and public policy.

'Theory' is a disputed term. If you think about how each writer you study might define the word, you will soon see how they might position themselves in ongoing disciplinary debates about the uses, nature and foundations of theory.

Taking it **FURTHER**

IR is a vast and complex discipline of study, so naturally a course in IR theory will reflect that size and diversity. It is testament to the scale of the task at hand (theorizing the world to put it simply!) that we have so many theories, so many ways of explaining the field of international relations. Studying the subject at undergraduate level will provide you with a flavour of the key debates and key areas of research interest in the field today, and the onus is on you to do as much wider reading as you see fit to expand your knowledge base.

Common pitfall

Many students tend to 'play it safe' and concentrate only on the essential textbook reading for their course. It is advisable to go that extra mile and seek out wider reading as a way of helping you develop your critical capabilities.

With that limitation in mind, I have included 'Taking it further' sections throughout the book, adding material which may well lie outside the scope of your course but which add depth to the themes covered in each chapter.

Taking things further in this way is useful for you for three main reasons. First of all, *following up wider debates* and points of interest will help you understand more about how the individual theories you examine on your course fit together to make the discipline of IR.

Second, *you will learn more effectively* about this subject – any subject for that matter – if you actively engage with the underlying disputes about how to study a subject, what 'counts' as evidence and how to present your findings appropriately. Taking time to reflect on what you have learnt and reading around a topic will help you understand the material you cover on this particular course, as well as helping you think through the big philosophical and theoretical issues associated with research and debates in politics and the social sciences more generally.

The third reason is perhaps the most important to you at this stage of your studies: *showing your module tutor that you have actively engaged with IR theory.* Having an active and informed dialogue with yourself and your peers about the nature, value and role of IR theory will come across clearly to your tutor when they mark your work. The average student might know what each of the theories says about IR, whereas the better student will be able to dissect the assumptions of each theory and be able to critique the theories using information they have taken from reading around the subject. In exams you will not necessarily be expected to show the same level of depth and critical capability, but trying to gain an overall impression of the big disciplinary and theoretical debates will help develop your intellectual abilities no end.

Although your course is an essentially theoretical one, it is important that you do not forget that the theorists whose work you study have been influenced by events in the world at their respective times of writing. Try and identify the influence of practice on theory when you read academic books and articles.

Questions to ponder

When doing the lecture and seminar reading for your course in IR theory it is helpful to consider the kinds of questions that you might have to answer about the material you are covering, either in exams or in essays. The obvious place to find the key themes and issues that might crop up is in past exam papers, so check your course materials early on in your studies and scrutinize them carefully. Assuming they change each year, your course tutor may also be willing to let you have copies of past essay titles if they are not included in your course resources from the outset. These will show you the kinds of themes, issues, concepts and ideas that you will be tested on in the course written work.

The nub of the matter is to take an *active* approach to your learning about IR theory. That is, you can learn from books and articles not just about the particular theory you are covering that week, but all sorts of other things. For example, think about the questions that spurred the authors you read to put pen to paper – what do *you* think about their response? Is it valid, fair, based on sound evidence and argued effectively? How would *you* prepare an answer to the question they set themselves and where would *you* look for evidence? What issues might *you* have covered to help that author make his/her argument, or to help the author knock down rival theories? Are there any case studies from the contemporary world of politics and international affairs that shed light on the theoretical problems being explored?

At the end of each chapter I set down a few key questions that arise from the material covered in that chapter. I suggest some ways in which you might approach answering them but I leave it up to you to flesh out my suggestions with further detail. These questions are designed to encourage you to engage with the issues discussed and to help you see how important it is to be an active consumer of academic literature rather than a passive receiver. Learning to take an active approach to reading and digesting this material will help you not just on your course in IR but on all the modules you study at university.

References to more information

Your course tutor will recommend a series of textbooks, journal articles and other resources to help you learn about theories of IR. Different tutors organize course material differently. On the one hand, you might have a reading list that is divided up theory by theory, lecture by lecture, or seminar by seminar, making it easy for you to locate the relevant reading for each week. On the other hand, some tutors prefer to give you a long list of readings and let you choose from them which sources you want to read in preparation for each of the lectures and seminars. Both approaches to course design have their strengths and weaknesses. The first approach puts the readings on a plate, so to speak, quickening your search for the appropriate texts by saving you having to root around in the library to find the relevant material from an aggregate course list. The second approach puts more onus on you to find the relevant sources for each week, so while it takes more time, it enhances your information retrieval and wider research skills. However your course reading lists are designed, there are certain core textbooks that are absolutely invaluable as aids to the study of IR theory and that I frequently refer to in this course companion.

These books come with online resource centres and are aimed directly at undergraduate students:

BAYLIS, J., SMITH, S. AND OWENS, P. (EDS) (2008) *The Globalization of World Politics: An Introduction to International Relations*, 4th edn. Oxford: Oxford University Press.

DUNNE, T., KURKI, M. AND SMITH, S. (EDS) (2007) *International Relations Theory: Discipline and Diversity*. Oxford: Oxford University Press.

JACKSON, R. AND SØRENSEN, G. (2007) *Introduction to International Relations: Theories and Approaches*. Oxford: Oxford University Press.

These books are aimed principally at undergraduates:

BROWN, C. (2001) *Understanding International Relations*, 2nd edn. Basingstoke: Palgrave.

BURCHILL, S. ET AL. (2001) *Theories of International Relations*, 2nd edn. Basingstoke: Palgrave.

PETTIFORD. L. AND STEANS, J. (2004) *Introduction to International Relations*. Harlow: Pearson Education.

These books are aimed at both undergraduate and postgraduate students:

BROWN, C., NARDIN, T. AND RENGGER, N. (EDS) (2002) *International Relations in Political Thought: Texts from the Ancient Greeks to the First World War*. Cambridge: Cambridge University Press.

CARLSNAES, W., RISSE, T. AND SIMMONS, B.A. (EDS) (2006) *Handbook of International Relations*. London: Sage.

DER DERIAN, J. (ED) (1995) *International Theory: Critical Investigations*. London: Macmillan.

GROOM, A.J.R. AND LIGHT, M. (EDS) (1994) *Contemporary International Relations: A Guide to Theory*. London: Pinter.

HOLSTI, K.J. (1995) *International Politics: A Framework for Analysis*, 7th edn. Englewood Cliffs, NJ: Prentice Hall.

LITTLE, R. AND SMITH, M. (ED) (2006) *Perspectives on World Politics*. Abingdon: Routledge.

NICHOLSON, M. (2002) *International Relations: A Concise Introduction*, 2nd edn. Basingstoke: Palgrave Macmillan.

SMITH, S., BOOTH, K. AND ZALEWSKI, M. (EDS) (1996) *International Theory: Positivism and Beyond*. Cambridge: Cambridge University Press.

STERLING-FOLKER, J. (ED) (2006) *Making Sense of International Relations Theory*. Boulder, CO: Lynne Rienner.

VASQUEZ, J.A. (EDS) (1996) *Classics of International Relations*, 3rd edn. Upper Saddle River, NJ: Prentice Hall.

VIOTTI, P.R. AND KAUPPI, M.V. (EDS) (1999) *International Relations Theory*, 3rd edn. New York: Macmillan.

WEBER, C. (2005) *International Relations Theory: A Critical Introduction*, 2nd edn. London: Routledge.

It is useful when studying IR to have a working knowledge of international history at least since 1945 and preferably back to 1900. The following books will give you the gist of the story:

BEST, A., HANHIMAKI, J.M., MAIOLO, J.A. AND SCHULZE, K.E. (2004) *International History of the Twentieth Century*. London: Routledge.

CALVOCORESSI, P. (2009) *World Politics Since 1945, 4th edn.* London: Longman.

GATHORNE-HARDY, G.M. (1964) *A Short History of International Affairs 1920–1939*. London: Oxford University Press.

KEYLOR, W.R. (2001) *The Twentieth-Century World: An International History*, 4th edn. Oxford: Oxford University Press.

MARTEL, G. (EDS) (2007) *A Companion to International History 1900–2001*. Oxford: Blackwell.

REYNOLDS, D. (2000) *One World Divisible: A Global History since 1945*. New York: W.W. Norton.

YOUNG, J.W. AND KENT, J. (2004) *International Relations since 1945: A Global History*. Oxford: Oxford University Press.

If you want more general guides to settling in and succeeding at university, I would recommend:

BECKER, L. (2003) *How to Manage Your Arts, Humanities and Social Sciences Degree*. Basingstoke: Palgrave Macmillan.

DAVEY, G. (2008) *The International Student's Survival Guide*. London: Sage.

RUGG, G., GERRARD, S. AND HOOPER, S. (2008) *The Stress-Free Guide to Studying at University*. London: Sage.

> *All textbooks naturally concentrate on some theories at the expense of others and treat the theories they do cover slightly differently, although they will all cover core sets of issues associated with the nature of theory, the strength of their claims to knowledge about their IR and their overall contribution to the development of the discipline. They tend to use examples from the 'real world' of politics and international affairs to bring the theories to life. This book is a companion to your textbooks rather than a replacement for them, so make sure you use your textbooks to put the flesh on the bones of what I say here.*

There are lots of journals devoted to the study of IR and IR-related issues. Here are some of the most popular. Increasingly you can access articles from the latest and recent issues of these journals online: *Alternatives, British Journal of Politics and International Relations, Ethics and International Affairs, European Foreign Affairs Review, European Journal of International Relations, International Affairs, International Feminist Journal of Politics, International Organization, International Relations, International Security, International Studies Quarterly, Journal of International Affairs, Millennium, Political Studies, Review of International Studies* and *World Politics*.

There is a lot of reading out there about IR and its theories and one of the skills you need to learn is knowing when you have done enough to understand the basics of each theory and how you might critique that theory. Make sure you have a thorough knowledge of your module guide and attend all the course lectures and seminars as they will give you a good insight into what your tutor expects from you. Every student reads differently, works differently and thinks differently and there are no hard and fast rules on how much preparation is enough for each of the seminars and coursework assignments you will do on your course. It is important that you work out for yourself as soon as you can in your university studies how *you* work best and how you best prepare for handing in assignments and revising for exams. This course companion will help you develop what are known as these transferable skills as well as helping you come to terms with the vast, complex, sometimes infuriating but always enjoyable world of IR theory.

No two courses in IR that I have experienced either as student or tutor look the same. In the module guide for your course your tutor will set out exactly the topics you will be studying and the expectations he/she has of you in terms of workload, attendance, participation, coursework assignments and exams. It is crucial that you orientate yourself to the demands of your particular course as soon as you can, and your first task will therefore be to read everything about your course as soon as it is available to you.

The differences between courses in IR make it impossible to write a book that speaks directly to one course alone and this book has intentionally been written at one remove from the specifics of your module organization and schedule. Instead, we move up a level to orientate you to the general field of study with which you will be engaging on your course, and to the big questions that have motivated so many writers over the years to study this complex subject. It is useful to try and think about the big questions about any field of academic study because understanding the context within scholars work helps you get inside their heads. Academics like students to do this, first, because it helps you understand what drives writers to put pen to paper and, second, it equips you with the weaponry to critique their ideas and opinions on their terms rather than with the benefit of hindsight. Reading this book will encourage you to develop both these skills: understanding academic theories and critiquing them.

This part of the book is organized around two big sets of questions about the discipline of IR. In Chapter 1.1 we introduce the hotly contested subject matter of IR. In Chapter 1.2 we add in the contested issue of theory. Chapter 1.3 makes some general remarks about tutors' expectations of students taking IR courses. Chapter 1.4 returns us to the central theme of the book: theoretical disputes about IR. We emerge the other side with a whole host of uncertainties: this is a field of study in which no-one can really agree either on the appropriate subject matter, or on how best to study it. If you can grasp the reasons for these disputes and show evidence that you have a position on them you are likely to succeed at your course because you will be able to actively engage with each theory at quite a sophisticated level.

Core areas:

1.1 Introduction to International Relations
1.2 International Relations theory
1.3 Your course in IR theory
1.4 Theoretical debates

1.1

introduction to international relations

First, in order to have a theory, you'll have to have a subject matter, because you can't have a theory about everything. There's no such thing as a theory about everything. (Kenneth Waltz, quoted in Kreisler 2003)

It is difficult to build a **theory** about any academic subject, whether it be in the social sciences like IR or in the natural sciences like physics, biology or chemistry. Theories by their nature are simplified versions of a complex reality. By developing them, we are paradoxically trying to make sense of this complexity by breaking it down into manageable chunks. Necessarily, therefore, theories tend to fall prey to criticisms about their coverage, their depth and their applicability to the 'real world'. It is worth remembering that all theories come with a health warning: no theory can explain everything about the world ... and we should not expect them to!

Theoretical disagreements are common even within disciplines where all scholars are trying to theorize the same thing, the same event or the processes which they see happening in the 'real world'. What, then, if scholars disagree on the essence of reality, on what makes the world go round, on why humans behave the way they do? What, then, for supposedly comprehensive theories which enable us to make predictions about what might happen in the future on the basis of our existing theoretical knowledge about the world?

Engaging with the 'big' questions about the role, value and nature of theories of IR is intellectually worthwhile because:

- It helps you see the problem through the eyes of the authors you study
- It enhances your ability to critique each theory
- It helps you 'think' like an IR theorist.

On your course in IR theory you may well have the chance to study these kinds of **metatheoretical** issues in some detail. For example, you may have timetabled lectures and seminars on the nature, role and value of theory at the start and end of your course, and seminars will doubtless incorporate discussion not only about the substance of each IR theory but also the assumptions they make about how the world works. Certainly many of the textbooks you read will, usually in the introductory and concluding chapters, engage with these metatheoretical issues in some detail and having an awareness of them will help you begin to think like an IR theorist (for instance Dunne et al.; Jackson and Sørensen 2007). In this chapter I try and answer three big metatheoretical questions that motivate scholars to theorize IR. First, what is the world? Second, what are 'international relations'? Third, who or what are the major **actors** we need to study in IR? Answering these questions helps us understand more about the role of theory in studying a subject like IR, and we cover that in the following chapter.

> Metatheory is theory about theory, a philosophical reflection on the nature, role and practice of theorizing. Metatheorists look down upon all the competing theories about a certain topic and try to understand how all the theorists they study are making sense of their subject.

What is the world?

Any discipline of study needs a subject that will be the focus for that study. This statement might seem obvious but it has many intriguing ramifications for social science subjects such as politics, history, media and communications and sociology, because here we do not find a huge amount of agreement on what the 'core' of each discipline is, or should be. So when I ask 'what is the world?', I am trying to alert you to what I like to call the problem of the subject matter of IR: what are we actually theorizing in this discipline?

Here, we can take a cue from literature in the field of the philosophy of social science by comparing the study of the social (or behavioural) sciences on the one hand with the study of the natural (or physical) sciences on the other (see Scriven 1994). This will enable us to draw some preliminary conclusions about the problematic nature of the subject matter of IR and develop insights into the reasons why theoretical disputes are so common in this discipline.

> *If you have friends at university studying in different departments (social or natural sciences) try asking them about their respective disciplines: what do they study and how? Is the subject of their discipline and how to study it well agreed upon by scholars? Who decides these things? Compare their experiences to your experiences of studying Politics and International Relations.*

Let us start with simple, dictionary-style definitions of the principal natural sciences, biology, chemistry and physics:

- **Biology** – the study of living organisms.
- **Chemistry** – the study of the composition, properties and reactions of substances.
- **Physics** – the study of the properties of matter and energy.

These disciplines are clearly not monolithic, that is to say, they are divided into communities of scholars working across various specialized sub-disciplines, each with their own scope for inquiry. Think, for instance, about how physics breaks down into astrophysics, nuclear physics and quantum physics. Nor are the natural sciences immune from tortured debates about the fragmentation of the discipline and the ensuing absence of cohesion among their various practitioners (Physics Web 2002). The key point, however, is that while the disciplines might be fragmented in this way, there is still broad agreement among biologists, chemists and physicists on essential aspects of their work: on their object of study (or problem to be solved), on how to study it, on what counts as evidence, and on when theories or explanations have become obsolete. As Martin Hollis and Steve Smith describe the natural science model, 'the broad idea is that events are governed by laws of nature which apply whenever similar events occur in similar conditions. Science progresses by learning which similarities are key to which sequences' (Hollis and Smith 1991: 3). We can see how the wheels of a scientific discipline go round in Figure 1 which assumes general agreement in four areas: (1) the object of study; (2) how to study that object; (3) what counts as evidence; and (4) when theories about that object have been disproved.

Having established what the disciplinary wheel looks likes for natural scientists, the question that needs answering is: can we replicate this approach for disciplines in the social sciences? I am not sure we can for the very simple reason that the subject matter of IR is **essentially contested** – there is no agreement on what constitutes the basic subject matter of IR.

As you progress through your module on IR, make a list of all the essentially contested concepts, objects and ideas you come across. Why are they essentially contested and what does this mean for the scholarship about them and our understanding of them?

In the natural sciences, the objects we study tend to be physical things we can pick up, pin down, observe and measure, either with

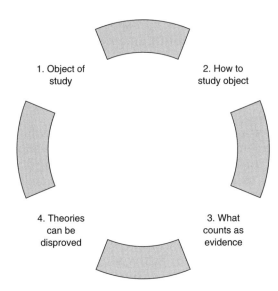

1. Object of
study

2. How to
study object

4. Theories
can be
disproved

3. What
counts as
evidence

Figure 1   How the wheels of a scientific discipline turn

our own eyes or with the help of a microscope or other audio-visual recording equipment. For example, a chemist can don a pair of safety goggles and drop a chunk of potassium into a basin of water to observe the reaction. A physicist can monitor the impact of temperature on solids by heating a strip of metal and watching the movement of molecules under a microscope. A biologist can test the impact of light on plant growth by measuring the relative speed of growth of the same plant in lighter and darker conditions.

In the natural sciences the tangibility of the subject matter helps researchers agree on the problem or object to be studied, on how to study it, on what counts as evidence, and to agree finally on when theories have become flawed or obsolete. Natural scientists can put things that interest them under a microscope and study their properties and behaviour in order to generate theories. Importantly, their experiments can be replicated by other scientists who can confirm the accuracy of the results and share ideas on what to study next. As the philosopher Karl Popper famously pointed out, most advances in scientific knowledge flow not from theories and explanations being proved true but from being falsified (Popper 1959, 1963). This process of falsification relies on each scientist's work being constantly tested and challenged by other scientists, and this is made easier by the existence of the physical objects that form the basis for experimentation in the natural sciences. We could say in very simple terms, therefore, that natural scientists generate knowledge the *empiricist* way. Like David Attenborough studying the behaviour of tree frogs in the Amazonian rainforest, natural scientists rely on having direct access to a 'real world'.

To put it in formal terms, knowledge in the natural sciences is held to be accurate and reliable when it:

- has a grounded **ontology** – theory connected with the things, properties and events that exist in the world, or what is out there to be investigated.
- is rooted in empiricist **epistemology** – theory about how we know things and what is regarded as valid or legitimate knowledge in a given discipline.
- flows from a robust **methodology** – rules and guidelines on how to set up experiments and interpret the data collected.
- is subject to **falsification** – a statement, theory or explanation might never be proved undoubtedly true but should be rejected when predictions derived from it turn out to be false.

Empirical scientific investigation tends to be the benchmark by which our claim to produce hard and fast knowledge about the world is judged. Do you think it is fair to judge social scientific knowledge production in this way?

We can now add these formal labels to the disciplinary wheel in Figure 2.

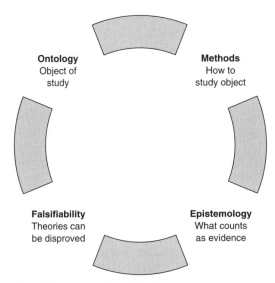

Ontology
Object of
study

Methods
How to
study object

Falsifiability
Theories can
be disproved

Epistemology
What counts
as evidence

Figure 2   The disciplinary wheel revisited

By now you will have twigged why I asked the question 'what is the world?' It needed asking because IR as a discipline is clearly concerned with investigating relationships between 'things' in the world ... and yet there is no agreement amongst theorists on what precisely it is that the discipline should study, on how to study it, on what counts as evidence, and on when theories have been proved false. This is why your course in IR theory covers so many theories – none of their authors ever admit that they are wrong because evidence can always be found to support an updated version of the theory. They cannot even agree on what it is that they are all studying.

Think about the differences between subjects that study 'tangible' things and those that study 'intangible' ones. What does this imply for the reliability of the theories developed in each field and what steps do you think we can take to develop methods of explaining intangible things more accurately?

Unlike in the natural sciences, where we can usually take physical objects for study and put them under the microscope for analysis, how can we possibly do this with 'the world', which is what scholars of IR necessarily try to do? In the following section we will start to see how this problem of the subject plays out in the study of IR theory by exploring competing definitions of 'international relations'.

What are 'international relations'?

In his book *Understanding International Relations*, Chris Brown explains why it is important to identify the scope of the field:

> The reason definitions matter in this way is because 'international relations' do not have some kind of essential existence in the real world of the sort that could define an academic discipline. Instead, there is a continual interplay between the 'real world' and the world of knowledge. (Brown 2001: 1)

Here, Brown adopts the same approach to the problem of the subject in IR that we did in the last section. His logic proceeds as follows:

- The development of academic disciplines is predicated upon there being a well-defined subject matter which organizes and focuses enquiry within that field.
- The field of IR does not have a subject matter that exists in the 'real world' of observable (physical) things.
- Therefore the subject matter of IR is in dispute.

- The subject matter of IR is made doubly hard to pin down because it is so bound up with contemporary developments in global politics and the *study* of global affairs.
- To put it another way: the world which scholars of IR are studying is constantly in a state of flux.

> In essays and exams you will be expected to be able to summarize key ideas in the field of IR. Note how we have taken Brown's argument apart step by step by examining his assumptions and the conclusions he derives from them.

Brown (2001: 1) goes on to suggest that the field of IR encompasses the study of some or all of the following:

1 **Diplomatic-strategic relations of states** – with a focus on war and peace, conflict and cooperation. This was the traditional subject matter of the discipline.

2 **Cross-border transactions of all kinds** – meaning the whole gamut of political, economic and social exchanges between **states**.

3 **Globalization** – of world communications, transport and financial systems, **multinational corporations**.

You can see from this all-embracing definition that when looking at international relations we are potentially looking at anything and everything that happens anywhere in the world. It seems as hard to nail down the subject of IR as it is to nail jelly to a wall!

Another writer who tries to solve the problem of the subject in IR by defining the scope of the discipline is Scott Burchill. In the Introduction to his collection on theories of IR (Burchill 2001a: 9) he notes that there is more to the study of this subject than merely looking at the relations between **nation-states**. His opinion is that the study of IR has four dimensions:

1 **Relationships** – not just those between states but those that cut across state borders both above and below the purview of the state. Such relationships include economic **interdependence**, Third World debt, international trade and the spread of multinational corporations, inequality in all its forms and regional economic and political associations such as the EU, the Organization of African Unity (OAU), the Association of Southeast Asian Nations (ASEAN) and the Gulf Cooperation Council (GCC).

2 **Actors** – nation-states, transnational corporations, financial markets, non-governmental organizations, **supranational** political communities, **sub-national** actors based on ethnic, religious or cultural affiliations, and **international organizations** (such as the North Atlantic Treaty Organization (NATO), the Red Cross/Red Crescent and the World Bank).

3 **Empirical issues** – here we come to specific themes and issues that are important enough in a global context to warrant understanding and explaining. Burchill highlights globalization, human rights, intervention and sovereignty, aid, refugees, ethnicity, women's issues (gender), the environment, HIV, drugs and organized crime.

4 **Philosophical issues** – all the questions we considered above about how to theorize IR: questions of ontology, epistemology and methodology and related issues which help explain why writers from different theoretical traditions disagree with each other over the explanation of state and other behaviour in the international system.

Brown and Burchill have different perspectives on the nature of the field of IR; this is largely down to the goals of their respective books. On the one hand, Brown's is a general introduction to the study of IR which he takes to mean the study of things 'out there' (empirical things) in the world of international affairs. On the other hand, Burchill's theoretical focus means that he has a broader remit which fits empirical issues into a wider framework, which under his heading of 'philosophical issues' allows for a consideration of the quality of the theoretical knowledge we can generate about issues and actors in the international system.

> *When doing your course reading, think carefully about the particular focus of the texts you read because this will help you understand the way authors approach the 'problem of the subject'.*

Burchill's inclusive approach to the theory and empirical study of IR is quite a common one. To take just one other example: in their edited collection *Handbook of International Relations*, Walter Carlsnaes, Thomas Risse and Beth Simmons (2006) split their work into three parts. Part one is on 'historical, philosophical and theoretical issues'; Part two is on 'concepts and context', including chapters on state sovereignty, power, diplomacy, bargaining and negotiation, interdependence and the link between domestic politics and international relations. Part three is on the substantive issues Brown majors on and which Burchill includes as part of his wider study: things such as war and peace, nationalism and ethnicity, international trade and finance, international development, the environment, law and human rights.

The upshot of all this is that there is no agreement on what constitutes either the subject area of IR or how to study it. Grayson Kirk's 1947 comment on the state of the discipline is as relevant now as it was then:

> the study of international relations is still in a condition of considerable confusion. The scope of the field, the methods of analysis and synthesis to be followed, the proper administrative arrangements to be made in college curricula, the organization of research – all these are matters of continuing controversy. (quoted in Schmidt 2006: 3)

Taking it **FURTHER**

International Relations or World Politics?

In their textbook *The Globalization of World Politics*, John Baylis, Steve Smith and Patricia Owens begin by outlining why they chose the term 'World Politics' rather than 'International Politics' or 'International Relations' in their title.

They chose 'World Politics', they say, because 'it is more inclusive than either of the alternatives. It is meant to denote the fact that our interest is in the *politics* and *political patterns* in the world, and not only those between nation-states (as the term international politics implies)' (Baylis et al. 2008a: 3). Their opinion on the appropriate title for their book shows the extreme power of language and labels and why it is important for us to take both seriously when studying at university level. Let us break down their argument into its component parts.

- 'International Relations' implies the study of relations between nation-states. For greater accuracy we might rewrite it 'Inter-national Relations'.
- 'International Politics' is similarly limited: 'Inter-national Politics'.
- Neither label does justice to what Baylis, Smith and Owens consider to be the essence of the field, which is both wider and deeper than the relations between nation-states.
- IR for Baylis, Smith and Owens is about the study of *politics* and *political patterns* in the world. To use Burchill's terminology from earlier in the chapter, Baylis, Smith and Owens are interested in explaining the web of connections and *relationships* between *all* actors in the world.
- Nation-states undoubtedly retain an immensely important place in the study of IR but they do not play the only or even most decisive part in global politics today.

Some good news!

Happily, to succeed at a course on IR theory you do not need to become a fervent historian of the discipline or have an expert knowledge of the different ways in which writers and teachers carve up the discipline for their students. However, it is useful for you to be aware of the ongoing disputes arising from the 'problem of the subject' because they intimately shape the theories you will encounter and how those theories generate and apply knowledge about the 'real world'. Ask yourself why it is that some actors and methods have conventionally been 'held largely silent' by the discipline while others have flourished and come to dominate the agenda (Watson 2006: 237). Forming some sort of opinion on this question will first of all help you understand the theories you cover on your course and, second, help you analyse the strengths and weaknesses of their respective claims to produce hard and fast knowledge about the world of IR.

Questions to ponder

"Can social scientists claim to produce the same kind of knowledge as natural scientists? Should they try?"

The first thing to do with this question is to consider some key definitional issues: how do we define 'natural' and 'social' sciences – give examples of fields or disciplines you consider to belong in each category. Maybe even include a small two-column table listing disciplines that belong to each category. Then think about defining the 'kind of knowledge' produced by each set of scholars: what are the similarities and differences? Is one more 'grounded', more certain, more reliable than the other and if so why? A simple way to introduce the differences would be to use ideas about the 'problem of the subject' in IR and the 'tangible/intangible' divide explored in this chapter.

Your second task is to come up with some way of judging the implications of what you say in the first part. Assuming social sciences do produce different forms of knowledge, do you think this is a good thing or a bad thing – and what do you mean by 'good' and 'bad'? Do you think the social sciences should try and emulate the natural sciences at all? The better students might here bring into question the whole idea of the natural sciences being a paragon of virtue as far as scientific knowledge production is concerned.

Common pitfall

When a question has two parts to it, students sometimes forget to answer the second part, especially when under pressure in exams. In the above, the second question 'should they try?' invites you to consider the knock-on implications of your answer to the first part. Not bothering with it will severely limit the mark you might obtain, however good your answer to the first part.

"Why is there so much disagreement about the subject matter of IR?"

This is slightly harder to structure than the first answer because it is open-ended, inviting you to consider any and every reason why writers disagree about the most appropriate focus for IR. You have to be absolutely rigid about narrowing your essay to just a few points. Given that you inevitably have time limits (if in an exam) and word limits (in an essay), one useful approach is to list all the reasons you can think of and then concentrate on, say, the three or four that your consider most compelling. You can then structure your answer around each of the points in turn. A possible list might include:

- Labels: 'Inter-national Relations' (narrower remit) or 'World Politics' (wider remit)?
- Which actors?
- What is 'the world'?
- The subject is ever-changing because the world is constantly changing
- Events or issues seen as important in one era will not necessarily seem so in another.

" '... there is a continual interplay between the "real world" and the world of knowledge' (Chris Brown). Discuss the implications of this statement for the study of IR."

This question is a slightly more specific take on the previous one. Your first task is to clarify what you think Brown is saying in the quote. What does he mean by the 'real world' and why has he put it in speech marks? What is the 'world of knowledge'? Are the two separate entities or over-lapping in some way?

Useful tip: when a word or phrase appears in speech marks in an exam or essay question, it is usually a cue for you to define what you think that term means, so that your tutor understands how you use it in your answer.

It obviously helps to know the wider context within which Brown makes this remark so hopefully you will have read that chapter of this book and can summarize what he believes the implications are. You can then weigh up the strengths and weaknesses of his opinion.

You can get analytical purchase out of this question by exploring how the study of IR closely follows events 'on the ground' out there in the real world of international politics, using case studies and/or examples of theories which are built on evidence from this 'real world'. You could, for instance, use Steve Smith's argument (2007: 4) that the dominance within the discipline of a theory like Realism flowed directly from 'often unstated, "common-sense" assumptions about the content of world politics'. Note also how the end of the Cold War in 1989 inspired many new theorists to take an interest in this field, some of them with radically different takes on what IR is and how to study it (see Chapters 2.5 onward in this book).

References to more information

Generally on the problems of studying Politics and IR:

SHIMKO, K.L. (2008) *International Relations: Problems and Controversies,* 2nd edn. Boston, MA: Houghton Mifflin Company.

Good introductory text which shows you where theory fits into the wider study of IR.

BLEIKER, R. (1997) 'Forget IR Theory', *Alternatives,* 22(1): 57–85.

Critical evaluation of the methods, practices and limitations of orthodox IR.

HALLIDAY, F. (1995) 'International Relations: Is There a New Agenda?', *Millennium,* 20(1): 57–72.

Examines the interplay between the global political agenda and how developments in the 'real world' of international relations affect the academic study of IR.

WALT, S.M. (2006) 'International Relations: One World, Many Theories', in R. Little and M. Smith (eds) *Perspectives on World Politics.* Abingdon: Routledge, pp. 386–94.

Reviews the impact of the end of the Cold War on theorizing IR.

HOFFMAN, S. (2001) 'An American Social Science: International Relations', in R.M.A. Crawford and D.S.L. Jarvis, *International Relations: Still an American Social Science?: Towards Diversity in International Thought.* Albany, NY: State University of New York Press, pp. 27–51.

TANSEY, S.D. (2004) *Politics: The Basics,* 3rd edn. London and New York: Routledge.

Chapter 1 provides a good introduction to the varieties of approaches and methods, while Chapter 2 introduces you to IR by exploring states and international institutions.

GOODWIN, G.L. AND LINKLATER, A. (1975) 'Introduction', in G.L. Goodwin and A. Linklater (eds) *New Dimensions of World Politics*. London: Croom Helm.

Contains a useful few words at the start on the distinction between 'International Relations' and 'World Politics'.

More advanced texts on the nature and role of theory:

HOLLIS, M. AND SMITH, S. (1991) *Explaining and Understanding International Relations*. Oxford: Clarendon Press.

Very good on empiricism and its implications for theoretical development.

MARTIN, M. AND McINTYRE, LEE C. (EDS) (1994) *Readings in the Philosophy of Social Science*. Cambridge, MA: MIT Press.

A series of excerpts from key writings in the field. I would particularly recommend Chapter 6 by Scriven, Chapter 9 by McIntyre, Chapter 18 by Lukes and Chapter 27 by Durkheim.

HERRMAN, R.K. (2006) 'Linking Theory to Evidence in International Relations', in W. Carlsnaes, T. Risse and B.A. Simmons (eds) *Handbook of International Relations*. London: Sage, pp. 119–36.

A defence of positivist thinking in IR together with a consideration of other approaches to connecting theory with evidence.

More general issues raised in this chapter:

BECHER, T. AND TROWLER, P.R. (2001) *Academic Tribes and Territories*, 2nd edn. Buckingham: The Society for Research into Higher Education and Open University Press.

See Chapter 3 for an account of how academics from across disciplines see their work and how this helps us define the concept of a 'discipline'.

KUHN, T.S. (1996) *The Structure of Scientific Revolutions*, 3rd edn. Chicago: The University of Chicago Press.

Ostensibly about the natural sciences, this path-breaking book boasts a wealth of information about the ideological foundations of all academic knowledge.

NEUMAN, W.L. (2007) *Basics of Social Research: Qualitative and Quantitative Approaches*, 2nd edn. New York: Pearson Education.

In Chapter 1, Neuman argues that knowledge generated by 'scientific' research is more reliable than knowledge gained by other means.

BARNETT, M. AND DUVALL, R. (2005) 'Power in International Politics', *International Organization*, 59(1): 39–75.

Gives you an idea of how to map disagreements between different IR traditions and explains the causes of some of their disputes.

1.2

international relations theory

[W]e are all theoreticians and the only issue is what kinds of theories should we adopt to guide us in our attempts to understand the subject matter. (Joynt and Corbett 1978: 102)

What *is* theory? Why do we have to bother with theory – can't we just study IR on its own? Can't we just look at the facts? These are just some of the questions you might legitimately be asking yourself as you set out on your journey through your course in IR. I want to answer them now by way of introduction, and then in Chapter 1.4 we will return to some of the core issues raised and develop them using the language and tools as they might appear in your course lectures, seminars and assignments.

What is theory?

Theories provide intellectual order to the subject matter of international relations. They enable us to conceptualise and contextualise both past and contemporary events. They also provide us with a range of ways of interpreting complex issues. (Burchill 2001a: 13)

We saw in the last chapter that the subject matter of IR is essentially contested, meaning that all scholars working in this field have different views on what constitutes the 'essence' of IR. Disputes run even deeper than that, however. Not only do experts disagree on what to study, they differ over how to study IR and what counts as appropriate evidence in this field. With all this complexity and dispute in mind, it seems logical for rational human beings (assuming that's what academics are!) to seek to navigate some sort of logical path through this mire of uncertainty. This is where IR theory comes in.

> *Think about when you encountered a 'theory' or theories in your previous studies at school or college. What was the purpose of those theories? What did theorists try and achieve by developing them? Did they help you understand more about the subject and how? What were their strengths and weaknesses?*

Burchill's neat summary of the part theory plays in the study of IR gives us good ground on which to begin our consideration of what theory actually is (in fact, his list of the values of theorizing IR goes on). The crucial words he uses are 'intellectual order'. Theories take complexity and try and simplify it. How theorists do this, and their relative levels of success, is less important to us at this stage than recognizing the goals theorists set themselves. Let us take a range of opinions from across the discipline:

- **Martin Wight** (cited in Burchill 2001a: 8): A tradition of speculation about relations between states. Theory in IR is all about unpicking state-to-state interactions and state behaviour. You can see here how Wight solves the problem of the subject by taking a popular line on the appropriate subject matter of IR: it is nothing more, nothing less than a study of relations between states.
- **Kenneth Waltz** (cited in Burchill 2001a: 8): Theories explain laws which identify invariant or probable associations. Waltz's use of highly specialized, technical language shows that he sees the goal of IR theorists as being the pursuit of explanations using the methods of the natural sciences.
- **Hollis and Smith** (1991: 62–3): Theories perform three functions. They abstract (group together events, situations or objects which are not identical). They generalize (identify what these things which are not identical have in common by virtue of analysis of the available facts). And they connect (identify cause and effect). This definition starts to move us away from considerations of how 'scientific' theory should or should not be and into the realm of the nature and uses of theory. Abstraction, generalization and connection are, for Hollis and Smith, the basic prerequisites of any theory in any academic discipline.
- **Baylis, Smith and Owens** (2008a: 4; emphasis in original): *'a kind of simplifying device that allows you to decide which facts matter and which do not'*. This definition undermines those who believe processes of theorizing in IR can or should mimic processes of theorizing in the natural sciences. Theory, they assert, is not simply 'some grand formal model with **hypotheses** and assumptions' (Baylis et al. 2008a: 4). Instead we should be less ambitious by being more realistic about what we can expect theory to deliver and more aware of the presuppositions and biases we bring to the study of the social world.
- **Robert Jackson and Georg Sørensen** (2007: 54): 'We always look at the world, consciously or not, through a specific set of lenses; we may think of those lenses as theory.' Theory, according to this interpretation, is the world we live in; it makes the world and constructs it for us whether we realize it or not.
- **Cynthia Weber** (2005: 2): 'IR theory makes organizing generalizations about international politics. IR theory is a collection of stories about the world of international politics. And in telling stories about international politics, IR theory doesn't just present what is going on in the world out there. IR theory also imposes its own vision of what the world out there looks like.' Weber pulls us

even further from the realms of IR theory as natural science. Look at the language she uses. Words like 'story' imply imagined and imaginative elements to theories developed in the field of IR. She is in full agreement with writers such as Baylis, Smith and Owens when she collapses the distinction between a 'world' of IR and the 'world' of the observer.

We have here an array of perspectives on theory. From the natural science 'formal model' interpretation of Hollis and Smith to Weber's view that we are intimate parts of the theories we devise, no two IR authors quite agree on what IR theory is or should be. In Chapter 1.4 we will revisit the debate about the impact of these debates about the nature of theory. For now, all you need to have clear in your mind is that these differences exist and they materially influence the work that goes on in the field of IR. In the next section we will take a step back and consider an even more basic question: why bother with theory in the first place?

> Whenever you come across a definition of 'theory' or 'IR theory', make a note of it in a theory checklist. It will provide an invaluable source of differences among writers for use in essays and exam answers.

Why bother with theory?

You are not alone if you doubt the 'value added' that theory brings to the study of academic subjects. In this section we will review both sides of the argument by looking first of all at the positions taken by those writers who doubt the utility of theory. We move on then to consider those writers who trumpet the value of theory – not just because they believe it is intrinsically useful to us but because it is inescapably everywhere, always shaping our study of the world whether we care to admit it or not.

The 'take it or leave it' approach to theory

In the field of history, there is a book by Keith Windschuttle (1996) called *The Killing of History: How Literary Critics and Social Theorists are Murdering our Past*. In the book Windschuttle describes how the discipline of history, traditionally concerned with the narration of events in the past using archival documents and other remnants from the period in question, 'is now suffering a potentially mortal attack from the rise to academic prominence of a relatively new array of literary and social theories' which question traditional historical practices and the knowledge produced by them (Windschuttle 1996: 10). There is 'history', Windschuttle implies, and there is 'theory' and it is dangerous for the two to get mixed up because the former deals with the real world of the past while the latter throws up needless conjecture about the reliability of all this knowledge: 'The central point upon which history was founded no longer holds: there is no fundamental distinction any more between history and myth' (Windschuttle: 10).

The same kinds of debates rebounded throughout the social sciences in the 1990s, especially with the rise in popularity of the intellectual movement commonly known as postmodernism (see Chapter 2.9). It is interesting to note in this context that IR as a discipline has long been involved in such disputes, and reviewing some of the key positions will give us some useful insights into how writers treat the question 'why bother with theory?'

Windschuttle's opinion is that we can have facts or we can have theory. We do not profit from mixing the two. In IR, this 'take it or leave it' approach to theory can be exemplified using the words of Noam Chomsky: in the analysis of IR, he says, 'historical conditions are too varied and complex for anything that might plausibly be called a "theory" to apply uniformly' (quoted in Burchill 2001a: 1). Theory, for Chomsky, unnecessarily simplifies the workings of the real world, making it intelligible only at the expense of over-simplification. Chomsky's judgement is that in order to grasp the complexity of the subject matter of IR we are better off reading lots of detailed historical case studies about events/personalities/decisions and so on because they give us a truer account of how the world really works.

The 'theory is inescapable' approach

Many writers disagree with the 'take it or leave it' approach to theory exemplified by Windschuttle and Chomsky. Writers who hold this 'theory is inescapable' opinion push the idea that theory is everywhere, and therefore that understanding theory is not an option but is rather forced on us by the very conditions of our human existence.

A review of the literature in this area reveals two interconnected propositions about the role and value of theory. The first and arguably best known is associated with writers such as Steve Smith and Ken Booth and features in some form in all their books on IR theory you are likely to encounter on your course. The clearest rejection of the 'take it or leave it' line comes in Baylis, Smith and Owen's Introduction to *The Globalization of World Politics*:

> It is not as if you can say that you do not want to bother with a theory, all you want to do is to look at the 'facts'. We believe that this is simply impossible, since the only way in which you can decide which of the millions of possible facts to look at is by adhering to some simplifying device which tells you which ones matter the most. (Baylis et al. 2008a: 4)

For them, unlike Windschuttle and Chomsky, the element of choice in saying we can either embrace theory *or* ignore it simply does not exist, and here they agree with other writers who consider the relationship between facts and theory. One such is Fred Halliday who argues that theory performs three functions with respect to facts: it helps us decide which facts are significant and which are not; it helps us explain how the same fact can be interpreted differently; and it helps bring to the fore questions of morality which cannot be decided by an appeal to the facts alone (summarized in Burchill, 2001a: 13).

When watching television, listening to the radio and reading newspapers think about the number of times you hear the words 'fact'. Why are the 'facts' of a story prized so highly? What is it about 'facts' that makes them so important to us?

Why do these writers see a world in which theory is inescapably everywhere? The answer lies in a second proposition about the key role theory has played, unwittingly or not, in the actual conduct of international relations. As Stephen Walt puts it:

> Even policymakers who are contemptuous of 'theory' must rely on their own (often unstated) ideas about how the world works in order to decide what to do. It is hard to make good policy if one's basic organizing principles are flawed, just as it is hard to construct good theories without knowing a lot about the real world. (2006: 386)

It is only by knowing theory that we can improve practice and by the same token theoretical sophistication comes from knowing about the world policy-makers inhabit.

Our goal here is not to evaluate the persuasiveness of this argument (I leave that up to you as you progress through this book and your course), but rather to set out a range of opinions which you might find interesting points of departure. Steve Smith (1995: 3) puts the theory–practice overlap in its sharpest relief by writing that 'international theory has tended to be a **discourse** accepting of, and complicit in, the creation and re-creation of international practices that threaten, discipline and do violence to others'. He points to the role that theoretical assumptions associated with the Realist tradition (explored in Chapter 2.2 of this book) played in moulding superpower foreign policies during the Cold War from 1945–89, particularly in terms of the nuclear arms race. In playing an active part in the development of aggressive American and Russian foreign policies, they suggest, Realist IR theory can be held partially accountable for some of the many horrors and catastrophes the world witnessed during that period.

> Theories are by definition partial, incomplete and context-specific and this should give you great heart when studying them because there are usually several grounds on which they can be dissected and criticized in your essays and exam answers.

Tim Dunne and Brian Schmidt agree that policy and theory are intimately connected, especially as far as realism goes: 'From 1939 to the present, leading theorists and policy-makers have continued to view the world through realist lenses' (Dunne and Schmidt 2008: 92). Francis Fukuyama likewise suggests that Realism has provided 'the dominant framework for understanding international relations and shapes the thinking of virtually every foreign policy professional today in the United States and much of the rest of the world' (quoted in Little 1995: 71). Martin Hollis and Steve Smith give us an excellent summary of the 'theory is inescapable' approach:

> [M]any International Relations scholars are directly involved in the US foreign and defence policy community. They try to use their theories to improve policy-making and they search for theories which will be relevant and useful for this purpose ... Hence the truth of International Relations theories has something to do with which theories are known and applied in the process they purport to analyse. (Hollis and Smith 1991: 70–1)

We come to discuss the tenets of Realist theory later. The point for now is to note how often that theory is cited by writers seeking examples of the theory–practice overlap (see also the examples given in Burchill 2001a: 10).

> Is it just coincidence that Realism is so often used as an illustration of the interplay between the theory and practice of international relations? As you go through your course see if you can find other examples from the literature where writers cite a direct connection between theory (any theory) and practice.

Contrary to the 'take it or leave it' approach, writers in the 'theory is inescapable' tradition are very clear about the pervasiveness, the 'everywhere-ness' of theory. For them, there is no such thing as choosing to use a theory or not because it is a fundamental part of life. And if that is not enough, they argue, look at the reasons why IR was founded as an academic discipline (explored further in Chapter 1.4 below). It was set up in the aftermath of the First World War (1914–18) to help us understand and explain (theorize) the relations between states, so that the futile carnage of the Great War could be avoided in the future. The theory–practice overlap has not just come about by chance but by design. As Scott Burchill (2001a: 6) explains: 'The very purpose of intellectual endeavour was to change the world for the better by eradicating the scourge of war. This was really the only function international theory had.' If we accept the 'theory is inescapable' approach in general, then in the field of IR its ramifications are doubly important because it is a discipline and a practice that deals directly with war, conflict, death and destruction.

 Taking it **FURTHER**

Ray Winstone on facts and theory

As I write this book, there is an advertisement currently running on television and in the cinema for a new cereal fronted by British actor Ray Winstone. In it, Winstone complains that 'When it comes to food there's a bit of a nanny culture thing going on. Don't do this. Don't do that. That is very bad for you. This is for your own good.' He goes on to say that we should be free to choose for ourselves how we live and what we do to our bodies. 'We're old enough and wise enough to just be given the facts, so this is a new cereal called Optivita. It contains oatbran which can help actively reduce cholesterol. Now, it's up to you to reduce cholesterol – or not.' In the final scene Winstone makes it clear he is not trying to bully us into making a decision. 'Well don't look at me: I'm not gonna tell you what to do.' The decision, it seems, is ours.

There are many interesting points about this advert, not least the idea that you might choose to ignore the advice of a well-known 'hard man' such as Winstone! But the crucial point for us lies in the moves the advert makes to sell us this product. Winstone tells us that there is a 'bit of a nanny culture thing going on' when it comes to food. This is asserted as the truth (a 'fact' if you like) but the nature of that 'nanny culture' is neither defined nor elaborated upon – as if we all plug into what he is talking about straight away. There is a long libertarian tradition in Britain of railing against an overwheening 'nanny state' which unnecessarily interferes in the daily lives of 'ordinary people'. The advert was broadcast at a time when British Prime Minister Tony Blair was promoting the idea of 'social marketing' which relied on food companies giving the public more information on health and diet because he felt that consumers are more likely to believe companies than the government (Wainwright and Carvel 2006). The 'fact' of the matter was that Britain was becoming *less* of a 'nanny state' just when the advertisers told us that it was becoming *more* of one.

Thus, the 'nanny culture thing' is not a fact about the world but a theory. It is one interpretation or 'take' on the government's policy to promote corporate and social responsibility for healthy living. If we do not accept the theory of the nanny state as far as healthy eating goes, then the rationale for both the cereal and the advert go out of the window. The idea that there are theory-free 'facts' about the world might not be as accurate as we might want to believe.

Can you think of other advertisements which rely on theories about how the world works presented as straightforward facts about how the world works?

International Relations theory on film

Scholars of IR are not alone in debating the value – or otherwise – of theory and in doing so they show how deeply interconnected IR as a discipline is with the wider cultural context within which scholarship is practised and disseminated. If we take this view seriously it has potentially radical consequences. Gone are the days of the lonely scholar sitting in an ivory tower writing huge tomes which only get read by a handful of other professors working in the same field, but of marginal importance to society as a whole.

> There is a popular phrase 'it's only academic', used to refer to something that has theoretical relevance but no practical relevance. In the study of IR is it feasible to say that the books and articles we read are ever only of 'academic' relevance?

One writer who well makes this point is Cynthia Weber (2005) who shows us how we can use popular films both to make sense of, and critique, key IR theories. At first sight this might seem a strange thing to do. Is not IR a distinct discipline of study with its own language, ideas, set of concepts, and 'great debates'? Is it not the case that early IR theorists and their successors today pride themselves on working in a separable, if not separate, social scientific discipline which they have worked for years to demarcate from history, law, philosophy, politics and economics (see Chapter 1.4)? What can films tell us about a theoretical, abstract subject like IR?

Your answers to these questions very much depend on your view of what makes an academic discipline and what makes for a valid approach to studying IR theory. Let us take a look at the reasons why Weber believes it is possible and enlightening to study IR through film through two quotes from her book:

> IR theory can be studied as a site of cultural practice. IR theory is an 'ensemble of stories' told about the world it studies, which is the world of international politics. Studying IR theory as a site of cultural practice means being attentive to how IR theory makes sense of the world of international politics. (Weber 2005: 4)

> Popular films provide students with answers to the question How does an IR myth appear to be true? In so doing, popular films point to how politics, power, and ideology are culturally constructed, and how the culture of IR theory might be politically reconstructed. (Weber, 2005: 20)

The moves Weber makes here are fascinating. First of all, she argues that the development of IR theory tells us a great deal about the cultures within which those theories have developed (and vice versa). IR is assumed to be a site of 'cultural practice' which reveals theorists' unspoken assumptions about how the world operates. Second, the 'stories' IR theorists tell us about the world rely on the same plot lines we find in 'stories' told to us by novelists and film-makers. Third, theories have to rely on certain hidden assumptions to make them 'work'; they are 'mythical' in the sense that they purport to describe aspects of the 'real world' whilst simultaneously constructing aspects of that 'real world' for us (this is what goes on in the Ray Winstone advert considered above). Finally, since IR, like novels and films, is composed of 'stories' we tell about international politics, uncovering the assumptions and ideologies behind those stories enables us to rethink the basis of IR theories themselves.

At the Annual Convention of the International Studies Association in San Francisco in 2008, several speakers used film, literature or television shows to illustrate aspects of IR. For example, a panel convened on 27 March looked at the concept of **anarchy** as illustrated in *Lost*, Joseph Conrad and the emergence of International Studies and the IR of J.R.R. Tolkein's *Lord of the Rings* (ISANET 2008: 176). This strategy for studying IR is fascinating because:

- It helps us better **understand** IR theories by making a complex set of ideas and language more accessible to us as students.
- It helps us **critique** the theories as well us understanding them. Being able to critique theories is likely to be a vital part of the assessments you undertake on your course in IR theory.
- It provides us with a **new dimension to the 'facts versus theory' debate**. By arguing that theory is everywhere, even in Hollywood blockbusters such as *Independence Day*, these scholars give us further cause to think about theory's role in our efforts to explain international relations today.

You might be lucky enough on your course to spend time exploring how Weber uses film to deconstruct IR theory in timetabled sessions. If not, you can still get full value for money by renting or buying the various films, watching them, and then seeing how Weber makes use of them in her work.

Questions to ponder

"Why do we need theories about international relations when we can look at the facts?"

There are two promising approaches to answering this question. The first is to think about it in 'for' and 'against' terms. In this approach you would begin by setting out the case 'against' theory and 'for' facts, looking at writers who question the utility of theory. You should mainly concentrate on writers from within the discipline of IR who posit the 'take it or leave it' approach to theory. You might show knowledge of the wider social scientific debates by referring to writers from other disciplines who question the value or utility of theory. In the second part of the essay, you would consider the case 'against' facts and 'for' theory, using any of the key points about the 'everywhere-ness' of theory raised by writers such as Steve Smith and Cynthia Weber. All this would be framed by your own view on which body of writing you find most persuasive.

The second approach would be to present a numbered list of reasons why you believe we should bother with theory and deal with each in turn in a 'fat paragraph' (approximately 250 hundred words per point, depending on essay length). Taking this approach makes it slightly harder to achieve balance in the essay because your tutor would presumably want to see some consideration of the 'take it or leave it' approach and you would have to think hard about where to explore that interpretation. It might, for example, be useful to have a long introduction setting out the rationale for the assertion made in the question and then arguing that you intend to knock it down by exploring a series of points from the literature on the value of IR theory.

"How do IR theorists make sense of the world?"

Vague or open-ended questions can be both a curse and a blessing. To put it another way, they can be deceptively difficult to answer despite on the surface appearing to be fairly straightforward. The place to start is to try and pin down for your tutor what you take the different bits of the question to mean:

Which IR theorists? Can they all be lumped together? Do all of them view 'theory' in the same way? Are there differences between, say, a Realist and a postmodernist take on theory and if so how is this expressed in their ontological, epistemological and methodological approaches to studying IR?

What does 'make sense of the world' mean in this context? It seems to fair to take it to mean 'how do the theorists you have chosen study the world of IR?' That is, how do they make it intelligible to us as fellow students of international affairs? Here we get into issues raised in the previous chapter about how different IR theorists define their field of study.

One approach you might then adopt is to choose a case study which exemplifies how academics from obviously different theoretical traditions 'makes sense' of 'their world' of IR and draw conclusions from that.

> *The use of case studies can provide you with valuable ways of comparing and contrasting different theoretical approaches to IR. Always make it clear to the reader why you choose particular cases and make sure to tell the reader after presenting case study material what conclusions you draw from it. Do not expect the reader to be able to infer from your case studies why you chose them: make it explicit in the essay.*

References to more information

CARR, E.H. (1990) *What is History?* Harmondsworth: Penguin.

There are various reprints of the 1961 original. Especially thought-provoking is the opening chapter which rethinks the idea of 'facts'.

GOLDSTEIN, J.S. AND PEVEHOUSE, J.C. (2008) *International Relations*, 8th edn. New York: Pearson Education.

Usefully, from a student point of view, the book is liberally sprinkled with 'thinking theoretically' text boxes which help you think through theoretical explanations for different outcomes in the cases covered.

HAY, C. (2002) *Political Analysis: A Critical Introduction.* Basingstoke: Palgrave.

The opening two chapters introduce you to the problems of defining the field of Political Science (including the sub-field of IR) and to the problems we encounter in trying to study this subject 'scientifically'.

BURNHAM, P., GILLAND, K., GRANT, W. AND LAYTON-HENRY, Z. (2004) *Research Methods in Politics.* Basingstoke: Palgrave Macmillan.

Chapter 1 outlines big debates about how to study Politics which filter into discussions about how to study IR.

AXFORD, B., BROWNING, G.K., HUGGINS, R. AND ROSAMOND, B. (2006) *Politics: An Introduction*, 2nd edn. London: Routledge.

Chapter 14 by Rosamond introduces ways of thinking about IR and shows how the borders between domestic and international politics are in the process of dissolving.

NEXON, D. AND NEUMANN, I.B. (EDS) (2006) *Harry Potter and International Relations.* Lanham, MD: Rowman and Littlefield.

For fans of the novels and/or the films of J.K. Rowling, this book helps us see the parallels between the 'real world' of international relations and the fictitious world of Harry Potter.

STERLING-FOLKER, J. (2006) 'Making Sense of International Relations Theory', in J. Sterling-Folker (ed.) *Making Sense of International Relations Theory.* Boulder, CO: Lynne Rienner, pp. 1–12.

This short chapter usefully introduces you to the main contours of the debates about 'theory'.

JABRI, V. (2000) 'Reflections on the Study of International Relations', in T.C. Salmon (ed.) *Issues in International Relations.* London: Routledge, pp. 289–313.

Good on the nature of theory and the problems of defining the scope of IR as a subject area.

NEUMAN, W.L. (2007) Basics of Social Research: *Qualitative and Quantitative Approaches*, 2nd edn. New York: Pearson Education.

Chapter 2 covers general issues to do with the nature of theory.

HARDING, S. AND HINTIKKA, M.B. (EDS) (2003) *Discovering Reality: Feminist Perspectives on Epistemology, Metaphysics, Methodology, and the Philosophy of Social Science*, 2nd edn. Dordrecht: Kluwer Academic Publishers.

See especially the chapters by Eve Keller on gender and science.

ROSKIN, M.G., CORD, R.L., MADEIROS, J.A., AND JONES, W.S. (2006) *Political Science: An Introduction*, 9th edn. Upper Saddle River, NJ: Pearson Prentice Hall.

Part 1 introduces the 'science' debate and introduces basic concepts useful for the study of domestic and international politics.

1.3	
your course in IR theory	

Course structure

No two university courses on the same subject ever look the same for a variety of basically practical reasons. First of all, universities tend to carve up their teaching time differently. Some still use the three-term system but increasingly UK universities have moved to a two-semester system, the first running roughly from September to December and the second from January to May. Within these semesters some universities offer reading weeks mid-way through, others do not. Even within the same Faculty at a given university, departments differ on whether or not to give students reading weeks. An IR course spread over 10 weeks will look very different from one spread over 12 or more weeks.

Make sure you find out the structure of your course as early as you can so you can plan your time and work accordingly. It is particularly important to know when the busy periods of the course will be, especially around asessment time.

Second, because university courses are designed, written, administered and taught by individual members of staff (sometimes pairs or small teams of staff share the workload), the same course will look very different even if the teaching period is the same. In a field like IR where the subject matter is in dispute, it is only to be expected that different tutors will want to cover some topics and not others, to order them in a variety of ways and to expect students to achieve varieties of learning outcomes from the course. Whilst universities and outside agencies routinely regulate academic teaching quality and practice, it is still up to the individual tutors to put the courses together and therefore those courses are infused with, and representative of, tutors' various research interests and teaching styles.

You will be given a variety of materials when you begin a new module. Traditionally these are delivered to you as hard copies but many universities are now choosing to present course material electronically in a Virtual Learning Environment (VLE) such as Learn or Blackboard. Be sure to read everything your tutor gives you at the start of the course and refer back to it as often as you need throughout the course to keep up to date on where you need to be for lectures and seminars, what reading you are expected to be doing, and when assessments are due in so you can plan your preparation effectively.

A third reason relates to the place of theory on courses in IR. Some will cover a few theories but, like many popular textbooks (for example Baylis et al. 2008b), will also cover various 'themes and issues' in global politics today. Even on courses where IR theory is the sole focus, it is unlikely, given the proliferation of theories, that on your course you will cover all the theories included in this book. Your tutor will have developed the course content with specific aims and learning outcomes in mind and will have designed a lecture/seminar programme to help you achieve them. From courses where theory plays a 'walk on' or cameo role to those majoring on IR theory, you can be sure that you will need to develop all of the thinking and practical skills explored in this course companion to get the best out of your course.

The aim of this chapter is to provide you with a very brief introduction to the world of academic course design. I have written it to show you where courses come from (not thin air!) and to try and convey how important it is for you to be attuned from the very start of each and every course you study at university to exactly what the course aims are, and how your tutor expects you to achieve those aims through the lecture, seminar and assessment schedule. If you would rather concentrate on the subject-specific material in the course companion, feel free to skip this chapter and progress straight to the next chapter on theorizing IR.

Course aims and learning outcomes

What are the likely aims and learning outcomes of a course in IR theory? Here I will write from my own experience of teaching a course specifically on IR theory, but be sure to check the module specification for your particular course before it begins so you are comfortable from the outset what your tutor expects you to be able to achieve by the end of the course.

> Every course you study at university has what is usually called a 'module specification' explaining in one or two pages the main aims of the course, the student learning outcomes to be achieved by its assessment details and an overview of course content and structure. These are usually available electronically on your departmental website and in hard copy. Be sure you know where to find these specifications and read them thoroughly before the start of your studies so you are absolutely clear about what you can expect of the course.

Aims

The aims of an undergraduate course in IR that incorporates a theoretical component are likely to be:

1. To understand the interpretation of IR put forward by each theory covered on the course.

2 To understand the assumptions underlying each of those theories.

3 To evaluate the strengths and weaknesses of each theory covered on the course.

There are two points to note about these aims. First of all, you can see that they are pretty general building blocks for the course, helping tutors identify what they want students to achieve when they have successfully completed it. Plus there is a key word here: by saying that the first aim is to cover the 'main' theories of IR, I am stressing that tutors are unlikely to cover each and every IR theory. Tutors will actively encourage you to explore other theories not covered on your particular course should you wish to do so.

> *Students who read about other theories not specifically covered on their IR theory course usually gain vital additional subject matter expertise and get into good habits of wider reading.*

The second point is that these aims are designed to facilitate robust and fair assessment. An average student (achieving marks in and around the 2:2 classification, so 50–59 per cent) will demonstrate in an exam answer or coursework essay that they can achieve the first two aims: understanding the interpretations and assumptions of the theories. Higher achieving students (those achieving marks into the 2:1 and first bandings) will demonstrate not just knowledge of a particular theory or theories but will also be able to dissect the assumptions of the theory and to evaluate their relative merits by critiquing them.

Learning outcomes

Student learning at university is themed around discrete modules where you explore specific themes and issues relating to given events, historical periods, ideas and concepts relating to the subject of those modules. But the whole idea behind university education is to encourage you to develop a range of what are known as **generic skills** or **transferable skills** – skills to do with writing clearly, communicating effectively, presenting an idea and constructively criticizing different sides of an argument. All of these skills will be valuable in your later career and universities are the ideal place to learn how to enhance them.

> The wider aims of your degree programme should be set out in your departmental handbook: look for the section on transferable skills.

The skills you can expect to learn will be identified in the Learning Outcomes for each module (Figure 3).

A. Knowledge and understanding

On completion of this module students shoule be able to:

1 Understand the importance of theory to the study of International Relations as an academic discipline.
2 Identify the central tenets of a number of International Relations theories.
3 Analyse the points of debate between these theories.
4 Apply theoretical positions to the 'real world' of international relations.

B. Generic Intellectual Skills

On completion of this module students should be able to:

1 Gather, organize and deploy evidence, data and information from a wide variety of secondary sources.
2 Construct reasoned argument.
3 Synthesize and analyse relevant information.
4 Exercise critical judgement in relation to issues in IR theory and world politics.
5 Reflect on their own learning and make use of constructive feedback.

C. Personal transferable skills

On completion of this module students should be able to:

1 Communicate effectively in speech and writing.
2 Use communication and information technology for the retrieval and presentation of information.

Figure 3   Typical learning outcomes for a course in IR theory

Part A covers the subject matter skills, but the bulk of the learning outcomes relate to the generic intellectual and personal transferable skills in Parts B and C. Tutors at university always appreciate students performing well in coursework and exams, but even more than that they like to see students making the best of their abilities. If you treat each module as an opportunity to develop good working, organizational

What do I need to succeed?

- Communication skills
- Willingness to take intellectual risks
- Openness to new concepts
- A willingnesss to work …
- … hard!
- Reading/thinking/participation/reflection

Figure 4   The skills you will need

and time management habits, you will not go far wrong in terms of the overall impression you give your tutor of your personal qualities as well as your subject matter expertise.

Thinking long term from your first year is a good skill to develop. One attraction of putting everything into every module you study is that tutors tend to remember the names of hard-working students. This can be useful when you want references for jobs to enable you to go on to postgraduate study after your final year.

The skills you will need

Having explained the lecture programme, the rationale behind it, and how we are going to progress from start to finish I put up this slide in the first lecture on IR theory (Figure 4). Let us take them one by one:

- **Communication skills.** Developing your communication skills at university is essential. By 'communication' we are thinking of both oral (talking), aural (listening) and written (structure, logic, clarity, use of evidence, good English). Almost everything you do at university requires you to talk to people (for example, in seminars and individual or group presentations), to listen to people (in those same environments, plus in lectures) and to write clearly and persuasively (in exams and coursework assignments). This process of contributing a point, listening to others' contributions, discussing and being able to communicate your ideas in clear written English will underpin your success at your course in IR theory, like all the courses you take at university.

- **Willingness to take intellectual risks.** What are 'intellectual risks'? It is tempting when first attending university lectures and seminars to fall back on what you know – from your A-Level or International Baccalaureate, for example. It is equally tempting to re-hash essays you did in your secondary education as a way of saving time and presenting arguments with which you are comfortable, having rehearsed them several times before. The whole point about university education is that you throw yourselves into new subject areas, expose yourself to new ideas, new concepts, new theories and novel ways of viewing the world. Students who take intellectual risks willingly plough through the essential and desirable course readings, even if they have never studied the subject before. They, in fact, go beyond the core readings and actively seek out wider reading on a given topic. This tends to show through in the clarity of their thinking and the extensive evidence on which they are able to draw in exams and coursework essays.

> The word 'risk' has both negative and positive connotations. Rather than worrying about the possible negatives, think instead about the potential pay-offs in terms of marks and intellectual development if you throw yourself wholeheartedly into a course. Tutors will always reward a student they believe to be going that extra mile.

- **Openness to new concepts**. This follows on from the last point about being open to new challenges rather than shying away from them – it relates to your mindset regarding studying at university. At this level you will be constantly confronted with ideas, bodies of knowledge and sets of literatures with which you will be unfamiliar. This is not something that should frighten you. Challenging yourself to read a tough book or journal article, and getting used to meeting those challenges on a regular basis is part of what higher education is all about. It will sometimes be the case that you find a core text really tough going the first time around, in which case do not be afraid to read around the subject and then re-read it at a later date, either later in the same week, later in the course or during your revision time. You might be surprised how much you grasp of that difficult text the second or third time around.
- **A willingness to work ... hard**! The key difference between the school/college environment and the university environment is that at university your learning

is mostly self-directed. At university you have more time on your hands to do with as you wish, so you need to develop sophisticated, motivational time management and organizational skills to see you through each course. If you are taking a degree programme in the broad realm of Politics or International Relations, you will have only limited direct contact time with your tutor – typically one lecture and/or one seminar per week. But try to avoid seeing your courses as lasting for just these two hours every week: the calculations in Figure 5 demonstrate why.

The credit system and total student effort

- Assume an undergraduate IR Theory module carrying a credit weighting of 20 credits.
- Each credit equates to an average student effort of 10 hours.
- 20 credits x 10 hours' worth of effort = 200 hours total student effort for the course.

Hours per week on IR Theory

- A 12-week course.
- 2 hours per week contact time.
- Total contact time with tutor: 24 hours per course.
- Total student effort: 200 hours. Take from this the 24 hours contact time = 176 hours.
- 176 hours spread over the 12-week course = 14.66 hours per week.
- Each contact hour for IR Theory entails approximately 7 hours of student preparation time.

Figure 5   The credit system and student effort

Some basic mathematics shows just how much work is expected of students on a typical core course in the first year. The direct contact time in lectures and seminars is only the beginning! For each contact hour on this course students are expected to put in seven hours of effort out of the lecture hall and seminar room. Knowing how to get the best of this self-directed study time will be crucial to your success on each module.

Total student effort out of contact hours covers everything from information retrieval, to reading, thinking, reflection, preparing for the re-reading and organization of notes as well as meeting your tutor in his/her office after hours or out of class, individual essays and group assignments.

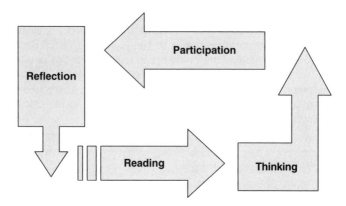

Figure 6   The learning cycle

- **Reading/thinking/participation/reflection**. These skills are closely inter-twined and mutually reinforcing (Figure 6). If you can get into a healthy cycle of reading widely, thinking about that reading before you attend lectures and seminars, actively participating in seminars and then reflecting seriously on what you learnt from the lectures and seminars, you will be in a strong position to succeed at your course in IR theory. You will also be developing a good habit of work which will stand you in good stead for your other studies at university.

References to more information

Here is a selection of the many university study skills books on offer:

MORAN, A.P. AND SUTTON, S. (2000) *Managing Your Own Learning at University: A Practical Guide*. Dublin: University College Dublin Press.

PALMER, S. AND PURI, A. (2006) *Coping with Stress at University: A Survival Guide*. London: Sage.

PRITCHARD, A. (2008) *Studying and Learning at University: Vital Skills for Success in Your Degree*. London: Sage.

RACE, P. (2002) *How to Get a Good Degree: Making the Most of Your Time at University*. Buckingham: Open University Press.

1.4

theoretical debates

In this chapter we deepen our understanding of the theoretical debates that have dominated the academic study of IR. In Chapter 1.2, we began by trying to define the problematic term 'theory' and discovered that there is no firm agreement among scholars on what theory actually is. If that did not make life difficult enough, we then encountered the debate that takes place between those scholars who question the utility of theory in explaining human affairs and those scholars who laud the achievements of theoretical perspectives in making sense of a complex world. We labelled the former approach the 'take it or leave it' approach to theory and the latter the 'theory is inescapable' approach.

In this chapter I want to pick up a few loose ends I left dangling in that chapter. In particular, I want to take these general debates about the nature, value and role of theory and show you how they have played out in the realm of IR theory. In order to do this I want to investigate a fundamental issue IR theorists argue about: the causes and conse-quences of anarchy in the international system. I will move on to explore whether we can tell a 'story' about the evolution of theoretical debates in IR. Finally, I will give an overview of different ways of evalu-ating the strengths and weaknesses of IR theories and explore the prospect of developing an IR 'super-theory'.

Anarchy in IR

What do IR theorists argue about? This question has partly been answered in Chapter 1.2 where we considered the 'problem of the subject'. The very fact that the discipline tries to explain anything and everything that might come under the general headings 'inter-national relations' and 'world politics' means there is no firm con-sensus within the discipline on what the subject matter of IR is or what it should be.

The sheer breadth of the discipline today, however, obscures the fact that in the early years of the discipline there was a bit more agreement on what IR scholars and students should study: how to manage inter-state relations. Everything else was secondary, if it was on people's radars at all. It seems fair to suggest, therefore, that in its formative years as a discipline the 'agenda' of IR was more limited than it is today. This had one crucial impact on the discipline: it placed the condition of international anarchy right at the heart of the discipline as *the* bone of contention between theorists.

> If you want to get into the heads of different IR theorists, try thinking about how they define anarchy and how they view its consequences for international relations. Is it central to their theories, and why or why not?

If you asked ten friends down the corridor in your hall of residence to define 'anarchy', they would probably mention a range of familiar themes: lawlessness, chaos, disruption, opposition to 'the powers that be' and violence might all feature in some combination in their answers. 'Anarchy' in its IR context picks some of these themes. So central is it to the study of IR that it is worth briefly exploring its **etymology** before showing how IR theorists have deployed it in their work.

Etymology

The word 'anarchy' comes from the Greek and has two components:

1. The prefix *An-* means 'without', 'not' or 'lacking' (Dictionary.com 2007a).

2. The suffix *–archos* (Dictionary.com 2007b) comes from the word *–archon*, meaning: one of the nine principal ruling magistrates of ancient Athens, or more generally an authoritative figure, a high official or a rule.

Putting the two parts of the word together and we find that the literal meaning of anarchy can be any or all of the following:

- No ruler.
- Without a high official.
- Lacking an authority.

In the study of IR, this is key because the central unit of analysis has tended to be the sovereign nation-state. **Sovereignty** is another word that can cause problems because of the various layers of meaning it has acquired over the years.

- Sovereignty is a politically charged term. You will probably know it best from debates about the advisability of British involvement in the European Union's (EU) various proposals for political and economic integration such as the European single currency. For Eurosceptics, such schemes are said to detract from British sovereignty, which has political and economic dimensions as well as a legal angle, because EU decisions then take precedence over British decisions (for more on sovereignty as seen in Britain's debates about European policy, see Axford et al. 2006: 484–5).
- In IR it means that different states in the international system are independent, territoriality defined and able to determine their own destinies (Dunne et al. 2007: 340).
- State sovereignty has internal and external dimensions. A state is internally sovereign 'when it exercises supreme authority over the affairs and people within its territory'; it is externally sovereign 'when it is recognized as such by the international community'; that is, when both its internal sovereignty and territorial integrity are respected and upheld (Jackson and Sørensen 2007: 313).
- In sum, sovereignty, says Ben Rosamond, is 'about the power to make laws and the ability to rule effectively' (Axford et al. 2006: 485).

We now have definitions of two fundamental terms in IR. Why are they fundamental? Well, it all comes down to the potential problems of having all these sovereign states existing together side by side in the **international system**. If each state is sovereign, who or what has the power/influence/authority/means to shape their behaviour so they can live peaceably together? What if one state, or a group of states, chooses to attack another state or group of states? What if one state or a group of states chooses *not* to recognize the domestic government or territorial integrity of another state? In the final reckoning, *who regulates state behaviour in an anarchic international system?* It is precisely this question that prompted IR theorists into action.

IR scholars take core tenets of the literal meaning of anarchy identified above and emerge with the following formulations:

- Hollis and Smith (1991: 7) argue that by calling the international system 'anarchic' we are suggesting 'not that it is chaotic but simply that there is no government above the states which comprise it'.

- Brown (2001: 4) likewise suggests that anarchy, in its IR context, 'does not necessarily mean lawlessness and chaos; rather it means the absence of a formal system of government'.
- For Weber (2005: 14), anarchy 'denotes *lack of an orderer*' (her emphasis) – there is no-one or nothing to impose order on the behaviour of states in a top-down way.

'Anarchy' is a central term in IR theory and is likely to feature in course-work and exam questions on your course. Find a succinct definition from an established IR scholar which you can use as your definition at the beginning of essays and exam answers.

As we move through the various theories in Part 2 of the book, you will see how anarchy and sovereignty play out in the various traditions we explore. For now, all you need to bear in mind is that these are not neutral concepts: they are loaded with meaning. Their implications for IR are constantly in dispute. Let us now take a look at how the discipline has unfolded over the years to debate these issues.

Theorizing IR

Telling a story about the development of a discipline such as IR is intensely difficult for a number of reasons. How do we write the history of an academic discipline? Who are the key actors? What are the key dates and events? How do we track and measure the comings and goings of academic debate over time? It is safe to say that a definitive disciplinary history is more or less impossible.

This has not stopped IR scholars from trying, however. In the literature you read on your course you will find many books and articles which tell the story of IR as one that developed around a series of so-called 'great debates'.

Some textbooks, for example, Jackson and Sørensen (2007) still like to begin with the story of the 'great debates'. Others, for example Dunne, et al. (2007), avoid this story until the very end. How does this affect their presentation of the 'story' of IR? What are the key themes these writers see running through the discipline today?

These 'great debates' have 'served to organize the discipline' (Wæver 2007: 299), giving it focus and helping it to regulate, categorize and 'place' scholarly writing within its borders. I will briefly review the gist of this story and then critique it using the work of Brian Schmidt (2006). From here we will develop a framework for understanding the nature of the theoretical disputes within the discipline which it will help to have at the back of your mind when you begin your analysis of each theory.

Taking _{it} **FURTHER**

Origins of IR as an Academic Discipline

The study of IR as a separate academic discipline began after the First World War (1914–18). Until that time, scholars from various disciplinary backgrounds had engaged in the study of international politics. Lawyers, historians, philosophers, political scientists and economists all had something to say about the conduct of international affairs and the relations between states. But there was no discipline devoted exclusively to the study of inter-state affairs. This all changed after the mass death, destruction and devastation of the First World War. Suddenly it seemed more important than ever to try and find answers to three key question: why do wars begin? What do wars achieve? What lessons can we learn from past wars to prevent future ones? When IR was founded, it was specifically tasked to generate answers to those tricky questions and drew on approaches, ideas and evidence from several other disciplines (Figure 7).

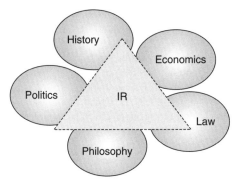

Figure 7   IR's creation as a discipline

> IR thus shares an intellectual affinity with many neighbouring disciplines: its disciplinary borders are quite porous. Pick up any IR journal today and you will see a proliferation of approaches, themes, issues and debates. This is a legacy of both its positioning in the academic marketplace and a reflection of changing times bringing new issues onto the international political agenda.

IR's great debates

- **Great debate 1: 'Idealism' versus 'Realism'.** This controversy is said to have emerged in the formative years of the discipline between the First and Second World Wars, 1919–39. The 'winners' of the debate were the Realists who managed to depict the Idealists as head-in-the-cloud dreamers who overlooked the true nature of power politics in modern world. While Liberal-minded politicians such as Woodrow Wilson (see Chapter 2.1) worked for global peace and security, the League of Nations collapsed around them and the world plunged into a disastrous second global war in the space of 25 years. It did not take too much effort to convince students of IR that Realism 'was superior in its ability to rationally explain the persistent and ubiquitous struggle for power among nations' (Schmidt 2006: 11. See also Jackson and Sørensen 2007: 31–9).
- **Great debate 2: 'Behaviouralists' or 'scientists' versus 'Traditionalists'.** This debate emerged in the 1960s – after the Realists had 'won' the first debate in and around the period of the Second World War. It pitted behaviouralists who believed that IR could best be studied using methods drawn from the natural sciences against traditionalists 'who argued that the study of the social world was not amenable to the strict empirical methods of natural science' (Schmidt 2006: 11). It was a rehearsal, in fact, of the big debates about methodology that reach to the heart of many debates in social science disciplines. As such, there was no clear 'victor', as in the first debate (Jackson and Sørensen 2007: 40–2).
- **Great debate 3: Neorealists versus the rest?** This is a far harder debate to describe, not least because we are not fully clear about who was involved or what they were arguing about! For Schmidt, the third debate developed out of a crisis within Realism in the 1970s, which found its core assumptions being challenged by events 'on the ground' in international politics, economics and security. Scholars increasingly attacked the state-centrism of Realism and noted that state relations were characterized as much by interdependence between states as by their **independence** from one another. Schmidt suggests that it was within the context of a focus on interdependency and economic relations between states that the sub-field of International Political Economy (IPE) emerged (Schmidt 2006: 11). Jackson and Sørensen (2007: 42–52) portray

the third debate as the product of a range of new theories, notably those inspired by Marx (see Chapter 2.6) and the English School (see Chapter 2.4), coming to feast at the IR table.

* **Great debate 4: 'Post-positivists' versus 'Positivists'.** I have called this the fourth debate but for some writers (see Schmidt 2006: 12), this is the *genuine* 'third debate'. The post-positivists came to prominence in the 1980s and they were critical of all prior mainstream approaches to IR. Feminists, Critical Theorists and postmodernists/poststructuralists (all of whom we explore in this book) critiqued the positivist approaches of the dominant theorists in the field. What they effectively say is that the alleged third debate is a non-debate because all the approaches identified above share the same commitments to doing IR the positivist way. This is much more of a debate, therefore, because post-positivists 'address methodological issues (i.e. about *how to* approach the study of IR) ... and substantial issues (i.e. *which* issues should be considered the most important ones for IR to study)' (Jackson and Sørensen 2007: 53. Their emphases).

Having outlined the focal points of each of the 'great debates' about IR, we can immediately see the problems of trying to write the history of the field. Everyone agrees that debates about IR have occurred and will continue to occur about all sorts of philosophical, theoretical and empirical questions. But no-one can agree on how to capture the essence of these debates over time (Holden 2002). As soon as we try to put chronological boundaries or dividers between the debates, something of the complexity of the field gets lost – and this can present real problems when it comes to educating students about the state of the study of IR today and how it has reached this point.

When doing your course reading, note all the different ways writers tell the story of the discipline. You might even think of different disciplinary histories as different theories about how to tell the story of IR. What does this tell you about the nature and value of theory?

From great debates to the positivist-normative distinction

Having told the story of IR's 'great debates', Schmidt sets about critiquing the idea that such a simple story can be told. Most damagingly, he writes, 'it is not evident that all of the three debates actually took place'. Second, he questions whether our contemporaneous 'stylized' versions of the debates can do justice to the complex nature of the disputes that took place. Third, by focusing on the 'great' debates, he says we ignore other equally important and interesting disciplinary controversies that were taking place at the same time. And, finally, by telling the history of the field in this way we risk giving coherence to it where in fact none has existed (Schmidt 2006: 12).

In this light, is there a framework for studying IR theory within which we might explore key points of contestation amongst its scholars which makes it intelligible but which does not claim to tell a simple chrondogical history of the field? Any such framework will be open to criticism, but one way I have found useful is to shift away from the idea of three or four 'great debates', and instead present the story of the discipline as the unfolding of an argument between two approaches: **positivism**, on the one hand, and **normative theory**, on the other. Let us look first of all at what these terms mean and then we can think about how we might categorize each of the theories you will cover on your course.

- **Smith and Owens** (2008: 176–7): explanatory (positivist) theory 'sees the world as something external to our theories about it' while constitutive (normative) theory 'thinks our theories help construct the world'.
- **Burchill** (2001a: 1) uses the previous distinction to argue that positivist theory is only one kind of international theory and that theory 'means more than scientific or positivist formulations'. Normative theorists, he writes, 'are concerned with the social and political purposes of knowledge, the cognitive interests and assumptions of the observer and the way in which the principal actors construct their images of the political world'.
- **Devetak** (2001a: 147) uses Max Horkheimer's categorization between traditional (positivist) and critical (normative) theory. In traditional theory the theorist is removed from the object of analysis; assumes an external world 'out there'; achieves objectivity by withdrawing him/herself from the object of study and leaving behind ideology, beliefs and values that would invalidate the inquiry. Critical theories, by contrast, are always embedded in social and political life; they 'allow for an examination of the purposes and functions served by particular theories'. In other words, normative theorists combine conventional theory (a study of an event/process/issue) with meta-theory (theory about theory).
- **Jim George** (quoted in Zalewski and Enloe 1995: 299) notes that positivism assumes 'a cognitive reaction to reality' rather than it 'being integral to its construction'. In other words, theory 'takes place after the fact'. For normative theorists, by contrast, 'theory does not take place after the fact. Theories, instead, play a large part in constructing and defining what the facts are.'
- **Kimberley Hutchings** (1999: xiii and 1–2): 'the theorist does not operate in abstraction from the object of analysis' (positivism); normative theories are 'concerned with how to criticize, change and improve the world as it is'.

Table 1   The positivist-normative distinction

Positivism	Normative theory
Also known as explanatory or traditional theory	Also known as constitutive or critical theory
A contested term	A contested term
Empiricist: sensory experience 'provides the only legitimate source of knowledge' (Dunne et al. 2007: 338)	Focuses on: (1) fundamental values of international life; (2) the moral dimensions of international relations; and (3) the place of ethics in statecraft (Jackson and Sørensen 2007: 310)
Naturalist: Social scientists can emulate methods of natural scientists	Critiques positivist belief in naturalism
Belief in separation of facts from values	Collapses fact/value distinction

Taking these definitions together we can summarize the differences between positivist and normative approaches as shown in Table 1.

Can we use this distinction between positivist and normative approaches to map IR theories according to their methodological, epistemological and ontological leanings? Quite possibly we can sketch things as shown in Figure 8.

Merits and flaws in the theory map

The merits of this framework are as follows:

- **Avoids history** – By moving away from the story of 'great debates' we avoid having to worry about whether or not we can or even need to tell a neatly packaged chronological story about the evolution of the discipline. As Schmidt argues, this approach does a disservice, a violence even, both to the range and the nature of the disciplinary debates in the field at any given moment in its past.
- **Freedom to choose** – The relatively simple positivist-normative distinction gives students scope to make up their own minds about the evolution (the 'story') of the discipline. Rather than we as lecturers telling you the story, you have more freedom using this model to place the theories where you see fit.
- **Nature of story** – If you do believe there is a story to be told about IR, then how important in your story is the positivist-normative dispute? Or do you think that the Great Debates capture the story well enough?

Positivist Theories   Normative Theories

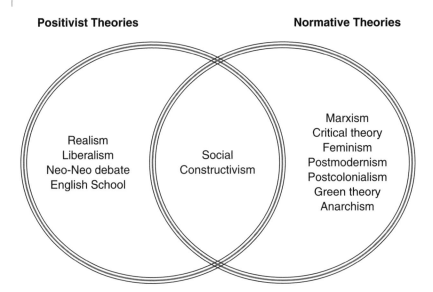

Figure 8   Mapping theories of IR

At the beginning of your course try setting out with my map in mind and as you go through the course try and identify writers within each theoretical tradition who might not fit my classification so easily. Use the map as a living document and move individual theorists around within it as you go.

There are two further questions that arise from a consideration of IR theory and its evolution over time; it is likely that some or all of them will appear in some form in the course of your lectures, seminars, coursework assignments and exams on IR theory. The first concerns how we judge the quality of competing theories and the second investigates the possibility of building an IR 'super-theory'.

How do we evaluate IR theories?

Neither the collapse of the Soviet Union, the Gulf War nor the ethnic conflicts in the Balkans were anticipated or adequately explained by any of the major traditions of speculation about international politics. (Burchill 2001a: 23)

Burchill's comment on the inadequacy of IR theories in predicting 'real-life' events raises big issues about our expectations for them. Should they be able to predict the timing and nature of the kinds of seismic international political events Burchill highlights? Or should we have more modest expectations about what theories can offer us by way of predictive capacity?

Comparing the relative strengths and weaknesses of theories is difficult. As Steve Smith puts it, 'they emerge from very different intellectual traditions' (2007: 8), making comparisons between them is tenuous at best and vacuous at worst. If all theoretical perspectives emphasize different facets of the world, centre their attention on different actors (in short, 'see' different worlds, 'read' the world differently), then Smith's point is well made. Choosing between theories comes down to a question of the tastes of the person doing the choosing because there is nothing inherent in the theories themselves that can make comparison in any way objective; it will be a subjective decision based on **aesthetics** as much as anything else.

Putting those admittedly acute problems aside, Burchill argues that in making our choice of which theory we prefer the following criteria need to be taken into consideration:

- understanding of an issue or process.
- explanatory power.
- success in predicting events.
- consistency and coherence.
- scope.
- capacity for critical self-reflection.
- engagement with contending theories.

At the beginning of your course, think carefully about which of Burchill's criteria you consider to be most important and why. Has he missed from this list any of the things we should expect of a valuable theory?

As you study each theory, score each of them out of 10 against the Burchill criteria. At the end of the course you will have a ranking order of theories you find most and least useful. Then ask yourself: why do I prefer the theories at the top of my list over those at the bottom? What does this tell us about the problems of weighing up competing theories? Is each of the Burchill criteria weighted the same, or are some more telling than others?

An IR super-theory?

After my lectures, students regularly come and ask me a deceptively simple question about IR theory. Assuming that no theory is perfect, they say, so that no theory can score a perfect 10 on the Burchill criteria above, can we take the best bits of each theory and put them together to make an all-in-one, comprehensive super-theory that would explain everything we need to know about world politics?

Smith calls this the 'pick and mix' or 'jigsaw' approach to thinking about IR theory. If we lay out the best bits of each theory, and leave aside their flaws, we can fit them together like a jigsaw puzzle which, when finished, gives us *the* definitive IR theory – we might use Realism to explain the persistence of inter-state conflict, Liberalism to explain inter-state co-operation in international organizations such as the EU, and Marxism to explain global economic exploitation of the underprivileged. Smith comments that this is an attractive idea and one that is extremely comforting for students who want to discover the 'right' answer (2007: 10–11).

Whether you think this a viable way forward depends once more on how you view the nature of the various IR theories on offer. On one hand, the jigsaw model assumes that all theories are **commensurable** – that they all see the same world but choose to expose and explain different aspects of it; in effect their ontological and epistemological positionings are the same. On the other hand, Smith's argument is that we should see IR theories as

> different coloured lenses: if you put one of them in front of your eyes, you will see things differently. Some aspects of the world will look the same in some senses, for example, shapes, but many other features, such as light and shades of colour, will look very different, so different in fact that they seem to show alternative worlds. (Smith 2007: 11)

The problem as Smith sees it is that no two theories are commensurable – they exist in different intellectual universes. Thus, piecing together a picture of the world from all the different theories is quite literally impossible.

The jigsaw model sets out an alluring way of discovering the ultimate IR theory – the one to beat all others. How valid do you think the model is? As you progress through your course try and keep the jigsaw idea in the back of your mind and note down key arguments in support of it and key arguments against. You will build up a bank of critical thought about the nature of IR theory that will be invaluable when it comes to 'big picture' essay and exam questions.

Questions to ponder

"Can we accurately tell the story of the evolution of IR as an academic discipline?"

This question invites one of several responses. Either you think we can tell a story about the evolution of the discipline, or we cannot, or that we can tell several stories in which case, your answer is both yes and no.

If you take either of the first two approaches, it is easy just to concentrate one side of the argument, but do not forget to include analysis of the counter-arguments. Knocking them down can you help make your case more convincing. More importantly, it will show your tutor that you have read around the subject and that you are aware of the broad sweep of the debate. Structuring an essay should not be too difficult because you can theme the opening part around the evidence to support your view; the second part will then be a deconstruction of the counter-arguments. The third answer (yes/no) is slightly harder to structure because you potentially have more to cover in the essay. Simply listing all the different types of story we could tell ('great debates'/positivism versus normative) will take a lot of words and could become merely a description of those stories. Think carefully about how you can fit in a serious engagement with the arguments of writers who challenge the idea of a neat story about the discipline.

Across all three types of response, the better student will show an appreciation of the importance of key words in the question, notably the ideas of 'accurately' telling a 'story'.

"How do you think we should judge the quality of different theories of IR?"

The key word in this question is 'quality'. Does it mean accuracy, scope, predictive capacity or empirical soundness? The question explicitly wants you to identify how *you* would go about judging such qualities, but do not feel compelled to devise a brand new set of criteria! You can happily draw on existing writers to make your case.

The obvious place to begin is with a writer like Burchill who lists his criteria and you could use that as a springboard from which to pull out the two or three criteria that you think are most important when evaluating theories. You might either or also (depending on the word limit and/or time in an exam) explore what practising IR theorists say about the nature and strength of their theories, as well as analysing their critiques of other theoretical traditions.

References to more information

BOOTH, K. AND SMITH, S. (EDS) (1995) *International Relations Theory Today.* Cambridge: Polity Press.
    Contains a thorough analysis (pp. 8–29) of the various ways in which we might tell the story of the discipline.
KUBÁLKOVÁ, V. (1998) 'The Twenty Years' Catharsis: E.H. Carr and IR', in V. Kubálková, N. Onuf and P. Kowert (eds) *International Relations in a Constructed World.* Armonk, NY: M.E. Sharpe.
    Includes a fascinating diagram (pp. 42–3) trying to map the discipline and considers the problems with doing this.
MORGENTHAU, H.J. (1972) *Science: Servant or Master?* New York: W.W. Norton.
    Explores the tensions between the worlds of academia (science; the pursuit of truth) and practice (the pursuit of power).
BUZAN, B. AND LITTLE, R. (2000) *International Systems in World History: Remaking the Study of International Relations.* Oxford: Oxford University Press.
    Thoroughgoing case for bringing history to the study of IR with an English School emphasis on how we theorize IR as 'international systems' (see Chapter 2.4 of this book for coverage of the English School).
REVIEW OF INTERNATIONAL STUDIES (2002) Interview with Kal Holsti by A. Jones, 28(3): 619–33.
    Holsti bemoans the fragmentation of the discipline of IR and as such acts as a counterpoint to the views of Steve Smith and others who see theoretical diversity as a source of empowerment.
TAUBER, A.I. (ED.) (1997) *Science and the Quest for Reality.* Basingstoke: Macmillan.
    See especially the editor's introduction and the chapters by Larry Laudan (on theories of scientific knowledge) and Hilary Putnam (on facts and values).
HENRY, J. (2002) *The Scientific Revolution and the Origins of Modern Science*, 2nd edn. Basingstoke. Palgrave.
RUSSELL, B. (1948) *Sceptical Essays.* London: George Allen and Unwin.

A work of philosophy which deals, amongst other things, with the value of taking a sceptical attitude to knowledge, 'dreams and facts', the super-stitions of science, rationality and the psychology of politics. Particularly useful if you have never read a 'straight' work of philosophy because it helps you think about the big issues in the human pursuit of knowledge.

OLSON, W.C. AND GROOM, A.J.R. (1991) *International Relations Then and Now: Origins and Trends in Interpretation*. London: HarperCollins.

BLAIKIE, N. (2007) *Approaches to Social Inquiry*, 2nd edn. Cambridge: Polity.

Written for a general social science audience, the second chapter is excel-lent on whether social scientists can or should borrow methods and approaches from natural scientists.

ZIMA, PETER V. (2007) *What is Theory?: The Concept of Theory in the Social and Cultural Sciences*. London: Continuum.

An advanced text exploring different understandings of 'theory', including positivist, constructivist and postmodern approaches.

WIGHT, C. (2006) 'Philosophy of Social Science and International Relations', in W. Carlsnaes, T. Risse and B.A. Simmons (eds) *Handbook of International Relations*. London: Sage, pp. 22–51.

A study of the sometimes uneasy status of philosophical questions within the field of IR.

WALTZ, K.N. (1979) *Theory of International Politics*, 1st edn. Boston, MA: Mcgraw Hill.

Especially the opening chapter on the nature of theory and how we test them.

part two

theories of IR

In Part 1 you were introduced to the big debates that have shaped the study of IR over its years as a formal discipline of academic inquiry. These range from the philosophical (the kinds of knowledge we produce about IR) to the empirical (what subjects IR should cover). Part 2 introduces you to all the main IR theories you are likely to encounter on your course. Feel free to dip in and out as you see fit and do not be afraid of looking into theories not directly covered on your course. The more widely you can read around the subject of IR, the more you will understand the debates these writers are engaged in and the better able you will be to express the disagreements between them in your coursework essays and exam answers.

A word of warning: each chapter below tries to summarize in a couple of thousand words theories about which millions of words have been written. I put forward my interpretation of each tradition in the knowledge that it can easily be contested, and in fact that has been part of the challenge for me when writing this book. I have had to answer two central questions you as students will face when putting together your essays and exam answers. How do I define each theoretical tradition? What do I leave out? So, I present my overview not just in the *expectation* that you will be able to challenge the story I tell you as you do more and more reading, but in the *hope* that you will. Bear in mind that this book is as much about how to think about IR theory as it is about delivering you knowledge about each theory, and it is in that spirit that I have tackled each theory.

These chapters on each of the theories can only give you a very brief introduction to them; it is up to you to delve further into each theory. There is no better way than reading the landmark texts – these give you a real insight into the hopes and ambitions for each theory set out by their leading exponents.

Core areas:

2.1

liberalism

Key terms:

Anarchy
State
Peace
Democracy
Co-operation
Interdependence
Progress

In this chapter we explore the founding theory of IR: Liberalism, which grew out of a much wider political theory. We will put this theory in context by considering first the Liberal tradition, second the impact of the First World War on thinking about IR and, finally, the Liberal resurgence after the Second World War.

The Liberal tradition

Like many theories you will study on your course, Liberal IR theory traces its roots back way beyond the establishment of the discipline in 1919. It draws on centuries' worth of political theory and political/economic philosophy and applies these to the study of relations between states. Inspiration for Liberal IR theory has come from various countries and periods and flows from the practice as well as the study of politics. Key Liberal thinkers you might encounter on your course include Erasmus (1466–1536), Hugo Grotius (1583–1635), John Locke (1632–1704), Adam Smith (1723–1790), Immanuel Kant (1724–1804), Jeremy Bentham (1748–1832) and Abraham Lincoln (1809–65).

Across the Liberal writers identified above we see many themes intertwining and recurring over time. To pick out some of the most significant for our purposes (see Dunne 2008: 112–16 and Burchill 2001b: 32–7), we can break Liberal ideas down into three categories (Figure 9). Having done

On war

- War is not the natural condition of international relations.

- Peace is normal.

- National interests safeguarded by more than military means.

On governance

- Democracy is necessary for the perfectibility of human beings to be allowed to develop.

- States not the main actors on the international stage.

- States not unitary actors.

- Interdependence between states a key feature of international relations.

On human nature

- Human beings are perfectible.

- Faith in the power of human reason.

- Faith in the power of humans to realize their inner potential.

- Belief in progress (scientific/ technological/moral/social).

Figure 9   The Liberal tradition

that we will trace how Liberal ideas were moulded into a distinctive theory of IR after the First World War.

Jackson and Sørensen's description (2007: 98) of the Liberal tradition in IR is that it is 'optimistic'. We can see why they say this from the above characteristics of Liberal thought. The unifying theme across all these writers is that progress is possible via 'modernization' – of economies, of technology, of human morality and of communication within and between states. Humans, Liberals assert, possess the crucial power of reason 'and when they apply it to international affairs greater cooperation will be the result' (Jackson and Sørensen 2007: 99). In this context, peace, progress and human advancement are all possible, even in a situation in which there are distinct entities known as states, each with their own languages, traditions, histories and political set-ups. As Jennifer Sterling-Folker puts it (2006a: 56, her emphasis), Liberal IR theorists take the same starting assumptions as Realist theorists (see Chapter 2.2) and investigate 'what *prevents* progress from being achieved, with the underlying assumption being that progress could be realized if we could uncover the barriers to collective action and promote their resolutions'.

Liberalism after the First World War

The study of IR after its 'founding' as an academic discipline in 1919 became closely enmeshed with a fertile period in Liberal thought about the relations between states in the aftermath of the Great War. What, people asked, had been the ultimate value of that conflict? How had states slid into such a disastrous war seemingly against their will? Why had these same states persisted in sending thousands of their citizens to their death for apparently minimal gains over the years 1914–18? Early scholars of IR set about trying to find answers to just such questions.

A key player in helping Liberal theory become central to the early study of IR was Woodrow Wilson, a former political scientist and President of the US when the country decided to intervene, decisively, in the First World War in 1917. In a speech to Congress in January 1918, Wilson said he wanted to make the world 'fit and safe to live in; and particularly that it be made safe for every peace-loving nation which, like our own, wishes to live its own life, determine its own institutions, be assured of justice and fair dealing by the other peoples of the world as against force and selfish aggression' (Wilson 1918). He proceeded to outline his 'Fourteen Point' programme which provides us with a vivid insight into how Liberals perceive international affairs.

To give you a flavour of his thinking he demanded:

- **Point I. 'Open covenants of peace, openly arrived at'** – a call for open and honest diplomacy; this would help get round the problem of secret alliances which entangled states in war seemingly against their better judgement.
- **Point III. Removal of economic barriers** – the establishment of free trade among all states consenting to the peace.
- **Points V–XIII. National self-determination** – incorporating a call for the dismantling of empires.
- **Point XIV. Association of nations** – coming together to guarantee 'political independence' and 'territorial integrity' (Wilson 1918).

Liberal Internationalism is sometimes known as 'Idealism'. You might also find it called Classical Liberalism or Utopian Liberalism. Keep a note of all the different labels you come across and the characteristics writers ascribe to those various theoretical positions.

The high contracting parties, in order to promote international co-operation and to achieve international peace and security

- by the acceptance of obligations not to resort to war

- by the prescription of open, just and honourable relations between nations

- by the firm establishment of the understandings of international law as the actual rule of conduct among Governments, and

- by the maintenance of justice and a scrupulous respect for all treaty obligations in the dealings of organized peoples with one another

Agree to this Covenant of the League of Nations.

Figure 10   Preamble to the Covenant of the League of Nations
Source: (Yale Law School 2007)

Wilson was a key player in the establishment of the League of Nations via the Paris Peace Conference of 1919. His view was that there was not necessarily a harmony of interests between states, but that international order could be constructed with the help, crucially, of international organizations, which would promote diplomacy, co-operation and the rule of law. The League of Nations is a concrete example of the widespread appeal and political influence of Liberal thought in the immediate aftermath of the First World War: note the Wilsonian leanings evident in Figure 10.

Crucially, the League was helped into existence via 'solid political backing from the most powerful state in the international system at the time': the US (Jackson and Sørensen 2007: 33). When American support for the League ebbed away in the coming years, it fell somewhat into disrepute, indicating that 'in practice states remained imprisoned by self-interest' (Dunne 2008: 114). It is a huge irony that the US decided, for domestic reasons, not to join the institution it had created and the League quickly became a 'talking shop' shorn of real international political clout and legitimacy. Adolf Hitler's aggressive diplomacy and military expansionism in the 1930s effectively exposed the League's weaknesses and, the story goes, 'dealt a fatal blow to Idealism' (Dunne 2008: 114).

> Note the connection between the rise of a theory and the international events occurring at the time it becomes popular. What does this tell you about the nature of IR theory?

Liberalism after the Second World War

There is an interesting parallel to be drawn between the real and lasting surge in Liberal thought after the First World War and the resurgence of those same ideas after the Second World War. After 1945, there was a renewal of Liberal efforts to create international organizations for the promotion of peace, prosperity and security at both the global and regional levels. However, Liberals had learnt that they needed to be a bit more hard-headed about what they said and did to take account of the realities of international politics, so after 1945 they spoke a more 'pragmatic' language of IR (Dunne 2008: 114). We will briefly explore the origins and nature of two such bodies, the United Nations (UN) and the European Union (EU), before showing how these renewed efforts to manage inter-state relations came from, and injected new lifeblood into, Liberal thought.

The United Nations

- **Origins.** Successor to the League of Nations which 'ceased its activities after failing to prevent World War Two' (UN 2005). The UN Charter was drawn up in 1945 by representatives of 50 countries, and the UN officially came into existence on 24 October 1945 when the Charter was ratified by China, France, the Soviet Union, the United Kingdom, the United States and a majority of the other 50 signatories (UN 2005). Compare the preamble to the Charter of the United Nations (Figure 11) with the preamble to the Covenant of the League of Nations (Figure 10).
- **Growth.** The number of states in the international arena has grown rapidly since 1945, helped by the decolonization of former Empires such as the British and the French, and the end of the Cold War in 1989. With the accession of Montenegro in June 2006, the UN membership totalled some 192 states (UN 2006a).

We the people of the United Nations determined

- to save succeeding generations from the scourge of war, which twice in our lifetime has brought untold sorrow to mankind, and

- to reaffirm faith in fundamental human rights, in the dignity and worth of the human person, in the equal rights of men and women and of nations large and small, and

- to establish conditions under which justice and respect for the obligations arising from treaties and other sources of international law can be maintained, and

- to promote social progress and better standards of life in larger freedom ...

Have resolved to combine our efforts to accomplish these aims.

Figure 11   Preamble to the Charter of the United Nations
Source: (UN 2005)

- **Aims and activities.** The activities of the UN are guided by its initial aims (Figure 11) and they have expanded along with the number and diversity of the political, economic, social and cultural issues that have forced their way on to the global agenda since 1945.

Take a look at the structure of the UN (2006b) and you can see its sheer presence on the world stage at all sorts of levels and in relations to all sorts of issues.

Media coverage of the UN's role in trying to resolve international disputes (for example, the question of the existence of Weapons of Mass Destruction in Iraq in 2001–3) can skew our impression of what the UN does. Using its website, make a list of some of the key economic, social and cultural programmes run by the UN and this will help you understand more about the breadth and scale of its activities.

The European Union

The EU as we know it today was formally brought into being by the Maastricht Treaty (1993). But the EU did not 'start' then. Maastricht (and subsequent revisions such as Amsterdam 1999 and the Lisbon Treaty 2008) extended and formalized processes of integration that had begun in the 1950s. It was this growth and development of institutions for European co-operation in the early post-war years that helped drive Liberal Institutionalism. We will briefly review these developments before summarizing what these two case studies tell us about this particular strand of Liberal thinking. Three key developments took place in terms of European co-operation in the 1950s:

1 **European Coal and Steel Community (ECSC)** – Based on the Schuman Plan of May 1950, in April 1951 six countries in western Europe (France, Germany, Italy, Belgium, the Netherlands and Luxembourg) announced that they were to pool their coal and steel resources and run those industries under a common management. Its aim was to end 'the frequent and bloody wars between neighbours, which culminated in the Second World War' (Europa undated).

2 **European Defence Community (EDC)** – In June 1950 France announced a further plan to place military forces from consenting states in Europe under a single command. The EDC had internal and external security dimensions. Internally it sought to ensure security in Europe by containing German forces within European as opposed to national military structures. Externally it sought to help defend Europe against possible attack from the Soviet Union by promoting military rearmament by leading European nation-states. The EDC collapsed in 1954 when the French parliament failed to ratify the treaty. Key among many concerns was the loss of French sovereignty or decision-making authority over its military forces (Ruane 2000).

3 **European Economic Community (EEC)** – Undeterred by the failure of the EDC, the six countries that developed the ECSC extended integration to many other sectors of their economies in 1957 with the Treaty of Rome, which aimed to enhance the free movement of people, goods and services across borders. As with the ECSC, the EEC used financial means to secure a political end: lasting peace and prosperity through economic co-operation. The EEC was renamed the EU in 1993 after the ratification of the Maastricht Treaty.

Liberal Institutionalism grew directly out of the efforts by states to co-operate by coming together in international organizations such as the UN and the EU. The latter provided particularly fertile ground for theoretical innovation and has come to be associated with two writers in particular:

- **David Mitrany**. Worked on the theory of **functionalist integration theory** after the First World War. 'Functionalism is concerned with the ways of creating... a working peace system. It involves a diagnosis of the problems of disorder in international society, and a prescription for ways of shaping a better world' (Groom and Taylor 1975: 1). Mitrany argued (1933) that state authority in the modern era has been challenged as humans have begun to find solutions to shared security, economic and political concerns across state borders, rather than working within the confines of those borders. Such efforts would increase as individuals saw the benefits of collective endeavours and this interdependence would then lead to peace and further integration across state borders through what has become known as the 'spillover' effect of integration.

Functionalists assume (Groom and Taylor 1975: 3–4):

1. Economic development promotes shared and recognizable values.
2. There is a need to develop mechanisms for the delivery of individual welfare across state borders.
3. That states are not necessarily the best way of organizing society.

- **Ernst B. Haas**. Developed Mitrany's ideas via **Neo-functionalist integration theory** after the Second World War. In *The Uniting of Europe* (2003, first published in 1958) and *Beyond the Nation-State* (1964), Haas argued that Mitrany had gone too far in theorizing integration at the global level. Integration at the regional level, however, could provide the kind of results Mitrany had predicted via spillover from lower levels of integration (economic/social) to higher levels (political). Such 'spillover' came from two forces. One was functionalist, as co-operation in one lower level issue led to co-operation in a related area. The other is political, as the creation of supranational organizations such as the UN and EU propelled integration forward into newer, possibly more politically sensitive areas such as defence and security.

The work on functionalism by Mitrany and Haas set about applying Liberal assumptions to the post-1945 world of international relations. Their ideas and associated work in the realm of interdependence, international institutions and international governance (most famously Moravcsik 1998) draw on centuries-old Liberal ideas about human nature, the organization of states, the causes of wars and how to manage inter-state relations in an apparently conflict-ridden international system. The major challenge to Liberal IR theory in the formative years of the discipline came from the Realists, and we will explore their take on IR in the next chapter. In Chapter 2.3 we will look in a bit more detail at the key developments that took place within each theory after the Second World War.

Questions to ponder

"Why did the First World War provide such an impetus to the development of Liberal IR theory?"

There are a couple of promising approaches you might take when faced with this question. One is to use the literatures on the origins of the discipline which we explored in Chapter 1.4 to trace the overlap between the worlds of academia and practice which came together in 1919 to produce the discipline of IR we know today. From here you would study the early agenda of the discipline as being normatively concerned with the promotion of peace, perhaps using a figure such as Woodrow Wilson as an exemplar of this early Liberal thinking. A second approach might be to focus more centrally on the Liberal agenda and key themes in Liberal IR theory in the inter-war years. This is a reverse of the first approach because you begin with the theory and work back to the impact of war, rather than the other way round.

> When answering questions containing references to momentous events like the First World War, it is tempting to 'pad' the essay out with lots of details about the event in question. In this example, the question does not ask for a history of the First World War, so only include as much as you need to make your point. You will get all your marks for demonstrating knowledge about Liberalism as opposed to the detail of the unfolding of the Great War.

However you answer this question you might also want to include elements of the Liberal agenda which pre-dated the war, helping you to a sophisticated argument that the war accentuated aspects of Liberal thought but did not provide their 'origins' in any simple sense.

"Does the existence of the EU bear out the accuracy of Liberal theories of IR?"

This question invites you to consider the relationship between the theory and practice of IR as far as the formation of international organizations goes. As with the previous question you will have to strike a balance between the detail you include on the history and development of the EU and the room you set aside for developing your response to the question. If you are ever in doubt about how much background material to put in an essay, a useful rule of thumb is: if in doubt, leave out. Your tutor will not want a history of the EU and all its treaties from 1957 to the present day. He/she will knock marks off if this forms the bulk of your focus in the essay and will be much kinder if your essay is balanced in favour of critical analysis of the questions.

Your answer will very much depend on your 'reading' of IR since 1945. Has the growth in the number and influence of international institutions like the EU (and the UN for that matter) stopped states from going to war, once and for all? Or have they only helped reduce the likelihood, without changing basic features of the international states system? Whatever you choose to argue, make sure you set your main case out in the introduction and follow it through logically in the rest of the essay towards a conclusion (see Chapters 3.3 and 3.4 on good essay writing). It is much easier to answer this question when you know about Realist IR theory which we are covering in the Chapter 2.2, because Realists criticize Liberals for placing too much emphasis on the power of international organizations to alter fundamental state interests in security and survival. In an essay you would want to mention this element of the dispute between the two traditions as a way of framing your own argument and giving critical depth to your answer.

References to more information

Inter-war Liberalism:

ANGELL, N. (1909) *The Great Illusion*. London: Weidenfeld and Nicolson.
Argued against the then popular view that war was profitable for states by showing how, in fact, it undermined prosperity by disrupting or destroying commercial and political ties between states.

WOOLF, L. (1933) *The Intelligent Man's Way to Prevent War*. London: Gollancz.
Encapsulates the essence of inter-war Liberalism. Note its gendered title (see Chapter 2.8 in this book).

CURRY, W.B. (1939) *The Case for Federal Union*. Harmondsworth: Penguin.

ASHWORTH, L. (2006) 'Where are the Idealists in Interwar International Relations?', *Review of International Studies*, 32(3): 291–308.

Argues lucidly against the conventional tendency in IR to identify the idealist tradition in IR between the two World Wars. For more historical context see also

Sylvest, C. (2005) 'Continuity and Change in British Liberal Internationalism, c. 1900–1930', *Review of International Studies*, 31(2): 263–83.

Overviews of the League of Nations, the UN and the EU:

KENNEDY, P. (2007) *The Parliament of Man: The United Nations and the Quest for World Government*. London: Allen Lane.

KNOCK, T.J. (1995) *To End All Wars: Woodrow Wilson and the Quest for a New World Order*. Princeton, NJ: Princeton University Press.

OSTROWER, G.B. (1997) *The League of Nations: From 1919 to 1929*. Garden City Park, NY: Avery Publishing Group.

PINDER, J. AND USHERWOOD, S. (2007) *The European Union: A Very Short Introduction*. Oxford: Oxford University Press.

BACHE, I. AND GEORGE, S. (2006) *Politics in the European Union*, 2nd edn. Oxford: Oxford University Press.

See Part 1 on theories of integration and Part 2 on the history of the organization.

HILL, C. AND SMITH, M. (EDS) (2005) *The International Relations of the European Union*. Oxford: Oxford University Press.

On Functionalism and Neo-functionalism:

GHÉBALI, V. (1975) 'The League of Nations and Functionalism', in A.J.R. Groom and P. Taylor, *Functionalism: Theory and Practice in International Relations*. London: University of London Press, pp. 141–61.

HAAS, E.B. AND WHITING, A.S. (1975) *Dynamics of International Relations*. Westport, CT: Greenwood Press.

Makes the case for the Liberal approach to IR; see especially Chapters 1–3.

ROSAMOND, B. (2000). *Theories of European Integration*. Basingstoke: Macmillan.

Overview of integration theories, including functionalism and neo-functionalism.

To give you a general flavour of what themes in IR exercise Liberals:

FRANCESCHET, A. (2001) 'Sovereignty and Freedom: Immanuel Kant's Liberal Internationalist "Legacy"', *Review of International Studies*, 27(2): 209–28.

MCGREW, A. (2002) 'Liberal Internationalism: Between Realism and Cosmopolitanism', in D. Held and A. McGrew (eds) *Governing Globalization: Power, Authority and Global Governance*. Cambridge: Polity, pp. 267–89.

Maps the Liberal tradition from the 1800s and unpicks its different strands.

BERTELSEN J. (ED.) (1977) *Non-state Nations in International Politics: Comparative Systems Analysis*. New York and London: Praeger.

A fascinating collection of essays on what are called in the book 'Non-state Nations': entities that operate as if they were nation-states but which are not confined to territorial borders, for example, the Palestinian Arabs, the Zionist Movement and the Basques. All serves to undermine the state-centricity of Realist IR theory and therefore offers much food for thought.

RISSE-KAPPEN, T. (1995) *Bringing Transnational Relations Back In: Non-State Actors, Domestic Structures and International Institutions*. Cambridge: Cambridge University Press.

Uses case studies in economics, about multinational corporations, security-building, and social and environmental movements to show that we cannot explain state behaviour without taking the cross-border activities of these non-state actors into account.

AXFORD, B., BROWNING, G.K., HUGGINS, R. AND ROSAMOND, B. (2006) *Politics: An Introduction* 2nd edn. London: Routledge.

Chapter 15 by Axford gives you a succinct overview of the processes and impacts of globalization, as well as a short section on backlashes against it which help you begin thinking about Marxist IR theory (Chapter 2.6 in this book).

2.2	
realism	

Key terms:

Anarchy
State
Power
Human nature
Interest
Reality

Liberal IR theorists tend to adopt an optimistic approach to explaining the relations between states in a condition of international anarchy. For Liberals, the potential for conflict between states is diminished, but not ruled out altogether, by a process of co-operation that results from states engaging in international organizations such as the UN and the EU. Such institutions act as forums for communication, open diplomacy and the peaceful resolution of disputes and they help engender adherence to peaceable norms of behaviour. The democratic organization of these bodies promotes the free expression of their members and, through that, permits the essential goodness of men and women in different states to be harnessed for the common good. For Liberals, international anarchy is a real and pressing concern, but it does not necessarily lead to states continually knocking against each other like balls on a snooker table.

Realists take a quite different approach, one that we might describe as pessimistic. They begin at the same place – explaining state behaviour in a condition of international anarchy. But the basic units of analysis and the central problem to be explained are the only things the two sets of theorists share. From here the two traditions diverge dramatically over the consequences for international relations: where Liberals see co-operation as the likely outcome, Realists see the perpetual threat of conflict and war (Figure 12).

Why do the two theories share the same beginning but end up with two almost polar opposite views of IR? Exploring the basic tenets of Realist IR theory will help us find out why.

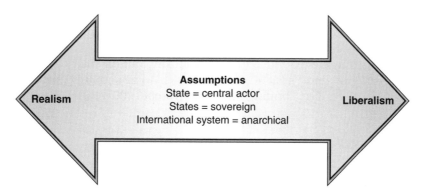

Figure 12   Same startpoint, different endpoints

Realists on human nature

We saw in our survey of the Liberal tradition that the essential goodness of human beings was the starting point for much Liberal thought. In order to understand state-on-state relations, Liberals extrapolate up from this essential goodness at the lowest level of international affairs to the level of the international system: people do not want to fight each other unnecessarily and if their opinions can be voiced democratically to their governments, co-operation can and will occur at the international level through the medium of international institutions. But what if human beings are not peace-loving? What if they are aggressive? What stops them if they wish to do harm to others? It is on this other side of the coin that Realist theory operates.

Hobbes and the state of nature

An excellent way to get to grips with the basics of Realist thought is to see how the English political and legal philosopher Thomas Hobbes (1588–1679) viewed the dynamics of political life. His 1651 work *Leviathan* contains an analysis of human nature which has become central to Realist IR theory. Hobbes tried to think through what the world would be like in a 'state of nature' – a world in which men and women live together but before the 'invention' of sovereign states.

In such a world humans revert to animalistic behaviour because this is a world in which no-one is safe from the potentially harmful behaviour of others. As Jackson and Sørensen put it (2007: 65) 'life is constantly at risk, and nobody can be confident about his or security and survival for any reasonable length of time. People are living in constant fear of each other.' In a state of nature there is nothing to regulate people's behaviour; no consequences for uncivilized behaviour towards others. This Hobbesian world of self-interested individuals only looking out for their own safety and security produces a 'state of war' in which, as he famously puts it, life is 'solitary, poor, nasty, brutish, and short' (Hobbes 2007: Part 1, Book 13).

Hobbes and the international state of nature

The Hobbesian world is not a nice one. Unfortunately, he argued, things do not get much better when people come together to try and get around the problems of living in this state of nature. In order to overcome their mutual fear, one approach is to create states in which men and women agree not to harm each other. These states are ruled by sovereign governments that have the 'absolute authority and credible power to protect them from both internal disorders and foreign enemies and threats' (Jackson and Sørensen 2007: 65). However, when different groups of men and women constitute themselves into distinct states to overcome their fear of each other, we then have the creation of a state of nature *between* all these different states. Where before it was people living in fear for their own livelihoods and security, it is now states experiencing this same fear. This is the classic Realist **security dilemma**: the enhancement of security at the domestic level (within states) goes hand in hand with the creation of insecurity at the international level. Anarchy within states is replaced by anarchy at the international level.

Hobbes gave IR theorists two key concepts: self-help and security dilemma. As you go through your course make a note of how each theorist you study uses (or not) these concepts. What do they mean by them and why are they more important in some theories than others?

Why is it different at the international level – why can states not come together to resolve their mutual security issues as men and women can? The main difference is in the parties to the contract. Whereas individuals are happy to give up some of their independence to a state government in return for a resolution of their personal security dilemmas, 'sovereign states are not willing to give up their independence for the sake of any global security guarantee' (Jackson and Sørensen 2007: 66). Why is this? Because the international state of nature is not perceived to be as threatening to states as the original state of nature is perceived to be to men and women living in it. States are better placed to provide for their security than are the individuals in a state of nature because they are less vulnerable – Jackson and Sørensen point out, for example (2007: 66), that unlike men and women states do not have to sleep, they can be permanently on the alert and have more means by which to fend off potential attackers.

Hobbesian or classical Realism attributes human characteristics to states: it is **reductionist**. How realistic do you think it is to explain state behaviour in the same way we explain human behaviour? What do the two have in common – or is the state of nature the main influence on the behaviour of both?

Realists on power

If you are a human living in the original state of nature or a state existing in the international state of nature, it is obviously useful to have 'power' of some kind to help you out, either to protect you from the aggression of other humans/states or to enable you to extract what you want from other humans/states.

'Power' is another of those IR terms that crops up in many theories. Make a note of all the different ways in which it is understood by theorists. How many different definitions can you find and why is it such a popular word in IR?

Where does the interest in power come from and how does it feature in Realist IR theory? We can find out how by looking at how three Realist writers, one classical and two modern, use power to inform their explanations of IR.

The 'timeless wisdom' of Thucydides

Thucydides was a fifth century Athenian general who wrote *History of the Peloponnesian War* between Athens and Sparta in 431–04 BC (Thucydides 2004). This work of history has inspired many a Realist to take a 'tragic view of life and politics' across a period of over 2,500 years (Lebow 2007:54.) Claiming a timeless wisdom to Thucydides' work gives Realists a real propaganda coup when it comes to attracting support for their theories because they can portray them as being applicable far beyond 'any condition or attribute of the modern world... but... as a central feature of prior epochs as well' (Sterling-Folker 2006e: 15).

Thucydides tells a story of an age of a few 'great powers' and many lesser powers, an inequality that was 'considered to be inevitable and natural' (Jackson and Sørensen 2007: 62). Thucydides' harsh dictum was that in order to survive and prosper, states of all sizes had to adapt to the reality they found themselves in and conduct themselves accordingly to stay safe – from here you can trace a line to Hobbes' international state of nature. Here, Thucydides opened the way for a discussion of morality and justice in the conduct of foreign policy that later Realists such as Hans Morgenthau would build upon (see below).

Most textbook treatments of Thucydides concentrate on the same passage from the 'Melian dialogue' of 416 BC where he highlights how power relations played out between the powerful Athenians and the weaker Melians. Yet it is not simply what Thucydides said but his whole approach to writing his history that should be of interest to you in terms of your understanding of the Realist tradition in IR. Gregory Crane makes this point well by writing that 'Thucydides' *History* exhibits four characteristics common to many "realist" schools of thought—not only political, but literary, artistic, and scientific' (Crane 1998, Chapter 2). Realism, like all IR theories you will cover, is much more than a list of foreign policy maxims. It is a way of seeing the world and of writing about it and studying Thucydides can be doubly instructive for that very reason. Let us take each of Crane's observations in turn (Crane 1998, chapter 2).

1 **Procedural Realism**. Thucydides 'insisted upon a high level of observational accuracy', involving 'careful observation and precise reporting'. He castigates previous historians (such as Herodotus on the Persian wars) for inaccuracies and located himself firmly in what we know as the positivist tradition of assuming a world external from him which he could experience and report on accurately.

2 **Scientific Realism**. Follows from procedural realism. Thucydides was well aware of the methodological problems he encountered in trying to report accurately the evolution of the Peloponnesian War, but was convinced that such a task was possible. He wrote of examining 'the facts themselves' to get at the truth of this long conflict.

3 **Ideological Realism**. In setting his account against less faithful or accurate histories, Thucydides could claim that only he had 'a monopoly on truth'. He placed his work directly in opposition to 'idealism', which he took to mean 'the pursuit of an attractive, but ultimately ill-founded, vision of the world'. By stressing his emotional detachment, Thucydides could claim a special authority for his work that he denied to fanciful histories not rooted in observed facts and faithfully reported. Unlike those imagined histories Thucydides dealt with the 'real world'.

4 **Paradigmatic Realism**. Using a word popularized by the philosopher of science, Thomas Kuhn, Crane suggests we should see Thucydides' self-proclaimed advances towards objective history as a shift in **paradigm**. Thucydides set down a new method for history and set new benchmarks by which histories should be judged. But in doing so, things got lost, methods forgotten, facts overlooked. For example, Thucydides privileged military and political history; he ignored the role of

women in Greek society and the conduct of the war. Thucydides' new paradigm claimed objectivity, completeness and impartiality, but like all paradigms of scientific inquiry, we find that we perhaps see what we want to see. Can social scientific inquiry ever be impartial?

Realism in the inter-war years

Echoes of both the style and the substance of Thucydides' *History* are to be found in much subsequent Realist literature. Two writers are of interest to us in this regard: E.H. Carr and Hans Morgenthau.

E.H. Carr

Carr's opinions on international relations were held in high regard because of his connections to both the political and academic worlds. He worked as a diplomat in the British Foreign Office between 1916 and 1936. As we have seen already (see Chapter 1.4) these were tragic decades with regard to the First World War and its aftermath, and crucial years in the formation of IR as a distinct discipline of academic study. Carr's attitudes to international relations were strongly influenced by both sets of events. In 1936, Carr resigned from the Foreign Office to take up a Chair (Professorship) in International Relations at what was then Aberystwyth University. While a student at Cambridge University, it might well be noteworthy that Carr had studied Herodotus' account of the Persian Wars and was clearly acquainted with the work of Thucydides (Carr 2001b: xi, 81 and 104).

A 'sustained critique of the way in which utopian thought had dominated international relations in the inter-war years' (Hollis and Smith 1991: 21). This is how Martin Hollis and Steve Smith correctly summarize the crux of E.H. Carr's *The Twenty Years' Crisis* (2001a), which was first published in 1939. What did Carr mean by 'utopian thought' and why did he attack it? Carr was dissatisfied with the key tenets of inter-war Liberal thought we identified in Chapter 2.1. He branded it 'utopian' in order to contrast it with an approach he deemed more 'realistic' – Realism. According to what Carr took to be utopian thought, human progress is achieved by essential human goodness being allowed to flourish in democratic states. These democratic processes are replicated and enhanced at the international level through international organizations where disputes can be resolved peacefully through dialogue between states.

For Carr, however, *willing* world peace was not the same as *achieving* world peace. Practical products of Liberal thought, such as the League of Nations, did not take into account realities that had to be dealt with in the world of foreign policy-making such as power, cunning and the use of force. Thus, Carr argued that Liberals had got everything the wrong way round. Instead of developing a theory (of human nature and IR) and trying to mould reality to fit the theory, they should be looking at the reality and fitting the theory to explain it.

On your IR course you are more than likely to find Carr presented as a founding father of the classical Realist tradition in the UK and US, so it is well worth looking at the 2001 version of *The Twenty Years' Crisis*. This contains an excellent introduction by Michael Cox that interrogates the easy assumption that Carr was a Realist thinker.

Carr's context: a Realist reality

The reality of the interwar years in Carr's eyes was one in which the condition of international anarchy led inexorably to war and conflict in the international system. That his book was first published on the eve of the Second World War (1939–45) must have helped convince his audiences in the political and academic worlds that international reality in 1919–39 was a Realist rather than a Liberal reality.

Two issues in particular helped persuade Carr of this conclusion. First, the collapse of the League of Nations undermined Liberalism's explanation of international political relations. Established in accordance with Wilsonian principles in 1919, the outbreak of the Second World War confirmed what many had feared for many years previously – that the League did not have the diplomatic, political or military clout to prevent inter-state wars. The rise and actions of the Axis powers, Germany, Italy and Japan, further showed Carr the truth of the Thucydidean principle that 'might is right' – the powerful do what they want, the weak do what they can.

Second, the Great Depression in the US, and the global recession it produced, undermined Liberalism's claim that free trade would bring about harmonious international economic relations between states. Economic statistics from this period offer a glimpse of the scale of the depression: US unemployment rose from 3 per cent in 1929 to over 25 per cent in 1933 (Darby, cited in Schenk 1997–2006). Over the same four-year period, US

Gross National Product halved from well over $100 billion per quarter to just over $50 billion per quarter (Moore, cited in Schenk 1997–2006). In Carr's view, interwar international economic disorder on this scale showed the frailty of the assumption that letting the free market do its work would promote global economic harmony as the Liberals suggested. What was called for was new economic thinking, and this meant interventionist policies to promote full employment, equality and social justice. Carr was helped to this view by the success of the Russian five-year economic plans from 1929, which contrasted sharply with the downturn in the capitalist world over the same period.

Carr: summary

On both the political and economic fronts Carr did not see much evidence in the 'reality' he observed to support Liberal thinking in the years 1919–39. The League of Nations had failed to prevent self-interested states such as Germany run amok while free market principles had been undermined by the Great Depression. In both cases, Carr saw the case for new superstructures to be devised which would take account of the realities of insecurity, inequality and the uneven distribution of power in an anarchic international environment.

Realism after the Second World War: Morgenthau

As Robert Jervis has observed, 'the experience of Hitler was a greater sponsor of Realism than any written text could be' (Jervis 1994), and although Carr went a long way to expounding the core principles of the Realist tradition, it was left to Hans Morgenthau to develop them in a rigorous 'scientific' fashion.

Morgenthau was a German émigré to the US who arrived there two years before the outbreak of the Second World War, having spent his early career teaching public law in Geneva and Madrid. His major IR-related books were written while he worked as a political scientist in various US universities (*Encyclopedia of World Biography* 2005–6). His *Politics Among Nations*, first published in 1948, responded directly to Carr's call for IR to be studied 'scientifically' and he developed a series of six principles of political realism. The conduct of both domestic and international politics can be understood, Morgenthau argues (1985: 4–17), if we appreciate that:

1 **Politics has its roots in human nature.** This nature is essentially as Hobbes described it and it has not changed over thousands of years (Morgenthau elaborates in his third principle). If we take this as one of several 'objective laws' of politics, we 'must also believe in the possibility of developing a rational theory that reflects … these objective laws'. This possibility exists because we also assume that we can untangle 'truth' (deduced rationally from evidence) from 'opinion' (subjective judgement divorced from facts).

2 **Foreign policy-makers 'think and act in terms of interest defined as power'.** In international politics, power political considerations are everything whereas ethics, morals, economics and religion are all subservient. They might be used to 'dress up' foreign policies to make them palatable for public consumption but these policies should and will be all about preserving the national interest. This assumption 'infuses rational order into the subject matter of politics, and thus makes the theoretical understanding of politics possible'. We can only measure the quality of foreign policy decisions in terms of the extent to which they enhance a state's security, in other words, with regard to the extent to which they are 'rational' decisions.

3 **(i) Humans are basically self-interested, as are states.** Relations between humans and states play out via politics at the domestic and international levels respectively, and this is where their different interests are liable to collide. **(ii) A state's definition and use of power depend on the cultural and political context within which it is exercized.** Put broadly, power 'covers all social relationships which serve that end, from physical violence to the most subtle psychological ties by which one mind controls another'. Transforming the contemporary world means working with these enduring realities of international political life: interest and power.

4 **We can only judge the morality of a leader's actions on the basis of a careful examination of the choices open to him at a particular point in time.** There is no universal moral code by which we can judge such actions. 'The ethics of international relations is a political or situational ethics' (Jackson and Sørensen 2007: 70).

5 **No nation has the right to claim its moral code as the world's moral code, or to impose its ideology onto others.** Such folly 'is liable to engender the distortion in judgment which, in the blindness of crusading frenzy, destroys nations and civilizations'. In fact, one test of morality is the extent to which we respect the decisions of others to live and act differently from ourselves.

6 **Restatement of the autonomy of the political sphere with examples of how it works in practice.** 'The economist asks: "How does this policy affect the wealth of society, or a segment of it?" The lawyer asks: "Is this policy in accord with the rules of law?" The moralist asks: "Is this policy in accord with moral principles?" And the political realist asks: "How does this policy affect the power of the nation?" International politics is not for the feint of heart but we cannot wish human nature away.'

This chapter and Chapter 2.1 have provided a necessarily brief overview of the Realist and Liberal traditions in IR. It is up to you to generate a deeper understanding of them by reading as widely as you can about them on your course. Let us recap some of the key elements by way of summary: first, Realists and Liberals share key assumptions about IR; second, they draw on different sources of evidence for their arguments; third, where Realists see conflict, insecurity and the perpetual threat of war between states, Liberals emphasize the possibilities for peace brought about by co-operation and international institutions; finally, both theories make claims about how accurate/reliable they are based on appeals to history and tradition. In the next chapter we will see how both theories have been updated in the form of Neoliberalism and Neorealism.

> Realists tend to have a more pessimistic view of IR than Liberals. How would you describe your own view of IR: more optimistic or pessimistic? On what do you base this view?

Questions for discussion

" How relevant is Thucydides to the contemporary study of international relations? "

A good place to begin here is to set out the claims on behalf of Thucydides made by IR scholars – Realist scholars in particular. One way to do this is to make a note of all the writers who show direct knowledge of his work (for example, Carr and Morgenthau) and they can form the basis of one side of the argument, that Thucydides *is* relevant.

Equally, however, there will be writers who disagree. They proceed by questioning the utility of understanding contemporary international politics by looking at political relations between Greek city-states thousands of years ago, and attacking some of Thucydidean/Realist assumptions about human nature, security, power and morality. Here you can use Realism's traditional opponent, Liberalism, to make the case that it is not only Thucydides but the entire tradition inspired by him that misconstrues the nature of contemporary IR.

> David A. Welch has written an article entitled 'Why IR Theorists Should Stop Reading Thucydides' (2003). When you come across provocative articles like this, you should certainly read them – they are likely to provide you with a whole set of tools for challenging established theoretical positions.

Remember throughout the essay to make a central argument about 'relevance'. It is quite hard to set benchmarks so one approach when planning your answer might be to give Thucydides a very simple score out of 10. If you think he's a 9/10: why? If you think he's a 2/10: why? Presumably if you are a Realist, your score will be higher than if you agree more with other IR theories.

“What role does morality play in Realist IR theory?”

This question invites you to consider the core assumptions and arguments about IR put forward by Realist theorists, and to gauge the place they give morality in the conduct of international politics. To begin with, you will have to specify what you mean by 'Realist', so explain which theorist or set of theorists will you take to be representative of the tradition. In this chapter we have explored a few seminal writers but there are dozens to choose from.

You next need to highlight where morality features in, say, the works of three writers you take to be representative of the tradition. You could see how these writers approach questions of morality in the international sphere in a number of ways, for instance, by exploring their views on private and public morality and by considering how for writers such as Morgenthau there is no universal moral code – morality is to be judged in the context of particular decisions at particular times.

You might also think laterally by comparing how the 'average' Realist writer treats morality compared to the 'average' Liberal writer, emerging with the conclusion that morality plays less of a role in this theoretical tradition than in others – or perhaps it is more accurate to say a more ambiguous role.

References to more information

For coverage of the general themes and issues pertinent to the Realist tradition:
WILLIAMSON, D. (2003) *War and Peace: International Relations, 1919–39*, 2nd edn. London: Hodder and Stoughton.

HERZ, J.H. (1959) *International Relations in the Nuclear Age*. New York: Columbia University Press.

Shows the link between Realist thinking and events 'on the ground' during the formative years of the Cold War.

HIRST, P. (2001) *War and Power in the 21st Century*. Cambridge: Polity.

See Chapter 2 on the international system since 1648 and Chapter 4 debating possible futures for the international system.

On Thucydides and his legacy:

CHITTICK, W.O. AND FREYBERG-INAN, A. (2000) '"Chiefly for Fear, Next for Honour, and Lastly for Profit": An Analysis of Foreign Policy Motivation in the Peloponnesian War', *Review of International Studies*, 27(1): 69–90.

BAGBY, L.M.J. (1994) 'The Use and Abuse of Thucydides in International Relations', *International Organization*, 48(1): 131–53.

Argues that Realists deploy Thucydides rather simplistically and offers alternative readings that are more useful, especially to foreign policy practitioners.

MONTEN, J. (2006) 'Thucydides and Modern Realism', *International Studies Quarterly*, 50(1): 3–26.

A further reassessment of Thucydides' Realist credentials.

Critical work on key Realist figures:

BEITZ, C.R. (1979) *Political Theory and International Relations*. Princeton, NJ: Princeton University Press.

Elaborates the theory of **cosmopolitanism** through a critique of the state-centricity of Realism, especially its assumption that states exist in a Hobbesian self-help environment. Useful if you want to critique Realist theory.

COZETTE, M. (2008) 'Reclaiming the Critical Dimension of Realism: Hans J. Morgenthau on the Ethics of Scholarship', *Review of International Studies*, 34(1): 5–27.

Reassesses Morgenthau's credentials as a critical thinker about IR through a close reading of his work on truth, power and the ethics of scholarship. Similar in intention to Bain, W. (2000) 'Deconfusing Morgenthau: Moral Inquiry and Classical Realism Reconsidered', *Review of International Studies*, 26(3): 445–64.

GUZZINI, S. (1998) *Realism in International Relations and International Political Economy: The Continuing Story of a Death Foretold*. London: Routledge.

Considers the theory, practices and crises in Realist thought as well as the Neorealist response to these crises in the theory (see the next chapter in this book).

GILPIN, R. (2002) 'A Realist Perspective on International Governance', in D. Held and A. McGrew (eds) *Governing Globalization: Power, Authority and Global Governance*. Cambridge: Polity, pp. 237–48.

2.3

neorealism and neoliberalism

Key terms:

Anarchy
State
System
Balance of power
Rationality
Regimes
Political Economy

The debate between the Neorealists and the Neoliberals emerged in the 1970s and developed over the next two decades into the major theoretical controversy within IR. Each body of writing is strongly rooted in the 'classical' Realism and Liberalism we explored in the previous two chapters, but has developed those ideas in new directions. With the emergence of the Neo-Neo debate, as it is sometimes called, we see how theoretical innovations in the field of IR continue to take a good deal of inspiration from changes on the international political, strategic and economic fronts. We begin this chapter by considering Kenneth Waltz's brand of Neorealism and move on to the Neoliberal reaction which took a variety of forms.

Neorealism

In the previous chapter we pulled out key Realist assumptions, arguments and approaches by looking at the work of E.H. Carr and Hans Morgenthau. We saw that in the early Realism which emerged through the interwar years and took hold of the discipline especially tightly after the Second World War, inter-state war and conflict was explained on two levels of analysis:

- **Level 1: Human nature.** Inspired by Hobbesian ideas about human insecurity in a state of nature, writers such as Morgenthau added that man also has a lust for power which could be a further cause of conflict.

- **Level 2: State interests in a condition of anarchy.** By transposing Hobbes's state of nature up to the realm of the international we can explain international relations with reference to the quest for security and power on the part of self-interested and perpetually insecure states.

Waltz himself contributed to this classical brand of Realism with his *Man, the State and War* (1959), which echoed Morgenthau's and Carr's treatment of IR as a never-ending series of conflicts among states trapped in a condition of anarchy. Twenty years later, Waltz published his *Theory of International Politics* (1979) in which he sought to explain the causes of wars more systematically than Realists had previously managed, arguing that for a viable theory of international relations to exist we need to:

1 **Identify the units in the system.**

2 **Specify the comparative weight of systemic and sub-systemic causes of change in the system.**

3 **Show how forces and effects change from one system to another.**

Explaining IR via the behaviour of states took us some way towards a genuine theory, he argued, but there was a crucial dimension missing. He observed that the capitalist US and Communist USSR both sought out military power and influence and competed for strategic advantage, for example, by conducting 'proxy' wars in Latin America. The question that exercized him was *why* the similar behaviour when the ideologies of each state were so different? If international anarchy exists, yet we cannot explain state behaviour using either of the two levels previously identified by Realist writers, then we need to search for an additional factor. Waltz argued that this factor was the international system itself which compels states to preserve their security by constantly building up their power (Burchill 2001c: 86). Waltz's structural realism is captured in his concept of the **balance of power** (Waltz 1979: Chapters 4–6).

The balance of power and stability theory

'If there is any distinctively political theory of international politics, balance-of-power theory is it' wrote Waltz (1979: 117). He said that to explain international relations the idea of the *system* is all important. He defines a system as a set of interacting units exhibiting behavioural regularities and having an identity over time. In other words, a system and the changes in that system are both observable elements of international relations.

This system is where we need to focus our attention because its units – individual states – all do the same things in that system, regardless of where they are located, their prevailing ideology, culture, and so on. They only differ in terms of their relative capabilities, and as these capabilities change so the system changes. 'In other words, international change occurs when great powers rise and fall and the balance of power shifts accordingly. A typical means of such change is great-power war' (Jackson and Sørensen 2007: 76).

Waltz goes on to define two types of system:

- a **bipolar system** is one in which there are two major powers such as the US and the USSR between 1945 and 1989
- a **multipolar system** is akin to the international states system that preceded and followed the Cold War, where many powers co-exist.

> What kind of international system prevails today? Do Waltz's categories have it covered or is it something altogether different? How many 'great powers' are there in the world today?

In Waltz's view bipolar systems are more stable than multipolar systems 'with only two great powers, both can be expected to act to maintain the system' (Waltz 1979: 204) because it is in their respective interests to keep the status quo as it is. In a multipolar system there is less incentive for individual powers to act in this way both because the potential for control is far less and because the potential outcome of their actions is far less certain. Rationally calculating the outcome of state actions is easier in bipolar systems and successfully implementing those actions is easier too.

So what, in sum, are the continuities and changes between Realism and Neorealism?

- **Continuity** – Waltz assumes states are the key actors, that there is a condition of anarchy and that international relations are shaped by power politics.
- **Continuity** – Waltz assumes states are trapped in an international state of nature, leading them to focus only on their security and survival.
- **Change** – Waltz does not root his explanation of international relations in Hobbesian theories of human nature, *à la* Morgenthau.
- **Change** – Waltz's structured account gives far less room for state leaders to employ cunning and skilful diplomacy, qualities that Thucydides highlighted in

his *History*, and which Morgenthau said could provide benchmarks for judging leaders' foreign policy decisions.

- **Change** – Waltz critiqued previous (Realist) theories of IR for paying insufficient attention to the systemic level. 'Blurring the distinction between the different levels of a system has, I believe, been the major impediment to the development of theories about international politics' (Waltz 1979: 78). Neorealism is more like a 'proper' theory because it theorizes at the systems level as well as the unit level.

To summarize, we can use the words of Stanley Hoffman: 'The Waltzian synthesis is referred to as neorealism, to indicate both its intellectual affinity with the classical realism of Morgenthau ... and its elements of originality and distinctiveness' (Keohane 1986: 15–16)

Books such as Keohane's Neorealism and its Critics *are a great source of information for you because not only do they explain the nuts and bolts of each theory, they also include chapters by critics of the theory (and sometimes responses to the critics). It is like buying two books for the price of one.*

Neoliberalism

Just as Neorealism accepts the basic premises of Realism and pulls them in new directions so Neoliberalism has the same relationship with inter-war and early post-war Liberalism we considered in Chapter 2.1. Neoliberalism can be considered an attempt to explain developments in the global political economy that gathered pace after 1945, focusing our attention 'upon the central role of institutions and organizations in international politics' (Martin 2007: 110).

Particularly influential in this tradition has been the work of Robert Keohane (1982) and Stephen Krasner (1983). Their ideas developed around the observation that there was relative stability in patterns of international economic co-operation despite the relatively uneven distribution of international economic power (Martin 2007: 111). Such co-operation seemed all the more remarkable given the volatile nature of international relations in the 1970s brought about by such things as:

- **Economics:**

  - the collapse of the **Bretton Woods economic system** in 1971
  - a quadrupling in the price of crude oil brought about by steep price hikes by the Organization of the Petroleum Exporting Countries (OPEC) in 1973 and 1979.

- **Politics:**
  - the Yom Kippur War in the Middle East, 1973
  - the Vietnam War between North Vietnam and the American-supported South Vietnam, 1959–75
  - the Soviet invasion of Afghanistan, 1979-88
  - ongoing talks between the US and USSR over nuclear arms limitations.

The crucial advance they made on conventional Liberalism was to introduce the concept of **international regimes** to the vocabulary of IR theory. The idea of looking at regimes is that co-operation takes place in international organizations such as the EU but also in forums like the **General Agreement on Tariffs and Trade (GATT)** which were not international organizations with all the formalized rules and procedures implied by that term, but more basic international economic agreements that helped shape and regulate state behaviour.

Neoliberal thinking is founded on several main assumptions (see Lamy 2008: 132; Martin 2007: 111–12):

1 **States are the main actors** in the international system.

2 **States are rational actors,** weighing up the potential costs and benefits of different courses of action and choosing that course most likely to give them the highest net pay-off.

3 States operate in a condition of **international anarchy ...**

4 **... but co-operation is not impossible in an anarchic system** because states will 'shift loyalty and resources to institutions if these are seen as mutually beneficial and if they provide states with increasing opportunities to secure their international interests' (Lamy 2008: 132).

5 **The scope and depth of integration between states** is increasing at both the regional and global levels.

6 **'Absolute' gains are more important to states than 'relative' gains.**

Taking it ***FURTHER***

Absolute versus relative gains

A fundamental distinction between Neoliberal and Neorealist theories is over their respective approaches to the gains made by states when engaging with each other in the international setting. By 'gains' we mean 'benefits that accrue to participants that cooperate' (Jackson and Sørensen 2007: 118).

Neoliberals argue that international institutions not only facilitate co-operation but help states make more rational choices about the outcomes of their co-operation because states involved in these institutions are both less likely and less able to cheat by reneging on commitments. So for example, State A whose economy currently grows at an average of 1 per cent per year will co-operate with other states in an international economic organization if it predicts that by doing so it will increase its growth rate to 5 per cent per year.

Neorealists argue it is more about the relative place of states within the international system. States will be wary of co-operating if they fear other states may benefit more than they do. If we take our example from above, Neorealists would propose that if another State B with a current growth rate of 1 per cent predicted growth of 8 per cent per year by joining that international organization, then State A will be inhibited about co-operating because in *relative* terms it will be worse off inside the organization than outside it. It is the comparison/prediction element and the fear of lagging behind in relative 'power' terms that is key for Neorealists.

Critiquing the Neo-Neo agenda

To return to the 'problem of the subject' we identified in Chapter 1.1, there was very little problem for the writers explored in Chapters 2.1 and 2.2 in defining the subject matter of IR. It was all about the nature and level of state interactions in an anarchic system. Realists and Neorealists were much more pessimistic about the extent to which states could avoid conflict than their Liberal and Neoliberal counterparts. But while they disagreed in terms of outcomes, they shared a lot in terms of assumptions and procedures for investigating international relations.

Writing in 1995, Steve Smith had the following to say about the Neo-Neo debate which erupted in IR in the 1980s. 'The debate is a Western, even North Atlantic one. It hardly begins to deal with the concerns of the vast majority of humanity, and very effectively silences those who do not fit into this US view of what international political is all about' (Smith 1995: 24). In 2001, Chris Brown echoed Smith's concerns about the narrowing IR agenda at this time. He pointed out that scholars such as Robert Keohane essentially accepted all the basic assumptions of Neorealism, merely interpreting differently the extent of the possibilities for co-operation in an anarchic international environment. He summarized the dispute between the two as follows: the problem for Neoliberals is in maintaining co-operation, whereas for Neorealists the problem is getting co-operation going in the first place (Brown 2001: 49–50).

The upshot for Smith and Brown was that the two sets of 'neo' theories represented a dangerous narrowing of IR's disciplinary agenda. Not only did they share many of the same contentious assumptions about the main actors on the world stage, they assumed that states were rational actors and the task of each was to explain the extent to which states might or might not co-operate in international organizations and institutions, set up within the 'western' world after 1945. A further assumption was that these facets of international relations could be measured scientifically and therefore accurately.

The critiques levelled at the Neo-Neo debate highlight the fact that there were other things going on in the discipline from the 1980s – new ways of defining and studying the problematic subject matter of IR. In the following chapters we consider a whole array of other theories that you are likely to encounter on your course. We begin with English School theory.

Questions to ponder

" What are the similarities and dissimilarities between Neoliberal and Neorealist theories of IR? "

It is tempting with questions such as this to get caught in the trap of explaining one theory and then the other without addressing the core of the question. Clearly you will have to demonstrate knowledge of the basis of each theory, but how much detail you include in this regard involves a judgement call on your part.

One approach is to describe, first, Neoliberal theory, second, Neorealist theory and, third, weigh up where they overlap and where they differ. A possible problem here is that by leading off with a description of each theory, you leave yourself less time (in an exam) and space (in a coursework essay) to demonstrate to the marker that you can identify the similarities and differences between the two.

A second approach is to structure the essay in two parts: first, deal with the similarities and, second, the differences. This takes more planning, organization and knowledge of the respective traditions, but it will pay dividends because you will be getting to the heart of the matter right away. The very best answers will explain the similarities and dissimilarities and then go on to make some judgement about whether the one set outnumbers the other set. They may also take into account the metatheoretical critiques of the Neo-Neo debate by critics such as Steve Smith, who argue that, compared to many recent theories that hit the discipline, these two theories have many unfavourable qualities in common.

" Do you think Waltzian Neorealism successfully created a 'proper' theory of IR? "

Your answer to this question will have to address three distinct issues. The first is to identify what Waltzian Neorealism is. You can do this via a simple explanation of the key themes of his *Theory of International Politics,* majoring on such concepts as the international system and the balance of power and his structural account of state interactions in a condition of anarchy.

Having demonstrated that you understand Waltz's theory, you then have the slightly more difficult task of explaining Waltz's claims about this being a 'proper' theory of IR. Why does he say this? On what grounds? It all comes down to his aim of generating a science of politics and you can quote from his 1979 study and later work to support you here.

In light of all this, you then have to judge whether Waltz is right to present his theory as a 'proper' theory. What does 'proper' imply in the context of the question and how do we judge when a theory is 'proper' or not? The best answers will use this element of the question to investigate metatheoretical debates about the nature of theory and whether we can study IR as scientifically as Waltz suggests.

References to more information

On Neoliberalism:

KEOHANE, R.O. AND NYE, J.S. **(1977)** *Power and Interdependence: World Politics in Transition.* Boston: Little Brown and Co.

CLARK, I. **(1999)** *Globalization and International Relations Theory.* Oxford: Oxford University Press.

Shows how globalization unsettles existing IR theoretical categories and helps us rethink both the concept of globalization and the framework of the discipline.

MITRANY, D. (1975) 'A Political Theory for the New Society', in A.J.R. Groom and P. Taylor *Functionalism: Theory and Practice in International Relations*. London: University of London Press, pp. 25–37.

See also the chapters in this collection by Nina Heathcote (neo-functionalism), Michael Hodges and John Burton.

NYE, J.S. (1975) 'Transnational and Transgovernmental Relations', in G.L. Goodwin and A. Linklater (eds) *New Dimensions of World Politics*. London: Croom Helm, pp. 36–53.

Examines the actors in IR overlooked by state-centric theories and makes the case for integration theory and interdependence. See also the chapter by Richard Rosecrance.

On Neorealism:

BERRIDGE, G.R. (1997) *International Politics: States, Power and Conflict since 1945*, 3rd edn. New York: Prentice Hall.

On pp. 166–83 Berridge explores the Neorealist concept of the 'balance of power' and illustrates how it has featured in the international system. Ends the chapter with a good list of further reading.

KREISLER, H. (2003), 'Theory and International Politics: Conversation with Kenneth N. Waltz', Institute of International Studies, University of Berkeley, http://globetrotter.berkeley.edu/people3/Waltz/waltz-con0.html.

Waltz talks about his educational influences, about being a political theorist and about the Neorealist vision of international politics. You can read the interview transcript, watch it as a webcast or listen as a podcast.

MEARSHEIMER, J.J. (1990), 'Back to the Future: Instability in Europe after the Cold War', *International Security*, 15(1): 5–56.

Tries to update Waltz's Neorealist balance of power thesis to predict trends in international relations after the end of the Cold War.

LINKLATER, A. (1995) 'Neo-Realism: Theory and Practice', in K. Booth and S. Smith (eds) *International Relations Theory Today*. Cambridge: Polity Press, pp. 241–61.

ASHLEY, R.K. (1986) 'The Poverty of Neorealism', in R.O. Keohane (ed.) *Neorealism and its Critics*. New York: Columbia University Press, pp. 1–26.

REVIEW OF INTERNATIONAL STUDIES (2004) 'Forum on the State as Person', 30(2): 255–316.

<table>
<tr><td>

2.4

the english school

</td><td></td></tr>
</table>

Key terms:

State
System
Society
Order
Justice
Rules

> *The goal of explaining the high level of order which exists between political entities which are not subject to a higher authority pervades the entire rationalist exercise (Linklater 1990: 15)*

> *You can open essays or exam answers with relevant quotes like this to focus your reader's attention on the central issue(s) you will raise in your work.*

In this chapter and the next, we analyse two IR theories that are alike in some ways but very different in others: the English School and Social Constructivism. I've classified them as 'mid-range' in the sense that they sit between the positivist, science-like theories of Realism, Liberalism, Neorealism and Neoliberalism and the more critical, **post-positivist** inclined theories such as Critical Theory, feminism, postcolonialism, Green theory and Anarchism. Hence, when thinking about the 'place' they occupy in the broader canon of IR theories, you might see the English School and Social Constructivism as bringing to the table new themes and issues which had previously been ignored or overlooked by earlier theorists; in so doing, they opened the door for a more radical reassessment of what IR theory was all about.

Introduction to the English School

This theory is slightly oddly named in that it was formed by scholars of varying nationalities: 'the English School was never very English and is even less so today' (Dunne 2007: 128).

As you can see in the quote at the start of the chapter, English School theory also goes by the name 'rationalism' so bear this in mind when reading around this subject.

What is so attractive about English School theorizing is that it tries to sit between what appear to be extreme positions taken by Realist, Liberalist and Neo-Neo theorists, on the one hand, and post-positivist perspectives, which we cover later in the book, such as Critical Theory and postmodernism, on the other. Dunne judges that the English School avoids 'either/or' theorizing; it is a 'synthesis of different theories and concepts' combining 'theory *and* history, morality *and* power, **agency** *and* structure' (Dunne 2007: 128, his italics). In this chapter we will explore the English School approach to IR first by considering how Hedley Bull positioned it within prevailing IR theory and then by unpacking its major concepts: state, system, society and order.

Bull: *The Anarchical Society*

The very title of Hedley Bull's foundational English School text (1977) gives us clues about where he was trying to take IR theory. His deployment of the concept of anarchy shows that Bull was accenting a central theme of Realist and Liberal theories, where states exist in an environment where there is no orderer, no chief to regulate their behaviour at the international level. As we have seen, early Realists held that without an orderer, the potential for conflict between self-interested states was ever-present because they were trapped in an irresolvable security dilemma. Neorealists such as Kenneth Waltz built their theories around the concept of the balance of power, arguing that the causes of conflict lay not so much with the actions of the units (states) but at the level of the system itself. Liberal and Neoliberal theorists took the same assumption about the existence of anarchy but drew different conclusions. They argued that conflict did not have to be, and was not empirically, a permanent or necessary feature of international relations. Early Liberals eulogized the spread of democracy and good governance, while Liberal theory after the Second World War concentrated on the growth of international organizations/institutions and showed how these could help mitigate the negative effects of anarchy.

It is probably fair to suggest that Bull's work was Realist in inspiration and Liberal in aspiration. It was Realist in inspiration because he wanted to open up dialogue about the implications of accepting the two founding assumptions of IR theory: that sovereign states are the main actors and that they exist in a condition of anarchy. But from this Realist starting point he brought distinctively Liberal-inspired ideas about the nature of IR to the fore. We can see this by looking at his central case that 'a group of states, conscious of certain common interests and common values, forms a society in the sense that they conceive themselves to be bound by a set of rules in their relations with one another, and share in the working of common institutions' (Bull 1977: 13). A glance at some of the key terms in this statement reveals Bull's Liberal agenda:

- Common interests.
- Common values.
- Society.
- Rules.
- Share.
- Institutions.

The main distinction between Bull and Liberal/Neo-liberal theorists was his effort to theorize the term 'society' into existence. His belief was that 'order is part of the historical record of international relations; ... modern states have formed, and continue to form, not only a system of states but also an international society' (Bull 1977: 22–3). Or as Alex Bellamy puts it, English School writers share the Constructivist belief that 'states form an international society shaped by ideas, values, identities, and norms that are – to a greater or lesser extent – common to all' (Bellamy 2004: 2).

Bellamy's book International Society and its Critics *is another of the 'two-for-one' style books you should find useful. It helps you both understand and critique English School theory.*

They might only be two short words but Bull's notions of 'society' and 'order' were crucial to the development of English School thought. Let us now see how and why Bull worked so heavily with them, and how they informed his reading of IR.

From system to society

Bull built his theory around four key words: state, system, society and order. He uses these in specific ways to advance his argument that international relations are more ordered than Realists and Neorealists assume, and more like a society than Liberals and Neoliberals assume.

State

Bull defined 'state' similarly to Realists, Liberals and Neo-neo theorists. A state, he argued, has three attributes:

- sovereignty over a group of people;
- a defined territory;
- a government.

Bull was not satisfied with theories such as Neorealism which explained state behaviour at the level of the international system. Bull put more emphasis on the agency of states; that is on the 'diplomats and leaders who think and act on behalf of the state and its institutions.' (Dunne 2007: 132) With this move, Bull helped open up the study of IR to Constructivist theories which open up the 'black box' of the state by viewing IR as a social sphere, where what people and organizations *within* states believe are held to matter at the level of the international system through their influence on state foreign and defence policies. Bull suggested that the flow of influence was not, as Waltz had it, mostly top down (from system to states) but involved more complex interactions in which state behaviour could also work upwards to affect the international system (we return to the Constructivist case in the next chapter).

An interesting way to think through the differences between a 'system' and a 'society' is to play a simple word association game. Think of the first word or image that jumps into your head when you think of the word 'system'. Do the same for the word 'society'. Ask three friends to do the same. You should notice some interesting patterns in the responses that help you understand what Bull was trying to get at by envisioning international relations in societal rather than systemic terms.

System

Bull's conception of what makes for a system at the international level was essentially Waltzian. The very word 'system' implies functional co-operation without any sense of the shared purposes or interests that we find in an international society (see below). Bull argues that two or more states form a system when they 'have sufficient contact between them, and have sufficient impact on one other's decisions, to cause them to behave – at least in some measure – as parts of a whole' (1973: 9). Systemic interaction between states is thus fairly limited and comes down to state perceptions of their 'technical interest in manipulation and control as opposed to the practical interest in promoting diplomatic agreement and understanding' (Linklater 1995: 256). Unlike Waltz, however, Bull put the concept of a system to different empirical and theoretical uses by asking what the change from one system to another tells us about the possible existence of an international society through time.

Society

The term 'international system' was deployed by IR theorists to explain the structured nature of state interactions. The very word 'system' has natural science-like associations which helps us explain how things are ordered and how different parts or units in the system interact with each other. Think for example, about planets in the solar system or the component parts of a computer system. Bull did not believe international relations could be classified in this rather abstract, cold way. After all, the relations between states and nations are conducted by, and reliant upon, the actions of the individuals within them. An international society for Bull is more than a system but less than a civilization, in the sense that we might talk about the Greek or Roman civilizations in previous centuries, or Western civilization today. A society might be something that comes about for more pragmatic reasons, less organically, we might say, than a civilization. But it is certainly a stage on in terms of understanding the depth and scale of inter-state transactions than Realists would have us believe. We see here how Bull blended together elements of earlier IR theories: hard-headed Realist calculations about national interest combine with Liberal institutionalism to create a theory in which the anarchical international system creates the impetus for groups of states to work together to achieve common goals.

Order

How is order in international relations brought about and maintained? For Bull, **diplomacy** and a respect for international law (as agreed in international institutions) are the foundations of international order and the prerequisite for the promotion of justice. This order, moreover, could be generated and maintained even among states with diverse, even *opposed* political, economic and social traditions.

Take the period of the Cold War, 1945–89, when two rival power-blocs, one led by the Soviet Union, the other by the US, competed for economic/political/cultural hegemony over the international system. Even then, the threat of 'hot war' between the main protagonists was somewhat mitigated by their participation in common institutions such as the UN which helped diffuse tensions between them via regular communication and decision-taking on events of global political, economic and strategic significance. (Although it could be argued that this view largely depends on the 'theatre' we look at and that it ignores the 'proxy' wars that were fought out in continents such as South America.)

Taking it **FURTHER**

When states engage in wars or, more likely today, humanitarian interventions, these interventions are, in theory at least, rule-bound exercises. It is not a case of 'anything goes' in times of conflict. Most states are signed up to the UN Hague Convention on the Law and Customs of War and the Geneva Convention which concentrates on 'the rights of individuals, combatants and non-combatants, during war' (UN 2007). Even in times of 'hot' conflict, then, states order their interactions to such a degree that even something as apparently chaotic and violent as war demonstrates their shared commitment to sticking by the rules for the good of international society as a whole.

Perhaps this is why, today, the treatment of prisoners of war receives so much attention and why the abuse of Iraqi prisoners of war, such as in Abu Ghraib prison during the US-led intervention from March 2003 have been so widely vilified (Amnesty International 2004). Not only did the mistreatment lead to a dwindling of support for an already controversial intervention, but also the US military personnel involved were seen to be abusing basic human rights of the Iraqi prisoners. Contravening the rules of war and abusing the law of armed conflict can be seen as undermining both the official rules and the unofficial norms underpinning the international society in which we live.

> This chapter has illustrated English School theory mainly using the work of Hedley Bull. To get a feel for diversity and richness of the tradition, you will be expected to know texts by other key writers. Compare and contrast their approaches to the four key terms explored above.

Questions to ponder

"Why did Hedley Bull posit the existence of an 'international society'? Was he correct to do so?"

This question invites you to explain Bull's reasoning and then tell the reader what you make of it, so an essay in two parts would be logical. Clearly it is sensible to concentrate mainly on Bull, but if you want to illustrate the English School's position with reference to other writers in the tradition, then that would be fine. Make sure to keep Bull's ideas to the forefront though.

In the first part you have to explain the steps Bull took to move IR theory from considering systems, power and interests towards the idea that these relations constitute a society. As such, you are being asked to summarize the key facets of Bull's thought. You can legitimately narrow your essay to focus on one seminal text (*Anarchical Society*), or you could pick ideas from across his œuvre. The first option is probably the easier to sustain because it is a relatively self-contained work; you might tell the reader that Bull developed his ideas over time but that for the purposes of answering this particular question you are sticking to his first major foray into the subject. You could summarize *The Anarchical Society* chapter by chapter; but in order to remain within the recommended word limit for your essay you will surely be better off to take a thematic approach, using foundational quotes to illustrate your reading of Bull's work.

In the second part you have to give your opinions on Bull's ideas about the existence of an 'international society'. Here you should demonstrate a familiarity with criticisms levelled at the concept. These include: first, the vagueness of the distinction between 'system', on the one hand, and 'society', on the other; just when does the one become the other? Second, does 'international' in fact mean 'European', undermining the applicability of the theory to anything beyond the notional and rather limited borders of 'Europe' or the 'Western'? Third, did Bull's theory overlook the elements of a human 'world society' of values that exists among human beings as opposed to states; was he too state-centric? Realist theorists critique Bull for being insufficiently Realist; Liberals critique him for being too Realist, so you could couch your evaluation in these terms. What do you make of their attacks? You could answer this by considering what Bull would have said to his Realist and Liberal critics.

"How does English School theory differ from Realist and Liberal theories? Which theory do you find most convincing and why?"

Whereas the last question concentrated on just one theory, this answer requires a good working knowledge of three. That you potentially have to cover so much ground makes your response harder to structure, so good planning and organization are vital. If answering such a question in an exam, your time management will have to be rigorous so that you effectively address both parts of the question.

Let us deal with the first half of the question. On the surface it might appear that the best way to approach this question is to take each theory in turn, explaining their central tenets and then comparing and contrasting in a section at the end. The flaw in this approach is that it may be impossible to cram in all the information you need. Say you only have 2,500 words for your essay – how are you going to summarize three theories and then evaluate them in this limited space? And bearing in mind this is an English School-oriented question, it is worth showing your tutor you actually know a lot more about that theory than the other two! It may, then, be better to centre your analysis on English School theory, moving into the other two theories as and when necessary. You could, for instance, consider the use Bull and others make of Realist-inspired words like 'system' and 'interest' and Liberal words like 'institutions' and 'society'. That way you are showing the reader you can compare and contrast the theories without having to narrate them one by one. This approach is harder to manage because it assumes a strong knowledge base but it certainly should pay dividends in terms of demonstrating your ability to meet higher order learning objectives for the course.

In the second part you have to pick your favourite theory (assuming you have one). The examiner will be looking for you to justify your choice with reference to either or both of two benchmarks. First, the coherence of the theory *as a theory*. Are its assumptions valid? Is it epistemologically grounded? Does it fit the 'facts' of international relations as understood by the theorist responsible? Second, you might consider the applicability of the theory today by asking: have they stood the test of time? Do they explain things about contemporary issues in international relations? Your answer will depend on your view of what constitutes contemporary international relations. Many students will skip straight to the personal approach to evaluating the theories but my advice is to try and evaluate the theories first and foremost on their own terms. It is very easy to say theories are outdated, that they ignore many themes in international relations, and so on, but you should also show that you can critique the theories *as* theories, which involves empathizing with what the key writers all those decades ago were trying to achieve through their works.

References to more information

BULL, H. AND WATSON, A. (EDS) (1985) *The Expansion of International Society.* Oxford: Oxford University Press.

Analysis of the growth and development of European and, increasingly, global 'society' from the sixteenth century onwards.

ROBSON, B.A. (ED.) (1998) *International Society and the Development of International Relations.* London: Cassell.

A collection of essays by leading English School writers assessing where they think the concept of 'international society' has taken IR.

BUZAN, B. (2001) 'The English School: An Under-Exploited Resource in IR', *Review of International Studies*, 24(3): 471–88.

A forceful statement of the case that IR theorists neglect the English School at their peril.

DUNNE, T. (1998) *Inventing International Society: A History of the English School.* Basingstoke: Macmillan.

WIGHT, M. (1991) *International Theory: The Three Traditions.* Leicester: Leicester University Press.

Wight's lectures at the LSE in the 1950s.

SUGANAMI, H. (2000) 'C. A. W. Manning and the Study of International Relations', *Review of International Studies*, 27(1): 91–107.

BUZAN, B. (2005) *From International to World Society?: English School Theory and the Social Construction of Globalisation.* Cambridge: Cambridge University Press.

Chapters 1 and 2 are good on the weaknesses of English School theory and Chapter 6 on the institutions that constitute 'international society'.

GROOM, A.J.R. (1975) 'Functionalism and World Society', in A.J.R. Groom and P. Taylor, *Functionalism: Theory and Practice in International Relations.* London: University of London Press, pp. 93–111.

Shows the overlap between English School and Liberal thought.

GONG, G.W. (1984) *The Standard of 'Civilization' in International Relations.* Oxford: Clarendon Press.

A wealth of information on the changing faces of 'international society' through the ages by appreciating non-Western societies in China and Japan. Also useful as a precursor to postcolonialism (Chapter 2.10 in this book).

HOFFMAN, S. (2000) *World Disorders: Troubled Peace in the Post-Cold War Era.* Lanham, MD: Rowman and Littlefield Publishers Ltd.

Chapter 2 covers Hedley Bull; Chapter 4 is on world order beyond Realist and Liberal perspectives.

REVIEW OF INTERNATIONAL STUDIES (2001) 'Forum on the English School', 27(3): 465–513.

A series of six short articles. See also the same journal's (2002) five-article section on the English School, 28(4).

BUZAN, B. (NO DATE) 'English School of International Relations', University of Leeds. http://www.leeds.ac.uk/polis/englishschool/.

Contains links to conference papers, reading lists and contact lists for people working on the English School.

2.5	
social constructivism	

Key terms:

Anarchy
State
Self-help
Security dilemma
Identity
Interest
Constructedness

At the time of writing this book I have a nephew who is four years old and a niece who is two years old. Being the dutiful and generous uncle that I am,

I have spent considerable money and time over the past few years purchasing Christmas and birthday presents for them. Last Christmas I wanted to buy them each a t-shirt for the summer, so off I went to Mothercare to choose their respective tops. I emerged with a blue t-shirt for Joe and a pink one for Freja. My choice was made in part because of my preconceptions about what colours we associate with young boys and girls and in part it reflected the nature of the dominant colours in the boys' and girls' clothing sections in the shop I searched in. The girls' section contained lighter tones and more pinks and yellows, whereas the tones for boys' clothes were darker, with blues, blacks and browns more apparent.

As Joe and Freja grow up I will have great fun choosing toys for them as well as clothes. There will doubtless be many toys that both will enjoy playing with such as jigsaw puzzles and board games. But there may be specific toys that I would give Joe but probably not consider giving Freja such as water pistols, Action Men and footballs. By the same token Freja might prefer dolls, dressing up clothes and glitter make-up. You can probably see where this is heading. My choice of gifts for my niece and nephew is crucially shaped both by my own reading of what they might want, but more, no doubt, by my expectations of what they would want given *societal expectations* about what young boys and girls wear, and what toys young boys and girls play with.

> What appear to be natural, taken-as-read realities about the social world are in fact not natural or forever given to us, they are made by us.

This slightly simplified (and gendered – see Chapter 2.8) example works as a way in to thinking about the complex nature of social reality. My choice of colour for my niece and nephew's t-shirts could have been totally different had blue and pink not been the 'accepted' male and female colours of choice. Replace blue with red and pink with black as the dominant colours and my own choice might well have been red for Joe and black for Freja, not blue and pink. My change of colour preference would have been down to a combination of my own expectations about what colours boys and girls wear, but also a function of material reality; had these been the dominant colours, Mothercare would presumably have stocked more red and black clothes as opposed to blue and pink. The point is a simple one: things could have been different. For that reason, these socially constructed norms and practices can be un-made or transformed, and this is the crux of Social Constructivist theories about IR: things could be different.

Context

Social Constructivism in IR did not simply appear out of nowhere. It formed part of a wider intellectual movement within the social sciences from the 1980s onward and was simultaneously a response to key trends within the discipline of IR at that time. Let us take each stimulus in turn.

The normative turn

In this book we have already discussed the big social science debate between positivist and normative theorists. Positivists believe that the social world can be studied using methods drawn from the natural sciences; that facts can be disentangled from values; that regularities in the social world can be discovered in the same way that a natural scientist can discover regularities in the natural world; and that we judge truth claims on the basis of an appeal to our value-free facts (for more on the philosophy behind positivism see Giddens 1974).

Normative theorists question each and every positivist assumption and in so doing provide serious grounds for us to investigate both the epistemological status of positivist theory (its claims to produce accurate, testable and objective knowledge) and the methodological underpinnings of positivist research (its naturalist approach). Smith and Owens point out (2008: 178) that in the study of IR, normative theory, sometimes referred to as reflectivist theory, only began to challenge the disciplinary dominance of positivism from the late 1980s. First of all, normative theorists disagreed that the study of the world should (could, even) be all about the way things were. They pointed out that this was a small 'c' conservative position which entrenched rather than challenged existing power arrangements. Second, normative theorists raised the question of the values inherent in all theory – even theory which claims to tell us simply the way things are. Believing that one can do this is to adopt a normative position because you are masking the fact that in telling 'the way things are' you are in fact telling *your version* of the way things are. It might not be my version, and almost certainly won't be the same as Victoria Beckham's version, as George Bush's version or Michael Moore's version.

> Normative theorists doubt the existence of a single position from which we can either 'view' the reality of the social world or tell it in terms that are anything other than partial, skewed and relative to our own theories and preconceptions about the world and its workings.

The normative turn in IR

Normative theorists in IR raised awareness of their concerns about positivist research within the discipline by challenging some of the assumptions about how to 'do' IR theory which appeared in the most popular works in the field until the 1980s. For the purposes of your course in IR, you might see Social Constructivism and the more obviously normative theories we cover in the next few chapters as a reaction against Realism, Liberalism and their Neo-Neo off-shoots. Constructivist writers work from the premise that IR is a far more complex field than these theorists have led us to believe (Onuf 1998). A variety of factors led to this interrogation of the prevailing theoretical consensus (following Smith and Owens 2008: 176):

- **The sudden demise of Neorealism.** First of all, the end of the Cold War in 1989 severely undermined the Neorealist argument that the bipolar international system that had prevailed since the end of the Second World War would be an enduring feature of international politics. Suddenly, theorists wedded to explaining the 'facts' of the world as they saw them had to account for myriad 'facts' in the Soviet Union and its satellite states that were neither predicted nor well explained by prevailing Neorealist thought.
- **Globalization.** We could write a whole book on this phenomenon and still not explore each and every aspect of it! Take the term here to mean increasing political, economic, technological and cultural interconnectedness between peoples and states around the world. Until the 1980s IR theory was state-centric and not adept at explaining the rise and increasing influence of such non-state activity; by definition, such activity falls outside the scope of any theory which takes the state as the main unit of analysis. By the end of the 1980s, therefore, it was felt that many significant aspects of international activity were not being explained by core IR theories.
- **Ignoring other issues.** Globalization has not only increased the degree of interconnectedness between individuals, organizations and states around the world, it has intensified such connections and thereby increased our awareness of all sorts of issues and problems in the global arena. IR theory by the 1980s was seen to be ignoring major cross-border politico-social movements such as the women's movement, environmentalism, global inequality, oppression, exploitation, and ethnicity as both source of identity and cause of conflict in the post-Cold War era. Social Constructivism, like other normative theories you are likely to study on your course, provided a way of plugging these and another global gap in IR's knowledge base: that associated with the impact of *perception* on state behaviour.

Normative theories such as Social Constructivism, feminism, environmentalism and Anarchism have emerged in recent years to fill gaps scholars feel 'traditional' IR theorists left open. What does this tell you about the relationship between theory and practice in the field of IR?

Wendtian Social Constructivism

In 1992, Alexander Wendt published an article in the academic journal *International Organization* called 'Anarchy is What States Make of It: The Social Construction of Power Politics' (Wendt 1992). It helped raise the profile of what has since become known as the Social Constructivist theory of IR (earlier works in this tradition include Kratochwil 1989 and Onuf 1989). On your course you are likely to find Wendt listed as *the* essential reading on this theory so here we will concentrate on his 1992 article. By academic standards this is a long piece which develops the constructivist position by ranging over the theory and practice of IR; so how to summarize? I have broken the article down bit by bit and, to help you grasp and memorize the key steps Wendt takes, I have tried to summarize it step by step using the acronym CONSTRUCTIVISM.

> *I found it useful to try and capture each step in Wendt's argument using the acronym of the theory he developed. It compelled me to think of ways to first identify the key issues he raised and, second, to think about how I could express these positions using each letter of CONSTRUCTIVISM at the beginning of each sentence. Try doing the same for other foundational texts you study on your course: REALISM, LIBERALISM, FEMINISM, POSTMODERNISM, and so on. Each letter could even be the start of a pithy quote from the original book/article. However you choose to do it, the process will familiarize you ntimately with the texts you cover.*

All references below are to Wendt (1992):

> *C*ommitment to rationalism on the part of Neoliberals and Neorealists.

Rational choice is a social theory which treats 'the identities and interests of agents as exogenously given' (i.e. given to them rather than being created by them). Rational choice theory explains processes and institutions as impacting on behaviour rather than those identities and interests (pp. 391–2). Wendt wants to give identities and interests more of a say in the explanation for state behaviour and the outcomes that result from the interaction between states in the international arena.

> *O*ther theorists can help us bring identities and interests into the IR arena.

Cognitivists, feminists, post-structuralists among others all privilege identity and interest formation in their theories. These 'reflectivists' are also known as 'constructivists' and it is to these groups of scholars that Wendt turns for his ideas (p. 393).

Neorealists such as Waltz give too much explanatory weight to systemic factors.

They erroneously suggest that states operate in a self-help system which is mysteriously given to them 'by anarchic structure exogenously to process' (p. 394); it is as if states have no say over how they think and act. For Wendt, this structured view of IR is too **deterministic**.

Self-help and power politics are, for Wendt, not such fixed, unchanging certainties.

They 'do not follow either logically or causally from anarchy' (p. 394); they 'are institutions, not essential features of anarchy' (p. 395). If states exist in a self-help world, it is because of processes they themselves have brought into existence. '*Anarchy is what states make of it*' (p. 395, italics in original).

The distribution of power is significant, but its effects are unpredictable.

State calculations are based on more than the assessment of absolute or relative capabilities of other states. Leaders are also concerned with perceptions of their own and other states' identities and possible future behaviour: on 'conceptions of self and other'. These identity perceptions are not given but dynamic, context-specific and relational to the actions of those other states (p. 397). Put another way, the international system is more fluid than systemic theories would have us believe because states have a good deal of say over what goes on in the international arena.

Reifying anarchy prompts us to overlook uncertainties in international relations.

To **reify** an abstract entity is to treat it as if it had human or living existence. Wendt believes that previous IR scholars falsely did this with the abstract (non-existent) concept of anarchy. 'Actors do not have a "portfolio" of interests that they carry around independent of social context'; instead, they define their interests in the process of defining situations' (p. 398). Interests and identities are not given to states but are constructed by those states on the basis of learning from past experiences, the experience of present actions and expectations about the future.

Underspecified nature of Waltz's definition of structure.

Self-help is just one sort of institution among several. Wendt identifies three types of security systems: 'competitive' (Realist version), 'individualistic' (Neoliberal version) and 'cooperative' (Liberal version) (p. 400). If several types of security system have come and gone over the centuries, then how do we predict what type of system we might live in the future? It is all dependent on what states do now and in the future – nothing is predetermined. For Wendt, Waltz cannot help us here because his definition of structure overlooks identities and interests.

Case studies.

Wendt takes us back to the original 'state of nature', a time when one state ('ego') first encounters another ('alter'), to illustrate his argument that there is nothing fixed about what the nature of this and future encounters will be (pp. 404–5). He elaborates by asking how we would react to being contacted by members of an alien civilization. Our response, he argues, would be highly context dependent and shaped by our 'reading' of their various gestures (words/actions) towards us (p. 405). Again, nothing about our response is determined in advance of this first encounter (pp. 404–7).

*Theories of state behaviour to the 1980s ignored the question of **authorship**.*

An elaboration of the perils of reifying anarchy. Wendt argues that Neorealists reified anarchy 'in the sense of treating it as something separate from the practices by which it is produced and sustained' (p. 410). Anarchy is taken to be something given to us, as existing out there, something not produced by human beings and the states they govern. Wendt's view is quite the reverse: that anarchy is authored by states and therefore a social construct – 'what states have made of themselves' (p. 410). Things could be very different. States do not have to operate in a condition of anarchy.

Institutional transformations of power politics.

The title of part 2 of Wendt's article in which he examines sovereignty, cooperation and critical strategic thought. He highlights theoretical routes by which states might escape the supposedly all-conquering, all-structuring Hobbesian state of nature, and identifies how just such escapes have been put into practice in global politics since 1945 (pp. 410–21).

Variety of possibilities for systemic transformations.

Using the example of Soviet President Mikhail Gorbachev's 'New Thinking', Wendt illustrates the capacity for state leaders to engage in critical, self-reflective learning which helps them change the nature of the world political 'game' they play. Action at the domestic and international level is needed to transform embedded attitudes, institutional practices and perceptions of identity of 'self' and 'other' (pp. 419–22).

> Wendt's use of the experience of Gorbachev's Soviet Union shows the context-specific nature of our theories about IR. Gorbachev's actions led to the end of the Cold War and the demise of the bipolar international system, so academics started searching around for new explanations to replace theories such as Neorealism which suddenly appeared empirically flawed, out of date and behind the times.

International Relations theories are intimately connected to social theories.

In conclusion, Wendt restates his position and adds a few important caveats. His opening remark is that IR theories are not divorced from wider debates about the nature of academic knowledge and what we can ever 'know' about the world. These social theories 'structure the questions we ask about world politics and our approaches to answering those questions' (p. 422).

Sovereign states will remain pre-eminent.

Having spent an entire article trashing many assumptions and explanations put forward by Neo-Neo writers, Wendt then takes a step back from some of the potentially more radical aspects of his thought, as if he does not want to go too near the 'postmodern' position (see Chapter 2.9 in this book). Any of the possible transformations he talks about will, he says, have to be brought about and mediated by sovereign states. Ultimate responsibility for the nature of international relations will rest with them (p. 424).

Making a bridge between rationalism and reflectivism?

Wendt's article has been heralded as the cornerstone of Social Constructivist thinking in IR. However, his parting remark that 'I am a statist and a Realist' (p. 424) has been used by critics to undermine his claim to have built a real and lasting bridge between the two traditions.

Questions to ponder

"Critically evaluate Wendt's judgement that 'anarchy is what states make of it"

Answering this question successfully relies on two things: first, a solid understanding of Wendt's 1992 article; second, a familiarity with some of the key critiques levelled at this piece. Lower marks will go to students who show some familiarity with Wendt's position but who do not bother critiquing his position. The average student will spend a good deal of time exploring the nature of Wendt's argument and then skip through a critique or two fairly briefly at the end of the essay. To achieve marks at the higher end of the spectrum you should demonstrate an incisive understanding of Wendt's main position and then make sure you devote at least as much time exploring the critiques. The term 'critically evaluate' implies you are not just setting out those critiques but weighing up their merits (just as those writers weigh up the strength of Wendt's article). To this end, you might in your reading for this theory look for articles (for example, Wendt 2000) where writers including Wendt himself respond to the criticisms levelled at him. Using his own words is a good way of showing you have read around the subject and will reinforce your understanding of Wendt's position and how he has modified it over time.

"Do you think Wendt's brand of Social Constructivism helped build a bridge between rationalists and reflectivists?"

You will first of all have to know what kind of bridge Wendt was trying to build and be able to explain why he felt a bridge was needed. To illustrate what Wendt meant by 'rationalism' and 'reflectivism' you will briefly need to delve into the Neo-Neo debate and contrast it with the position of anti-foundational theories, so a working understanding of at least four theories will be needed to convince your tutor you are acquainted with the disciplinary context within which Wendt was writing. Your second step will be to assess the success of Wendt's efforts. Here you can use knowledge of all those theorists who critique Wendt from a metatheoretical perspective, before looking at the weaknesses in Wendt's own positioning within the wider debate between rationalism and reflectivism. While Wendt claims to take a middle position, is he in fact on the rationalist side of the fence? And, if he is, how can you realistically build a bridge if you never set foot on one side of the divide you are supposed to be crossing?

This question again invites you to concentrate on Wendt. However, you may think other Social Constructivist writers made a better stab at building this bridge so you could devote a section to these in the answer.

References to more information

CHECKEL, J.T. (1998) 'The Constructivist Turn in International Relations Theory', *World Politics*, 50(2): 324–48.

GERGEN, K.J. (2003) *An Invitation to Social Construction*. London: Sage.

ADLER, E. (1997) 'Seizing the Middle Ground: Constructivism in World Politics', *European Journal of International Relations*, 3(3): 319–63.

WELDES, J. (1996) 'Constructing National Interests', *European Journal of International Relations*, 2(3): 275–318.

Theorizes the concept of 'national interest' using Wendt's brand of Constructivism and uses a case study from US foreign policy during the 1960s Cuban Missile Crisis to illustrate the applicability of this approach to IR.

GASKARTH, J. (2006) 'Discourses and Ethics: The Social Construction of British Foreign Policy', *Foreign Policy Analysis*, 2(4): 325–41.

Like Weldes, uses a case study to illustrate the applicability of Constructivism to the study of IR.

KATZENSTEIN, P.J. (ED.) (1996) *The Culture of National Security: Norms and Identity in World Politics*. New York: Columbia University Press.

See Chapters 2 (co-authored by Wendt among others), 12 and 13 where the big theoretical questions are addressed.

PRICE, R.M. AND REUS-SMIT, C. (1998) 'Dangerous Liaisons: Critical International Theory and Constructivism', *European Journal of International Relations*, 4(3): 259–94.

STERLING-FOLKER, J. (2000) 'Competing Paradigms or Birds of a Feather?: Constructivism and Neoliberal Institutionalism Compared', *International Studies Quarterly*, 44(1): 97–119.

SUGANAMI, H. (2002) 'On Wendt's Philosophy: A Critique', *Review of International Studies*, 28(1): 23–37.

ZEHFUSS, M. (2002) *Constructivism in International Relations: The Politics of Reality.* Cambridge: Cambridge University Press.

SMITH, S. (2001) 'Foreign Policy is What States Make of It: Social Construction and International Relations Theory', in V. Kubálková (ed.) *Foreign Policy in a Constructed World.* Armonk, NY: M. E. Sharpe, pp. 38–55.

FIERKE, K.M. AND JØRGENSEN, K.E. (EDS) (2001) *Constructing International Relations: The Next Generation.* Armonk, NY: M. E. Sharpe.

PRÜGL, E. (1998) 'Feminist Struggle as Social Construction: Changing the Gendered Rules of Home-based Work', in V. Kubálková, N. Onuf and P. Kowert (eds) *International Relations in a Constructed World.* Armonk, NY: M. E. Sharpe, pp. 123–46.

Introduces you to the 'constructedness' of gender taken up in Chapter 2.8 of this book.

2.6	
Marxism	

Key terms:

Historical materialism
Class
World System
Imperialism
Capitalism
Inequality

The theories we have covered so far in this book form what you might call the 'core' of the discipline. Ask any man or woman on the street what they think makes the 'stuff' of international relations and their answers would probably include power politics, diplomacy, war and conflict, alliance building, the work of international organizations, including international negotiations and treaties signed by states. The 'world' they described to you would probably resonate with many of the theorists whose work we have studied in Chapters 2.1–2.4. Realists would identify with the war/conflict and alliance building elements; Liberals would identify with the emphasis on negotiations and treaties; while the ears of English School writers would prick up at hearing your interviewees mention laws, rules and the resulting order that develops out of them.

In the last chapter we saw Alex Wendt trying to work some of the themes left neglected by this conventional agenda. He tried to bring the study of 'identity' into the mainstream study of IR but simultaneously he underscored the place of states in our understanding of who 'makes' IR by using these as our units of analysis, so in effect we found his alleged departure from the mainstream was not as decisive as he promised. Several other theoretical traditions have sought to make more of a decisive break from the mainstream of IR and in this chapter and the next we consider two of the best known of these: Marxism and feminism.

Marx and Marxism

Karl Marx's key works were written well before the discipline of IR was founded. The two main works you will probably have heard of were both published in the nineteenth century: *The Communist Manifesto*, co-authored with Friedrich Engels, appeared in 1848 (Marx and Engels 1998) and the three volumes of *Capital* appeared in 1867, 1885 and 1894 respectively (Marx 2008). Here, Marx sought both to explain the evolution of the capitalist system of economic production and to diagnose its ills. His normative goal was to bring about revolutionary change by highlighting what he considered to be the exploitation of the masses (what he called the 'proletariat') by a privileged few (the 'bourgeoisie').

To grasp the triangular relationship between Marx, the writers inspired by him and IR, it is helpful to bear in mind three features of this body of work:

1 **Capitalism as a 'system'.** We have seen the word 'system' used before by IR theorists. Marx saw in capitalism a different type of system, and in global capitalism in particular he saw forces structuring state interactions which Realists and Liberals totally ignored (Hobden and Wyn Jones 2008: 144). Within this system capabilities and interests are not defined in raw power terms, as in Realist theory, but in terms of whether you are a member of the bourgeoisie (owning the means of production and creaming off the profits) or a member of the proletariat

(selling your labour but not receiving in terms of payment the full value for the labour you give). 'World system' theorists used this terminology to explain IR in economic structuralist terms, as we shall see below.

2 **Economics as politics.** As Steve Hobden and Richard Stephen Wyn Jones explain, writers influenced by Marx hold a 'materialist conception of history' whereby historical change reflects the 'economic development of society ... economic development is effectively the motor of history' (2008: 145–6). Advances in technology change the nature of the productive process and in turn this prompts changes in the means of production as producers try to get on board with new technology and make the most of their enhanced productive capacity. Marxist writers not only see economics and politics as intertwined, as the one *necessarily* affects the other, they go further in seeing economics 'as the driving force of world politics' (Sterling-Folker 2006c: 200), as developments in the economic realm shape social arrangements and configurations. For Marxist writers, economic relations determine the content and conduct of domestic and international political action.

> Note how Marxist writers change our view of what makes the subject matter of IR: from politics and security in a condition of anarchy to economic relations in a global capitalist system.

3 **Normative theory.** Andrew Linklater cogently captures the essence of Marxist work: 'Transforming global society to eradicate alienation and estrangement has been the fundamental political aspiration of the Marxist tradition' (Linklater 2001a: 121). Marxist writers tend quite openly to blend elements of positivism with a normative agenda. In tracing the development of the capitalist system Marx was also thinking through how that system could be changed. He wanted to benefit the oppressed masses of workers whom he felt were not being paid sufficiently for the labour they sold to the owners of the factories where they worked. Marxist writers are generally quite comfortable about putting forward such agendas for change.

The key point here is that Marx's economic focus is starkly at odds with the ideas and goals of mainstream IR as I have presented its development after 1919. Conflict for Marxist writers is not the product of insecurity or other problems caused by an anarchic international arena; rather, it is the product of 'competition between capitalist classes of different states' (Jackson and Sørensen 2007: 187). Capitalism entails an endless search for new markets and resources and capitalists can inadverteneth draw states into conflict as they trawl the globe looking for new ways to expand their profit margins. Let us now have a look at the two main ways in which Marx's ideas have been used to explain international relations.

World System Theory

We saw in Chapter 2.3 how Neorealist writers such as Kenneth Waltz used the idea of an international system to explain the nature of the interactions between states. For Waltz, state behaviour in this system was shaped by the relative power of each state, power in this case being defined mainly by military capabilities. The system evolves from state choices about how best to survive in a condition of permanent insecurity and entails moves like alliance-building, power-balancing, and so forth.

World System Theory (WST) developed around the work of Immanuel Wallerstein, particularly his three-volume *The Modern World System* (Wallerstein 1974; Wallerstein 1980; Wallerstein 1989). Wallerstein had a new take on the idea that state interactions are shaped by unseen systemic forces, the Marxist twist being that the system is not shaped by relative power but by the workings of the global capitalist economy. A state's behaviour in WST is shaped by the position it occupies in the global capitalist system, and it is this position that affects that state's 'capabilities, identities and interests' (Freyberg-Inan 2006: 225).

Remember Marx's idea that political life within states was defined by the fraught relations between the bourgeoisie (exploiters) and the proletariat (exploited masses) (Figure 13). In Marx's view, wealth creation in the capitalist system tends to flow from the proletariat to the bourgeoisie: in Figure 13, the darker the shade, the wealthier the class, so here we can see wealth concentrated in the hands of very few capitalists. It is also noteworthy how the capital tends to reside in the hands of few in society at the expense of many, hence the pyramidal structure. Moving from the level of domestic society to the international level, in the global capitalist system, states can be grouped into three categories which broadly map onto the class division Marx identified in the domestic arena (Figure 14).

In WST, the classic Marx model has been adapted so that 'bourgeoisie' equates with 'core' states and 'proletariat' with 'periphery' states. The

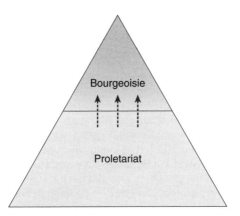

Figure 13   Marx's class system

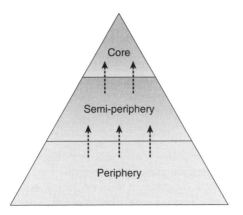

Figure 14   Marx's class system at the international level

crucial difference, however, is the existence of a group of countries called the 'semi-periphery' which sits between the two others.

- **Core states** – These states are the most advanced in economic terms, meaning they incorporate 'mass-market industries and sophisticated agriculture', ownership of which resides in the hands of an 'indigenous bourgeoisie' (Jackson and Sørensen 2007: 191). You might have heard these countries go by the name 'First World' – in economic terms they are 'the most prosperous and powerful' states in the international arena (Sterling-Folker 2006c: 202). The USA is the best example of a 'core' state today.

> It is important to note that the WST core–periphery model is dynamic: states can move between categories depending on changes to their political and economic structures over time.

- **Periphery states** – At the other end of the spectrum, we have states which export raw materials such as wood, grain and sugar to the core states (Jackson and Sørensen 2007: 191), and which sell unskilled labour to core producers (Sterling-Folker 2006c: 202). Core states manufacture goods using raw materials from the periphery and sell back the finished products to consumers in periphery states. The irony for periphery countries – we might call it the 'Third World' – is that they buy from core states goods made from the very labour and materials products they provided, but at marked-up prices which are far in excess of what it would have cost to manufacture them indigenously, had they developed the capacity to do so. Poorer states in Africa and Latin America, such as Malawi might today be considered periphery states.
- **Semi-periphery** – These states sit between the core and periphery, combining economic, political and social attributes from both of them (Sterling-Folker 2006c: 202). In the process of unequal exchange between periphery and core states, the semi-periphery states act out a crucial role as a buffer or 'shock absorber' (Jackson and Sørensen 2007: 191). Today, semi-periphery states might include Brazil and India.

> Make a list of countries you think belong to each of the three categories set down in WST. What are the common features across your groupings and can you find statistics to support your positioning of each state?

In sum, WST provides us with a structuralist account of economic exploitation in the global arena. It helps us both identify the position of various states within the system and theorizes the processes by which they find themselves in that position. WST offers a neat model of the workings of the global economic order often ignored or overlooked by proponents of Neoliberal IR theory. Marxist-inspired writers more often than not have a malign rather than benign view of ongoing developments in the international political economy, and this is well illustrated by the Marxist take on the phenomenon of 'globalization', as we shall see in the next section.

Taking it **FURTHER**

The exploitation of child labour in periphery states

The term 'sweatshop' has come to mean a factory where unskilled labourers are paid a pittance for their labour, and where they are treated appallingly in terms of pay, hours and working conditions. We often associate the term with multinational corporations that have their headquarters in core states but which profit from the cheap resources and labour located in periphery states (see, for example, Fuller 2006). The UN's International Labour Organization (ILO) reports that the problem goes much wider and deeper than factory labour alone while stressing that the problem is not confined to adult labourers. One estimate is that 250 million children between the ages of 5 and 14 are exploited for cheap labour. These children are sent down mines, are sold into prostitution, or are forced to work long hours on plantations or in the sweatshops (The UN Works for Fair Labour, undated). The ILO works among other things to eliminate child poverty and to improve equality in terms of pay and conditions for male and female labourers (International Labour Organization 1996–2008).

Writers in the Marxist tradition use all such statistics and stories supplied by agencies monitoring forced, exploitative, unfair or cheap labour. They use them to help advance our understanding of the subtle and sometimes not so subtle forms of coercion of the poor and weak by the wealthy and strong. The existence of sweatshops and the like would seem to provide support for the WST understanding of IR: they are empirically visible manifestations of the core exploiting the periphery. As Jackson and Sørensen explain: in the periphery, 'what little industrial activity exists is mostly under the external control of capitalists from other countries' (2007: 191).

Globalization or imperialism?

I could write a whole book trying to define the phenomenon of 'globalization' and still be no nearer a definitive account. It has many dimensions: political, economic, technological, social and cultural are just the main ones we tend to think of when we consider the ways in which the world is said to be shrinking under the effects of globalization. The term 'global village' has been coined to describe the cumulative effects of globalization (McLuhan and Powers 1989). The apparent paradox of combining reference to the entire globe with something as small as a village helps highlight the idea that today, in the supposed era of globalization, we know much more about events going on in the world than we did previously. This is partly due to the 24 hours a day news media, to new technologies such as the internet and portable satellite systems and to advanced communications such as mobile phones. In short, we experience more of the world more often and can travel around it faster than we used to, whether it be in the air or by surfing the net.

For our purposes here we only need consider the economic implications of globalization. For some, globalization is an inevitability, a phenomenon that modern states have to adapt to and take advantage of, but also work *with* to solve cross-border problems such as environmental degradation, the credit crunch and pollution. As former British Prime Minister Tony Blair put it in a speech to the Australian Parliament in 2006: 'Globalisation is a fact ... This is the age of the inter-connected. We all recognise this when it comes to economics, communication and culture. But the same applies to politics' (Blair 2006). For Neoliberals such as Blair, globalization exists, it is real, we can see and feel its effects and we can choose to embrace and work with them or ignore them. But we ignore them at our peril because they will affect us anyway; after all, we live in a 'global village' and are therefore always affected by goings-on elsewhere in our global neighbourhood.

> Globalization is one of those politics and IR buzzwords. In any essay or exam question where it features you will need to show knowledge of its essentially contested meaning.

Marxist writers have a quite different take on globalization. Where Blair sees it as a benign force posing challenges, yes, but also offering the hope of solutions, for Marxist writers, globalization is not something that happens to us but something we have created. In a highly constructivist take on things, a Marxist might argue that globalization is something that we in the West, or in WST terms, the 'core', have *authored*. Globalization in its economic guise has been driven by the spread of multinational corporations, by cross-border financial transactions and all supported by an international financial and regulatory regime led by international organizations such as the International Monetary Fund (IMF) and the World Bank. To illustrate this point, let us take a look at three examples of how a Marxist might respond to Blair's globalization thesis:

Globalization is not new

Hearing policy-makers talk of globalization we may labour under the impression that there *was* a beginning to it – some year or event (never defined) that marked the beginning of the process. A Marxist would ask: can we pinpoint the 'start' of globalization? No, because like any ongoing process, locating its origins are intensely problematic. This is key because whereas policy-makers believing in globalization theory might want to present the era of globalization as 'new' or 'different' from previous eras, Marxists can place globalization in their longer story about the evolution of modern capitalism going back hundreds of years.

Christopher Chase-Dunn, for instance, contends that what we are seeing today are 'continuations of trends that have long accompanied the expansion of capitalism'; the only difference is that we notice them more now (quoted in Hobden and Wyn Jones 2008: 220). Furthermore, since globalization has become 'part of the ideological armoury of elites within the contemporary world', and a driver of domestic and foreign policies in many states around the world, globalization is being used as the rationale for diminishing workers' rights as states seek to help their national businesses stay competitive (Hobden and Wyn Jones 2008: 221). Noam Chomsky presents a damning indictment of the Neoliberal consensus on globalization by suggesting it is no more than a rhetorical smokescreen: 'it should be stressed that the economic doctrines preached by the powerful are intended for others, so they can be more efficiently robbed and exploited' (quoted in Burchill 2001b: 53. For more on Chomsky see Chapter 2.12 of this book).

Globalization is a new form of imperialism

Just as the British, French, Dutch and other European states conquered empires by force, a Marxist take on contemporary military interventions by leading Western powers would be that these are expressions of imperialist exploitation by a different name. Just as Chomsky pointed out that economic free trade doctrines are masks for economic exploitation of the periphery by core states, so interventions for humanitarian reasons or to promote democracy can be read in the same way. Work on the Kosovo intervention of 1999 (Cafruny 2006) and the contemporary War on Terror (Rupert 2007: 159–62) both point out that energy security (keeping open oil and gas pipelines and flows from of these vital natural resources Russia Central Asia and the Middle East) surely played a huge role in the decision to intervene in these regions.

In fact, argues Cafruny, the Kosovo intervention was partly predicated on a long established supposition by US and European policy-makers that they needed to diversify their sources of oil supply to counter the challenge from Middle Eastern exporters and 'ensure continued dominance of international oil markets' (2006: 217). Mark Rupert, meanwhile, suggests that the 'war on terror' has the longer-term goal of making the world safe for penetration by US businesses, a geopolitical explanation with evidence reaching back decades into American foreign economic and political conduct (2007: 161–2).

Which account of these interventions do you believe? Do we have to choose? Can we combine elements of the Marxist take on them with elements of the policy-makers' justification to generate a multi-causal explanation?

International organizations entrench institutionalized inequalities between states

Ngaire Woods well captures the Marxist take on international institutions such as the UN, the World Bank and the IMF, stating:

> Existing multilateral organizations are still hierarchically arranged. Their authority and effectiveness depend on the will and actions of their most powerful members and, as the most powerful states balance up the advantages of stronger and more effective institutions against possible losses in their own control and sovereignty, they repeatedly come down on the side of the latter. (1999: 9)

While ostensibly these bodies work to reduce poverty and enhance the integration of less developed states into the global economy, a Marxist views them quite differently: as covert agents helping to enmesh these states further into the exploitative structures of the capitalist system.

Contrary to Blair's idea that globalization exists and that it is a benign transformative force shaping the modern world, you can see that Marxists take a different view. They interpret economic, political and military interventions by core states in periphery states as starkly at odds with the high sounding moral rhetoric about preventing humanitarian disaster and advancing liberal democratic ideals about which we hear so much. The very globalization thesis, in the Marxist view, is severely open to interpretation because it is a 'concept' not a 'fact'.

Questions to ponder

" Do Marxist texts provide a valid theoretical intervention into IR when they are so obviously 'positioned'? "

The fundamental issue raised by this question is one of theoretical validity which we discussed in Chapter 1.4. There are many ways in which we might judge the quality of a theory: it needs to be reliable, to be evidentially sound, to be falsifiable, and perhaps to have predictive capabilities. One way to think through this question might therefore be to set out the basic Marxist position with reference to key exponents such as Wallerstein or Marx himself. The better answers will challenge the assumption that there is one coherent 'Marxist' tradition by making clear the variety of agendas pursued by different writers influenced by Marxist ideas: some are more positivist and attempt to be more 'scientific' than others. Wide reading and preparation will alert you to the competing styles within this broad church.

The question is also alluding to the big debate within IR between positivists and normative theorists – the give-away is that the word 'positioned' is in quotes. Think about what it means to say a theory is 'positioned' – do you think a theory can ever be anything other than 'positioned'? However much we might aim to be scientific and objective – can we really be?

" 'Men make their own history, but they do not make it as they please' (Marx). What is the significance of this quote for the study of IR? "

The first task here is to demonstrate that you understand where Marx wrote this and what he meant by it. You do not need to spell out his ideas on each and every aspect, but you should demonstrate a familiarity with key concepts such as Historical Materialism and the capitalist forces Marx saw as guiding the progression of history over time.

From here you might go on to consider the issue of structure. The structure/agency debate is a big one within IR and you could reference other writers who engage in it (especially Waltz versus the Constructivists) and then show what Marxist IR writers meant by concentrating on global economic structures. You could deploy WST to back your case and/or explore a case study in the application of Marxism to military interventions such as Kosovo (for example from the Sterling-Folker book) to back your case about Marxists reading world political events through the lens of (usually sinister) economic forces. It is then up to you to say how significant you think the Marxist emphasis on structures is.

We have not yet covered Feminism in this book but note the gendered nature of the quote ('men' not 'women' or 'people'). The better student may well mention Marx's oversight here and in the process demonstrate good knowledge of other IR theories.

References to more information

MARX, K. (2008) *Capital: A New Abridgement*. Oxford: Oxford University Press.

Marx's works have been published and reprinted many times over and you can find books containing the full text and abridged versions. The first volume of *Capital* is probably the best known so the above text is very useful, containing almost all of Volume 1 and extracts from Volume 3.

COX, R.W. (1987) *Production, Power and World Order: Social Forces in the Making of History*. New York: Columbia University Press.

WALLERSTEIN, I. (2004) *World-Systems Analysis: An Introduction*. Durham, NC: Duke University Press.

An updated version of WST giving you the nuts and bolts of the theory and its application today. Will save you ploughing through the lengthy and densely written historical material in the original three volumes!

AXFORD, B. (1995) *The Global System: Economics, Politics and Culture*. Cambridge: Polity.

See Chapter 2 on Marxism, Imperialism and Wallersteinian World System Theory.

BURBACH, R. (2001) *Globalization and Postmodern Politics: From Zapatistas to High-Tech Robber Barons*. London: Pluto Press.

Part 1 is especially recommended because it sets out neo-Marxist interpretations and responses to globalization.

CALLINICOS, A. (2002) 'Marxism and Global Governance', in D. Held and A. McGrew (eds) *Governing Globalization: Power, Authority and Global Governance*. Cambridge: Polity, pp. 249–66.

JENKINS, R. (1970) *Exploitation: The World Power Structure and the Inequality of Nations*. London: MacGibbon and Kee.

KUBÁLKOVÁ, V. AND CRUICKSHANK, A.A. (1980) *Marxism-Leninism and the Theory of International Relations*. London: Routledge.

BUSH, R., JOHNSTON, G. AND COATES, D. (EDS) (1987) *The World Order: Socialist Perspectives*. Cambridge: Polity.

See the chapter by Ankie Hoogvelt which gives empirical support to claims for the existence of a 'world capitalist system'. Hoogvelt has expanded and updated this thesis in **A. HOOGVELT (1997)** *Globalisation and the Postcolonial World*. London: Macmillan.

ARONOWITZ, A. AND GAUNTNEY, H. (EDS) (2003) *Implicating Empire: Globalization and Resistance in the 21st Century World Order*. New York: Center for the Study of Culture, Technology and Work, Graduate School and University Center of the City University New York.

CHANG, H. (2003) 'Kicking Away the Ladder – Globalization and Economic Development in Historical Perspective', in J. Michie (ed.) *The Handbook of Globalization*. Cheltenham: Edward Elgar, pp. 385–94.

2.7	
critical theory	

Key terms:

Communicative action
Legitimacy
Capitalism
Hegemony
Order
History
State
Emancipation

Critical Theory (CT) is closely allied to, but seeks to go well beyond, the Marxist theories we explored in the previous chapter. It is also interesting in that it has an affinity with some of the postmodern approaches we study later in the book, as well as containing elements of Constructivism. All in all, CT is difficult to 'place' as a neatly self-contained theory about IR because in both its scope and its methods it transcends many of the other theories of IR you will study on your course. Here is just a flavour of the problems IR theorists have 'placing' CT:

- Mark Rupert identifies CT so strongly with Marxism that they share a chapter in his book (Rupert 2007).
- In Jackson and Sørensen (2007: 189–92), CT is referred to as 'neo-Marxism' and integrated almost seamlessly into a chapter on Marxism.
- Sterling-Folker (2006d) puts CT nearer the postmodern end of the spectrum and includes it in a chapter with that approach to IR.
- Hutchings (1999: 88) helpfully suggests that we use CT in the singular to refer to the Marxist and/or neo-Marxist variant explored in this chapter but reminds us that it can be used in a plural sense to cover any 'non-orthodox' theoretical perspective. This is why CT also goes by the name 'International Political Theory' because its methods can be used to study international politics and social and political theory more generally.

Summing it up, Hutchings observes that that the terminology used to refer to this array of critical perspectives 'can be somewhat confusing' (Hutchings, 1999: 88, note 3). You will have to be careful in essays and exam answers to state exactly what you mean by CT and how you see it relating to other positivist and normative theories of IR.

This chapter begins by introducing you to the origins of CT with an emphasis on the work of Jürgen Habermas. It goes on to study how CT has been accented in IR using the work of Robert Cox and Andrew Linklater.

Introduction to CT

To use the terminology we have been working with throughout this book, CT is most definitely a normative theory. As Richard Devetak puts it, quoting J. Maclean in the process, 'Behind critical international theory lies the conviction that "international relations could be other than it is at both the theoretical and practical levels"' (2001a: 145). Here we see the normative element shining through, as well as an element of Constructivist thought in the sentiment that things could be different if we think and act in ways that go against custom, convention and social norms. Like Marxism, feminism and postmodernism, Devetak writes later in the chapter, CT concentrates on the concept of exclusion and how to overcome it and 'sets itself the task of understanding the conditions under which emancipation in world politics is possible' (2000a: 166).

First generation CT emerged in the years between the First and Second World Wars in Germany among the so-called Frankfurt School of writers, which included thinkers such as Max Horkheimer, Theodore Adorno, Walter Benjamin, Herbert Marcuse, Erich Fromm and Leo Lowenthal.

Note how CT emerged in Germany at exactly the same time as E.H. Carr and others were expounding the virtues of Realist thought over Liberal thought in the UK. Why do you think CT took so long to make itself felt within the discipline of IR?

The broad aim of these writers was 'to salvage Marxist thought from its orthodox, political manifestations' (Sterling-Folker 2006d: 158), which were restricting its emancipatory potential by centring the debate almost exclusively on economic relations. The concern for the Frankfurt School was, rather, 'to comprehend the central features of contemporary society by understanding its historical and social development and tracing contradictions in the present which may open up the possibility of transcending contemporary society and its in-built pathologies and forms of domination' (Devetak 2001a: 146). Production, they argued, is more than a function of economic relations: ideas, intersubjective meanings, norms, institutions and social practices all influence the production of material goods (Sinclair 1996: 9). In other words, the Frankfurt School wanted to use Marxist ideals but to build upon them in new ways to challenge the view that the state was the natural or normal basis on which societies should be organized. In short, they interrogated how we have come to *think* about the state.

Second-generation CT is associated with the work of Jürgen Habermas and his conception of 'legitimacy'. His logic is as follows (all from Lynch 2006: 183–4).

1 There are two types of action: 'strategic' and 'communicative'.

2 Strategic action is undertaken to manipulate another person or state via 'threats, incentives or rhetoric'. For example, states use strategic action when they use military force to coerce (force an opponent to do something they might not otherwise do) or deter (prevent an opponent from doing something they might otherwise do).

3 Communicative action occurs 'when actors set aside their self-interest, their relative power, and even their identities in order to seek truth – or at least consensus about the right course of action'.

4 Strategic action produces only temporary agreement because it is imposed by one actor on another. Communicative action, by contrast, is more legitimate because both actors have engaged in rational argument in an environment in which 'all affected actors are effectively able to speak and be heard'.

For Habermas, legitimacy in the international arena is only gained for a specific action if there has previously been a full and frank discussion by all actors likely to be affected by that course of action, for example a military intervention. In this forum it is not Realist power or force that wins the day, but 'the rationally more convincing argument' (Sterling-Folker 2006d: 164). According to Habermas, such 'ideal speech acts' are possible and the benchmark by which we judge states' behaviour is as much based on *how* they reach decisions as what those decisions are. Habermas's work on communicative action is wide-ranging and complex. It is a form of social theory which mixes philosophy, ethics, politics and linguistics to help us see the potential for a genuinely international public sphere to emerge. Critical Theorists do not just want to explain the world but to critique it and contribute to human betterment by encouraging open and equal exchanges of views about matters of contemporary importance. We shall now see how these variants of CT have been applied to the study of IR.

Critical Theory in IR

Both the traditional Frankfurt School and the second generation work of Habermas have been felt within the study of IR for at least two decades. We will use the work of two scholars to illustrate this impact: first, Robert Cox, whose major intellectual debt is to Marxism, and, second, Andrew Linklater, who draws more on Habermas' theory of communicative action to chart the possibilities for us to transcend the Realist logic of the state system (Hutchings 1999: 66, 70).

Cox on societies, states and order

As described by Timothy Sinclair, Cox's research programme has two elements to it. On the one hand he wants to understand how a relationship, institution or process operates on a day-to-day basis. On the other hand, Cox wants to understand the wider ramifications of the processes by which these things work, 'the contradictions and conflicts inherent in a social structure ... and the nature and extent of structural change that is feasible' (Sinclair 1996: 8).

> Note here how Cox combines positivism (understanding the nature of a relationship/institution/process) with a normative agenda (how can we alter that relationship/institution/process in the future?)

CT is all about understanding aspects of the prevailing order but also taking a much broader perspective which sees that initially contemplated part as 'just one component' and seeking 'to understand the processes of change in which both parts and whole are involved'. It is a guide to 'strategic action for bringing about an alternative order' rather than a 'guide to tactical actions' that sustain the existing order (Cox 1996b: 89–90).

In his article 'Social Forces, States and World Order', first published in 1981, Cox rethought what he saw as a narrow and overly deterministic Marxist conception of 'structure'. A structure, he suggests, does not wholly determine individual actions; people have more room for manoeuvre than that. Sure, individuals cannot ignore structures but they can resist and oppose them in ways that may bring about structural changes. Here is the Constructivist element to Cox's thinking.

What is a 'structure'? For Cox, 'Three categories of forces' interact in a structure (all from Cox 1996b: 98–9), the direction and strength of the interaction being dependent on the particular case at hand.

1 **Material capabilities** – The Marxist element: 'technological and organizational capabilities' including natural resources and the wealth that commands all of them.

2 **Ideas** – Two kinds. To begin with, we have intersubjective meanings that shape our views of the world at a fundamental level. These are historically 'durable' ideas such as the idea that the world is made up of states. Then we have ideas about the world held by different groups within societies. Whereas the first set of ideas are common throughout a particular historical structure, these competing

sets of ideas continually hold out the prospect for change through the establishment of new structures or the transformation of existing structures.

3 **Institutions** – Are used to stabilize and perpetuate a particular order. They are the embodiment of all the power relations that prevail at their point of origin; 'are particular amalgams of ideas and material power which in turn influence the development of ideas and material capabilities'.

Having identified the components of a structure, Cox then goes on to set out his method of 'historical structures' (Cox 1996b: 100–1). The essence of this approach is to establish the nature of the sphere of human activity from a 'study of the historical situation to which it relates' and then to look for rival structures 'expressing alternative possibilities of development.' We do this on three interrelated levels:

1 **Social forces** – flowing from the organization of production and the production process.

2 **Forms of state** – as derived from a study of the nature of state/society at the particular historical juncture.

3 **World orders** – the make-up of forces that shape the interactions between states.

The connections between levels means that developments in one area affect developments in the other two. The task of the Critical Theorist is to capture the totality of the historical process that led to the present configuration of structures on each of these levels and then to ascertain the possibilities for change in the future arising from possible structural change within each level and at the macro levels themselves. Adapting Cox's own diagrams (Cox 1996b: 98 and 101) we might present the gamut of relationships between and within the levels as shown in Figure 15.

In Figure 15 we see the flow of influence between the three spheres of activity he suggests we use the method of historical structures to uncover. Within each level its component structures (ideas, institutions and material capabilities) are constantly interacting with each other and for this reason the possibilities for transformations in human activity are endless, given the circulation of ideas, institutions and material capabilities across levels as well as within them.

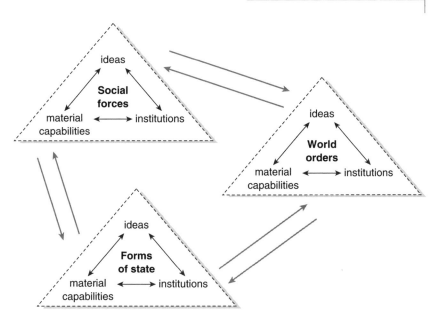

Figure 15   Cox's levels and their internal structures

Cox sets out an ambitious research programme which invites the student of IR to be a good positivist in order to be a good normative theorist, and this raises interesting questions about the relationship between the two types of theory.

In the rest of the article (Cox 1996b, 102–13) Cox shows how to apply his method of historical structures to understanding the global order prevailing under the ***pax Americana***. Rather than detail the moves he makes here I will leave you to read up on this, and turn instead to his second key article, 'Gramsci, Hegemony and International Relations', first published in 1983, where Cox developed the concept of **hegemony** in IR in two stages.

The first part of the article was devoted to a reconsideration of the concept of hegemony using the work of Antonio Gramsci. Cox began by arguing that hegemony is not 'dominance of one country over others' or another word for 'imperialism' (1996a: 135). The first definition makes it too focused on state-on-state relations; the second is too far from the Gramscian meaning to make it relevant.

> *Keep a list of different definitions of 'hegemony' as you come across them in your reading. They will be useful when it comes to writing essays and exam answers on global order and its critics.*

The only way we can understand the meaning of 'hegemony', Cox suggests, is to study when it is that periods of hegemony begin and end (and therefore when historical epochs can be called 'nonhegemonic'). His categorization of recent international history is as follows (Cox 1996a: 135–6):

- **1845–75: hegemonic** – A world economy with Britain central and holding the balance of power in Europe.
- **1875–1945: nonhegemonic** – Reverse of Period 1. Many other powers challenged British supremacy, two global wars erupted and global free trade collapsed.
- **1945–65: hegemonic** – A world economy with the US central, but arguably not as stable as during Period 1.
- **1965–83 (Cox's 'present' at the time he first published the article) nonhegemonic** – A fracturing of the US-centred period of hegemony after 1945 (ibid.: 135–6).

The crux for Cox is that hegemonic periods are not based on naked exploitation or coercion of weak states by the strong, but are formed when the order created is 'universal in conception'. Moreover, hegemony is about more than state-on-state relations but about civil society operating 'on the world scale' (Cox 1996a: 136).

The tool for this spread of legitimacy behind the dominant mode of production is international organizations which aid 'the process through which the institutions of hegemony and its ideology are developed' (Cox 1996a: 137). International organizations facilitate hegemony in five ways (Cox 1996a: 138–9):

1. **Rules** – International organizations make, enforce and change the rules, notably in areas of monetary policy and trade relations. The GATT, the IMF and the World Bank are such institutions operating today.

2. **Products** – International organizations are generally set up by the state that establishes the hegemony, or at least they have its support. This informal structure of influence might be seen in the role the US plays in IMF decision-making and the role the Permanent-5 play in decision-making in the UN Security Council.

3 **Ideology** – International organizations set the parameters for policy discussions, legitimating the approaches and practices of the 'dominant social and economic forces'. The neoliberal agenda at the IMF could be one example of the ideological legitimation function performed by this organization, linking to the Marxist critiques of international institutions noted in Chapter 2.6.

4 **Elites** – Brought in from peripheral states, they may wish to change the ideological *status quo* but end up co-opted by it. Thus, writes Cox, 'Hegemony is like a pillow: it absorbs blows and sooner or later the would-be assailant will find it comfortable to rest upon.' Part of the process of creating a social class that transcends state borders.

5 **Absorption of counterhegemonic ideas** – A bit like the co-option of elites in that new ideas or approaches can be sucked into the organizational machinery and regurgitated as hegemony-supporting policies which say one thing but which actually do another.

> *Try and bring Cox's model up to the present day by pinpointing periods of hegemony/ nonhegemony since 1983. Where would the end of the Cold War fit in? How would you define the world today: hegemonic or nonhegemonic?*

Through his work on social forces, order and hegemony, Cox invites us to get inside the workings of states in order to better understand their internal dynamics and, from an IR perspective, the interactions between them. Using his method of 'historical structures', Cox hopes to show that many of the things we take for granted as existing 'out there' in the world, like states themselves, are not social 'facts' but things we build ourselves. Even though Cox's greatest debt is to Marxism, we can see a strongly Constructivist turn to his thinking. Oddly, as we saw in Chapter 2.5 of this book, it would be several years before Constructivist ideas made a real and lasting impact on the discipline.

Beyond Realism and Marxism: Linklater

The work of Andrew Linklater comes from a slightly different but related tradition of inquiry into the state of normative theory in IR and how to develop it. We will briefly summarize the essence of his argument to show you how he builds his brand of CT.

Linklater set out to write 'a critical international theory which endeavours to incorporate and yet to supersede the main achievements of realism and Marxism' (1990: 7). His rationale was that the three dominant traditions in IR at his time of writing had taken the discipline so far, but that none alone had really solved the conundrum of explaining outcomes in IR as the product of interactions between states and the systems within which they operate. For Linklater (1990: 10–27) the flaws in each tradition were obvious:

- **Realism**. Focuses on the causes and consequences of war within an anarchical system but overlooks other important webs of relations between states, such as their economic relations. Lacks any sort of emancipatory agenda, seeing a system that perpetually reproduces itself from Thucydides to the present and into the future.
- **Rationalism (or the English School)**. Incorporates the best features of Realism in a larger framework that accounts for order as well as conflict. In the Rationalist account, world politics is formed out of more than 'strategic competition' between states (Linklater 1990: 15. see Chapter 2.4 in this book). However, it is Western-centric and ignores the possibility that global values and other sources of order and disorder might exist.
- **Revolutionism (or Marxism)**. Sees conflict in the international system not as the outcome of nation-state insecurities but as the product of tensions within the international system of economic production which cuts across state borders. Revolutionism therefore underplays military insecurity and conflict – taking us back to the merits of Realism. Plus it was dealt a huge blow by the end of the Cold War which undermined the possibility of forming a 'socialist' world state system.

Having detailed the state of the discipline, Linklater's conclusion is that elements of the first and the third approaches (from Realism: geopolitics; from Marxism: capitalism) are vital to a comprehensive understanding of IR, but that in isolation each is insufficiently attentive to the fabric of global history to have the explanatory force their proponents claim for them. As he put it, 'a critical theory of international relations can only be developed by moving beyond the realist and Marxist perspectives' (Linklater 1990: 165).

The 'world' Linklater sees is neither that of the Marxist nor the Realist. It is a more complex world in which states share the world stage with all sorts of other social forces.

For Linklater, the 'critical' element of CT comes from it seeking to extend our understanding of 'community' through a reinvigorated Marxism, one that takes into account all the drivers of human norms and relations between societies rather than just class struggle (Linklater, 1990: 171). His broad concept of IR chimes in nicely with the general drive behind CT identified in this chapter: it takes old concepts and looks at them afresh; it invites us to de-naturalize things about the world we take for granted; and it holds out hopes for a new international ethics which would work for all in the world rather than a privileged few.

Questions to ponder

❝Are we living in a period of US hegemony? Answer with reference to Cox's work on world order.❞

There are at least two steps you will have to take to answer this question successfully. First of all you have to define 'hegemony'. Knowledge of the two articles by Cox explored in this chapter will be key but you can refer to any of his books/articles as long as they are relevant to the question set. Cox does a lot of the work for you in both dismissing populist definitions of 'hegemony' and then setting out his preferred definition. The better answers will supplement Cox's work with a range of competing definitions of 'hegemony' particularly by Realist writers. If you have made a checklist of these definitions, your task here should be fairly easy.

Having explained Cox's understanding of 'hegemony' you then have to judge whether the world today is hegemonic. You could do this in one of two ways. On the one hand, you could use Cox's analysis of the features that have made for hegemonic periods in history and those that have made for nonhegemonic periods and weigh up how the world today looks compared to these ideal type periods. On the other hand, you could avoid the past comparisons and go straight for analysis of the social/material/ideational/institutional forces you see prevalent in the world today and whether these constitute hegemony. The danger is that you pick and choose the 'facts' to suit your argument, so pay attention to: the start point of your selected period, its ideological underpinnings and the organizational fabric. The best answers will stay close to Cox's idea that hegemony rests on consent more than coercion/force so avoid offering accounts that major on US military action around the globe.

"Do the differences between Critical Theorists undermine our ability to call it a 'theory' of IR?"

This is a tricky question because it is inviting you to reflect both on the nature of CT as a form of inquiry into IR, as well as the nature of 'theory' more generally. Early on in the answer you will therefore have to scope your answer, pare it down to some basics. On CT, you might pick two or three writers as exemplary of the kinds of debates these theorists have among themselves. The same goes for theory: there are many perspectives on what this term means, so pick one that you think helps you best make your argument.

In terms of structure, you could go for a yes/no one. First of all, present the evidence that suggests fragmentation within a theoretical tradition undermines its claim to posit a coherent or unified approach to the study of IR. Then look at the converse view that these theories share enough in common to mark them out from other theoretical traditions in IR. The best answers will allude to the fact that all theoretical traditions have different wings to them and interplay with other theories. Overall, therefore, your argument will turn on your opinion of how much unity we can expect within *any* theory of IR.

References to more information

Generally on CT:

Stanford Encyclopedia of Philosophy (2005) 'Critical Theory', http://plato.stanford.edu/entries/critical-theory/.

Excellent overview of CT together with an insight into the divisions between writers in this tradition.

GIDDENS, A. (1985) *A Contemporary Critique of Historical Materialism*, Vol. 2: *The Nation-State and Violence*. Cambridge: Polity.

HELD, D. (1980) *Introduction to Critical Theory: Horkheimer to Habermas*. Berkeley, CA: University of California Press.

On CT in IR:

ASHLEY, R.K. (1981) 'Political Realism and Human Interest', *International Studies Quarterly*, 25(2): 204–36.

NEUFELD, M. (1995) *The Restructuring of International Relations Theory*. Cambridge: Cambridge University Press.

KEYMAN, E.F. (1997) *Globalization, State, Identity/Difference: Toward a Critical Social Theory of International Relations*. Atlantic Highlands, NJ: Humanities Press.

Applies CT to the study of globalization and points ahead to the chapters in this book on feminism, postmodernism and postcolonialism.

WYN JONES, R. (ED.) (2001) *Critical Theory and World Politics.* Boulder, CO: Lynne Rienner.

A comprehensive collection that showcases the work of both Marxist and more Habermasian-inclined theorists.

REVIEW OF INTERNATIONAL STUDIES (2005) 'Forum on Habermas', 31(1): 127–209.

Includes articles on the Frankfurt School as well as on Feminist Critical Theory.

REVIEW OF INTERNATIONAL STUDIES (2007) 'Critical International Relations Theory after 25 Years', 33, special issue.

YOUTUBE (2007) 'Jürgen Habermas interview', posted 1 February http//www.youtube.com-/watch?v=jB16ALNh18Q.

Short piece in which Habermas sums up the key themes of his research and how they relate to the contemporary world.

2.8	
feminism	

Key terms:

Gender
Masculine/feminine
Patriarchy
Sovereignty
Rationality
Security

Feminist scholarship came to the discipline of IR in and around the 1980s and 1990s. As with other openly normative theories we have covered in the last few chapters in this book, it was not IR that produced feminist scholarship. Feminism, rather, is a wider social and intellectual movement which has had a major impact across politics, academia and society over recent decades. In IR, a diverse array of feminist scholars have added a vital new term to the language of IR: **gender**. This has gone hand in hand, in many but not all cases, with a reassessment of the fundamental ways in which IR scholars try to make sense of their subject matter.

Feminists have therefore achieved two significant things in IR. First of all, they have 'added' women where previously they were overlooked or invisible in the study of IR. Second, they have reassessed definitions and re-thought methods of studying central IR concepts such as the state, security and sovereignty. As such, critical branches of feminism share affinities with theories such as postmodernism in that they seek to go beyond hackneyed ways of defining and studying IR. This chapter will begin by introducing the concept of gender and move on to highlight the different varieties of feminist scholarship you are likely to encounter on your course.

> As you read around feminism make a note of the similarities and differences between feminism and some of the earlier theories such as Realism and Liberalism in terms of: subject matter; methods; kind of knowledge produced about IR.

Gender

Of all the keywords in feminist scholarship, 'gender' is probably the most important for you to get to grips with. When we are filling out passport forms, opinion surveys, forms to get NUS cards, and so on, we are asked to tick one of the two 'gender' boxes: male or female. It is easy to tick the correct box because we all know what the differences between men and women are: men are 'male' and women are 'female'. But what is it, beyond biological differences, that distinguishes masculinity from femininity? It is precisely this question that critical feminist scholars seek to answer through analysis of the constructions of each category and their day-to-day ramifications in the practice and theory of IR.

> Feminists argue that IR has excluded/marginalized women empirically (by not seeing them as valid subjects for study) and theoretically (by constructing the conceptual building blocks of the discipline on concepts associated with masculinity).

Here are two of many definitions of gender from key writings you are likely to encounter:

- **V. Spike Peterson** (1992: 8): 'the socially constructed dichotomy of masculine-feminine (man-woman, maleness-femaleness) shaped only in part by biologically construed male-female dimensions'.
- **J. Ann Tickner and Laura Sjoberg** (2007: 186): 'a set of socially constructed characteristics describing what men and women ought to be'. Masculinity is associated with characteristics such as 'strength, rationality, independence, protector and public' and femininity with 'weakness, emotionality, relational, protected and private'.

Note the emphasis Peterson, Tickner and Sjoberg all place on the constructedness of gender categories we commonly take to be givens. Feminist scholarship tries to highlight the artificiality of these supposedly natural divisions and also shows how the masculine characteristics have been privileged or looked more favourably upon within IR than feminine characteristics – how international relations operates a **patriarchal** system that works for men at the expense (literally) of women not just in practical terms but in the very ways we see and talk about IR. As Daryl Jarvis puts it (2001: 105), gender is 'an indispensable ingredient in the study of international politics, a means of understanding not just the systemic basis of the international system, but of the power structures embedded in those relations'.

In the introduction to her edited collection *Gendered States*, Peterson (1992: 9–10) identifies four reasons why it is useful to 'gender' IR:

1 **It decentres biological explanations** – Conceptions of maleness and femaleness are not fixed over time or across national boundaries. Taking gender constructions as 'given' rather than 'made' obstructs our understanding of the subtle yet powerful part they play in the practice and study of IR. As Charlotte Hooper explains, 'historical and anthropological research suggests that there is no single "masculinity" or "femininity" and that both are subject to numerous and fairly fast-changing historical and cultural variations' (2006: 377).

2 **Interdependence of key words** – Peterson here concentrates on the inter-relationship of the terms 'masculine' and 'feminine' and their associated characteristics such as 'rationality' (masculine) versus 'emotionality' (feminine). They are not mutually exclusive but interdependent, meaning that our understanding of the one is necessarily dependent on the characteristics we attribute to the other. Usually, feminine characteristics are valued less than masculine ones and

this highlights the power *in* language to degrade the feminine at the expense of the masculine.

Feminism is not just about women or women's concerns. It crucially feeds into social theory and questions about our ways of 'being' in the world, male or female.

---

3 **Structure and agency** – Feminist scholarship is comfortable working on questions about the 'subjective, everyday' and relating these to historical or structural contents within which these day-to-day experiences are felt. There is no privileging of one level of analysis as we have, for example, in Neorealist theory which emphasises the structural determinants of state behaviour away from the identity/beliefs/idiosyncrasies of the states themselves and which downplays the human and ideational aspects of IR.

4 **Diversity** – Feminists take an inclusive approach to the subject matter of IR by speaking to all of the following issues: power, identity, culture, sexual relations, discourse, the international division of labour, poverty and militarism. This wide agenda gives feminists a distinctive handle on all of the big ontological, epistemological and methodological questions about IR as a discipline covered in Chapter 1.4 of this book. See Cynthia Enloe (2001) for a good example of the eclectic range of subjects to which this theory speaks.

Feminists are broadly interested in what makes IR work to exclude women and theorize them out of the discipline.

Feminist perspectives

By saying there are different strands to feminist thought we are not saying that these are mutually exclusive or that they are somehow in opposition to each other. However, there are distinctive approaches to feminist IR that are worth noting because they highlight the porous nature of the boundaries between the theories covered in the book and the capacity for one theoretical tradition to house a diverse array of perspectives. Something of this complexity is captured in Figure 16.

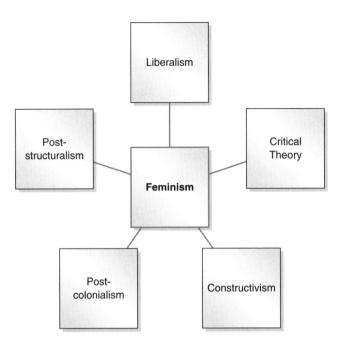

Figure 16   Feminism in IR Theory

Feminist scholars pick up aspects of wider work both in IR and the social sciences more generally. Here we will follow the work of Tickner and Sjoberg (2007: 188–92) who give a breakdown of how these myriad influences show themselves in feminist scholarship. Other textbooks do it differently (for instance, Smith and Owens 2008: 181–5). Note also that their choice of terminology, for example, poststructuralism instead of postmodernism, differs slightly from the terminology used in this book. However, the point is to note the overlap between the various theoretical traditions and this is as good a place as any to seek them out.

> That writers cannot agree on how best to capture the field of feminist scholarship says something about the breadth and depth of its concerns. Keep a note of all the variations for use in essays/exams where you have to define 'feminism'.

Liberal feminism

Liberal feminists basically accept the conventional framework of IR by looking to add women and women's issues to the IR agenda as it currently stands. This 'add women and stir' approach takes existing subject matters, methods and the positivist epistemologies and introduces women where previously they were either invisible or forgotten about. They do this by documenting 'various aspects of women's subordination' (Tickner and Sjoberg 2007: 188) in economic, political, legal, social and health terms. They seek out women's contributions to society and shine a light on them to show the contributions they have made and to make a call for greater equality. International organizations like the UN and pressure groups such as Human Rights Watch have collected vast amounts of data, statistics and reports on gender (in)equality and women's human rights around the world and they can be mined for information to help the Liberal feminist cause (UN 2008a; Human Rights Watch 2006).

Critical feminism

Critical feminists do more than add women and stir them into existing IR scholarship. Taking inspiration from the work of Marxists and Critical Theorists such as Robert Cox (see Chapter 2.7 of this book), they stress the part perceptions of the key word 'gender' play in moulding policies and practices in the world. Gender in the Critical perspective is another structure that shapes (often unwittingly) how men and women interact and how relations between them are infused with power inequalities. Critical feminists show how all this plays out in the form of material (economic) inequalities and the maltreatment and exploitation of women. After highlighting these structural inequities, Critical Theorists hope that they can be changed in the future, giving their work an emancipatory edge, or in Kimberley Hutchings' words, 'a productive impact on how international politics are to be understood and judged' (1999: 83).

> Critical, Constructivist and postcolonial feminists are more openly normative than Liberal feminists. Poststructuralist feminists want to bring about even more radical change to the world and our study of it.

Constructivist feminism

Following the Social Constructivists, feminist constructivists focus on the ideational rather than the material aspects of global politics. They 'focus on the way that ideas about gender shape and are shaped by global politics' (Tickner and Sjoberg 2007: 190) and are interested in discovering the causes of the ideas that shape our gendered world as well as in the language through which these ideas are expressed. Constructivist feminists work at de-naturalizing divisions between the genders by investigating the ideas that lie behind these constructions and asking: where have our ideas about gender come from; are they just; and how might they be altered?

Poststructural feminism

This is the widest, most thoroughgoing feminist perspective that questions the very ways in which we make sense of the world through our language, our theories and our 'scientific' ways of studying IR. We have previously seen that gender divisions are constructed around the interdependence of terms such as 'masculine' and 'feminine' and the characteristics we tend to associate with each gender. We further noted that these categories and characteristics are imbued with power relations in that the masculine characteristics tend to be looked upon as the standard for the rest of humanity to live up to: things masculine tend to be privileged over things feminine.

Poststructural feminists use the 'gender as power' idea in two important ways:

1 They rethink the very basis of the supposedly objective knowledge claims made by Western science. As Peterson points out (1992: 12–13), Western philosophy has tended to be the preserve of Western elite males where men's experiences are said to be representative of all human experiences; supposed gender differences have been institutionalized in the academy and policy practice; and the Western phallocentric order privileges masculine qualities over feminine ones (for example, masculine 'reason' is elevated above feminine 'passion').

One of the most famous feminist re-workings of practices in conventional IR theory was Tickner's reformulation of Morgenthau's six principles of Political Realism (1988). Work through her line of thought to see the depth of the critique poststructural feminists have of IR in its positivist Realist-Liberal guise.

2 They apply this line of thinking to IR by rethinking the ways in which the language of IR sets up artificial binaries between, for instance, 'civilized/uncivilized,order/anarchy, and developed/under-developed' (Tickner and Sjoberg 2007: 191). Think also about how often terms such as 'good/evil', 'state/failed state', 'secure/insecure', 'terrorist/freedom fighter' feature in the practice and study of IR. Poststructural feminists invite us to see the real-world implications of what are in fact artificial binary distinctions which implicitly privilege one of these terms over the other; they 'seek to expose and deconstruct these hierarchies' (Tickner and Sjoberg 2007: 191).

Can you think of other artificial binaries commonly used in the practice and study of IR? Which of the two terms is privileged? What are the consequences?

Postcolonial feminism

This branch of feminism makes two broad contributions to the study of IR. The first has an affinity with poststructural feminism and the post-colonial movement more generally (see Chapter 2.10). It highlights the structured nature of the oppression and/or invisibility of women in former **colonial** states. Even in states which have formally declared their independence from their former 'masters' (note the gendered terminology), postcolonial feminists argue that colonial constructions of 'self' and 'other' linger on and denigrate the 'other' as inferior (Tickner and Sjoberg 2007: 192). Like constructivist and poststructural feminists, they highlight the importance of binary categories and therefore see language as a site of oppression and dominance.

The second contribution is more a debate with other feminists. Postcolonial feminists unpick the fabric of the feminist movement. They argue that feminism has tended to be the preserve of elite Western women, who have made their concerns stand in for the concerns of all women around the globe. Just as feminists criticize the tendency for men's experiences to be held up as representative of humanity as a whole, so postcolonialist feminists take issue with feminist scholarship that confuses Western women's concerns with those of women from other parts of the world. There is, they say, no 'universal understanding of women's needs' and we need to be aware of cultural, religious and ethnic divergences (Tickner and Sjoberg 2007: 192).

Where Liberal feminists tend to add to the existing IR agenda, their Critical, constructivist, poststructuralist and postcolonialist counterparts point to major inequities not just within the world of IR as *practice* but in IR as *theory*. Feminism is not just about raising the profile of women in IR but about raising the profile of the gender-biased nature of IR as a field of the social sciences. Work on the philosophy of science, on the constructedness of gender and the discrimination in the very language of IR force us to rethink what it is that IR is all about. We have further cause to rethink these disciplinary practices in our encounter with post-modernism in the next chapter.

Questions to ponder

" Can 'gender' concerns be added to the existing IR agenda? Answer with reference to at least two feminist scholars you have studied on your course. "

Your first task with this question is to scope it by defining the key terms 'gender' and 'existing IR agenda'. With the former you need to give some sense of the constructedness feminists see in the term. Using definitions from key writers such as Peterson, Tickner and Sjoberg, and pulling out the implications, as we did in this chapter, is a good tactic for two reasons. First, it shows that your knowledge of the literature is wide and that you know the meaning of *the* key term in feminist IR. Second, you will immediately produce the names of at least two scholars as directed by the question. It is arguably trickier to define the 'existing IR agenda'. It is open to you to define it how you wish, and one good way is to use the conception of IR prevalent in feminist critiques of its limitations as a discipline. In doing this you are showing that you can empathise with the scholars you have read by seeing the world through *their* eyes.

Having scoped the essay, you need to come up with a response which will be dependent upon what you see as the mainstream IR agenda. You should ideally try and show that you are aware of arguments that gender and/or women are more than 'variables' which can simply be stirred into IR as part of an ever widening agenda (Liberal feminism). Reference to the more critically inclined variants of feminism will let you show that gender actually subsumes IR by providing a critique of Western philosophy of science as we conventionally understand it. An 'it depends' answer is no bad approach here because it allows you to talk about the significance of our interpretations of both IR and science as determinants of our position within this debate.

❝ 'Gender hierarchy is not coincidental to but in a significant sense constitutive of Western philosophy's objectivist metaphysics' (Peterson). Discuss the implications of this statement for IR theory. ❞

It is perennially difficult to structure answers to 'Discuss' questions. Some students fall into the trap of writing everything they know about some of the major terms raised in the question. To get past this erroneous approach try and think through why Peterson wrote what she did and how her ideas have been received by other feminists and critics alike.

Your first job is to summarize Peterson's argument: untangle the thrust of her case for your reader in a few hundred words. Ideally you would know where this quote comes from (Peterson 1992), but if not, you should have read enough of her work to be able to capture the essence of her argument. The implications are many and varied, and the number you include will naturally depend on the word and/or time limit you have. Normally at undergraduate level you will not be able to cover more than four or five points in depth in the body of an essay or exam answer. You want to try and showcase the point of view that takes 'conventional' IR theory as a sub-set of the positivist, objectivist view of science, and therefore that it can be critiqued on a number of grounds. Any of the following broad issues could be included and they would need breaking down: 'gender' and science (science as 'masculine'); feminism as a philosophy of social science; gender and the power of language; IR theory as a masculine pursuit (by men, about men, for men); IR, the public sphere of the international and the neglect of the private (women's realm); is 'gender' a variable? The best answers will do more than explore Peterson's intervention, they will pay some homage to writers who see gender either as irrelevant to, or pointless distraction from, the core concerns of IR as a discipline, so finding critics of the feminist approach in your course readings will help you out here.

| References to more information

On gender in IR:

TRUE, J. (2001) 'Feminism', in S. Burchill and others *Theories of International Relations*, 2nd edn. Basingstoke: Palgrave, pp. 231–76.
   Excellent overview of the contours of feminism and the contribution it has made to IR theory.

ELSHTAIN, J.B. (2006) 'Reflections on War and Political Discourse: Realism, Just War and Feminism in a Nuclear Age', in R. Little and M. Smith (eds) *Perspectives on World Politics*. Abingdon: Routledge, pp. 368–75.

A feminist deconstruction of the language and assumptions of Realist theory.

WHITWORTH, S. (1989) 'Gender and International Relations: Beyond the Inter-Paradigm Debate', *Millennium* 18(2): 265–72.

One of the landmark works in feminist IR scholarship.

WHITWORTH, S. (2005) 'Militarized Masculinities and the Politics of Peacekeeping', in K. Booth (ed.) *Critical Security Studies and World Politics*. Boulder, CO: Lynne Rienner Publishers, pp. 89–106.

Case study of Canadian peacekeeping illustrating how feminist concerns are central to the study of military values and practices.

TICKNER, J.A. (1988) 'Hans Morgenthau's Principles of Political Realism: A Feminist Reformulation', *Millennium*, 17(3): 429–40.

Classic 'standpoint' feminist study which rewrites Morgenthau's work from the perspective of women and in doing so shows the gender bias in this supposedly objective Realist account of IR. Textbooks in IR often feature Tickner's work so it is useful to have read the original.

TICKNER, J.A. (2006) 'Feminist Perspectives in International Relations', in W. Carlsnaes, T. Risse and B.A. Simmons (eds) *Handbook of International Relations*. London: Sage, pp. 275–91.

On feminism and gender studies more generally:

KELLER, E.F. (1985) *Reflections on Gender and Science*. New Haven, CT: Yale University Press.

Critique of the Enlightenment scientific project which equates 'objectivity' with 'masculinity'.

MERTUS, J. (2007) 'Liberal Feminism: Local Narratives in a Gendered Context', in J. Sterling-Folker (ed.) *Making Sense of International Relations Theory*. Boulder, CO: Lynne Rienner Publishers, pp. 252–67.

Good example of feminist theory being put into practice.

KRAUSE, J. (1995) 'The International Dimension of Gender Inequality and Feminist Politics: A "New Direction" for International Political Economy?', in J. Macmillan and A. Linklater (eds) *Boundaries in Question: New Directions in International Relations*. London: Pinter, pp. 128–43.

LLOYD, M. (2005) *Beyond Identity Politics: Feminism, Power and Politics*. London: Sage.

LANGE, L. (2003) 'Woman is Not a Rational Animal: On Aristotle's Biology of Reproduction', in S. Harding and M.B. Hintikka (eds) *Discovering Reality: Feminist Perspectives on Epistemology, Metaphysics, Methodology, and* *the Philosophy of Social Science*, 2nd edn. Dordrecht: Kluwer Academic Publishers, pp. 1–16.

Demonstrates how an appreciation of gender helps us think critically about the big questions in the philosophy of science and IR.

SPENDER, D. (ED.) (1981) *Men's Studies Modified: The Impact of Feminism on the Academic Disciplines*. Oxford: Pergamon.

BUTLER, J. (1999) *Gender Trouble: Feminism and the Subversion of Identity*. London: Routledge.

STEANS, J. (2002) 'Global Governance: A Feminist Perspective', in D. Held and A. McGrew (eds) *Governing Globalization: Power, Authority and Global Governance*. Cambridge: Polity, pp. 87–108.

BRAUNSTEIN, E. (2003) 'Gender and Foreign Direct Investment', in J. Michie (ed.) *The Handbook of Globalization*. Cheltenham: Edward Elgar, pp. 165–75.

CHINKIN, C. (1999) 'Gender Inequality and International Human Rights Law', in A. Hurrell and N. Woods, *Order, Globalization, and Inequality in World Politics*. Oxford: Oxford University Press, pp. 95–121.

Review of International Studies (2007) 'Forum: Women and Human Rights', 33(1): 5–103.

2.9	
postmodernism	

Key terms:

Power/knowledge
Statecraft
Sovereignty
Identity
Discourse
Genealogy
Deconstruction

> The postmodern vantage point is one of critique. Its aim is to unsettle, to jar, to challenge, and to subject our most fundamental beliefs and principles to intense critical scrutiny. (Shinko 2006: 168)

> Postmodernist theory calls for a radical re-thinking of how we think. (Hutchings 1999: 82)

As an intellectual movement, postmodernism swept through the social sciences in the 1990s. Some scholars jumped on board, liberated by the critical tools it offered them. Others have been left confused about what it all means and some are actively hostile to anything to do with the 'p'-word (Sterling-Folker, citing James Der Derian, 2006d: 165). Critics of postmodernism from within IR have variously called it 'evil', 'dangerous', 'bad IR', 'meta-babble' (Krasner and Halliday, cited in Campbell 2007: 210), or simply questioned the 'novelty of the arguments developed by the proponents of these allegedly new paradigms' (Navon 2001: 612).

Keep a record of the reasons why different writers you study are supportive of, apathetic about, or hostile to some of the 'newer' IR theories like postmodernism. What informs their views and what does this reveal about the nature of debates about IR theory?

The main thing postmodernism has in common with all the other theories covered in this book is that calling it 'theory' in the singular does it a disservice. There are many variants of postmodernism, just as there are many strands to Realism, Liberalism, Critical Theory and the English School. Moreover, postmodernism is like Marxism, feminism and postcolonialism in being a broad intellectual movement that cuts across disciplines. Some feminists are postmodernists, but not all; some Marxists are postmodernists, but not all; postcolonialist writers are renowned for their transgression of all these theoretical boundaries. IR is just one site for postmodern work among many.

Postmodernist works come under many names. On your course you might find it called 'poststructuralism' or 'post-positivism' because increasingly tutors are finding that 'postmodernism' is too broad a term or simply inapplicable in the context of IR theory (Campbell 2007: 211–12). It does not get any easier when we try and define postmodernism, for as Richard Devetak puts it 'Unfortunately a clear definition of postmodernism that will meet with general agreement is precisely what is not possible.' He classes as a postmodernist: first, anyone who regards their works as postmodern; second, anyone whose writing is referred to as postmodern; and third, anyone who avoids mention of the term but who theorizes in a manner informed by ideas and practices associated with postmodernism (Devetak 2001b: 181).

> I have chosen to use the label 'postmodern' in its broadly accepted IR sense to encompass poststructuralist and post-positivist works, even if their authors might take issue with being labeled postmodernists.

The first two categories are self-explanatory, the third more problematic. How do we identify postmodern works or do we just know them when we see them? Sterling-Folker goes some way to making this point when she writes 'The postmodern IR scholar also focuses on what the positivist would consider trivial or unrelated to IR, such as the spy novel, football, defense manuals, *Star Trek*, and popular culture' (Sterling-Folker 2006d: 162). It is not only the subject matter that defines postmodernism, however. Postmodernists draw upon an eclectic array of sources, ideas and practices to challenge ontological, epistemological and methodological conventions in IR. In this process, 'readings of Derrida and Foucault have been particularly important' (Hutchings 1999: 77).

As the two quotes at the start of this chapter make clear, postmodernists want to critique things we take for granted in IR, like the very idea of the state. In this regard they share affinities with Anarchist thinking (see Chapter 2.12 in this book). In so doing, they want to help us reassess not just the world as we see it but the very ways in which we think we see the world. While it has obvious affinities with Critical Theory and the stronger types of Constructivism, as well as an emancipatory agenda that chimes with other openly normative IR theories, postmodernism brings concepts and ideas all of its own to the IR table.

> If you find postmodernism challenging, difficult and unsettling then do not fear! Postmodernists jolt us out of cosy, established ways of thinking and invite us to think the unthinkable.

In this chapter we can only introduce you to some of the most influential ways in which postmodernism has been felt within IR. We will do this, first, by introducing the key concepts and methods associated with postmodernism and, second, we will take you step-by-step through a postmodern study of statecraft by Devetak (1995). By the end of the chapter you should be able to grasp the meaning of basic postmodern terms and be able to spot postmodern IR texts when you see them.

Postmodern ideas, concepts and approaches

Works of IR written in a postmodern vein are built on one, some or all of the following ideas, concepts or approaches inspired by the work of the French philosophers Michel Foucault (1926–1984) and Jacques Derrida (1930–2004).

Power/knowledge

Postmodernists investigate the ways in which power is generated by putting artificial closures or limitations on our understanding of the world and, following on from that, how the exercise of power is deeply intertwined with the production and transmission of knowledge.

This focus on power/knowledge comes directly from Foucault's understanding of power, which is quite different from the definition of 'power' many IR scholars work with. To use David Campbell's terminology (2007: 215–16), the conventional meaning of power (whether it be manifested physically in the form of nuclear warheads or ideationally in terms of a political speech, for instance) is essentially repressive – the imposition of limits or constraints on our thought and actions. Foucault sees power as being more productive than repressive. The power of which he speaks is the power to define and impose those limitations in the first place. How, he asks, is language used to limit our thinking about what is normal, legitimate and proper in the world? Who is it that gets to circumscribe our social 'truths'? Productive power shapes things, builds things, describes and categorizes them.

The X-Files gave us the positivist motto 'the truth is out there'. For Foucault, things are much more complicated. 'Truth is a thing of this world: it is produced only by virtue of multiple forms of constraint. And it includes regular effects of power. Each society has its regime of truth' (Foucault 1991: 72–3). Foucault asks what sources of power societies have erected under truth, behind truth and around truth to give it authority and legitimacy: to make it *function* as truth. How does an always *partial* truth about the world come to parade as *the* truth, to make it appear to hold across time and space?

Representation

Foucault's interest in discovering 'regimes' of truth led him to engage with issues of representation: how different regimes of truth call to mind the world to us through language. We are forever using words in the place of things. In the context of IR, 'we are engaging in abstraction, representation and interpretation' when we use words to try and make sense of international affairs (Campbell 2007: 204). Terms such as 'globalization', 'war on terror', 'freedom', 'international system', even 'humanity', by necessity, relate to objects, people and clusters of things that have happened, are happening and which will continue to happen in some form into the future. The point for Foucault is that our words can only ever *stand in* for or represent these essentially unknowable things; words can never *be* those things. Individual words in this interpretation are more like concepts: always slippery and prone to manipulation and misapplication.

Discourse

To summarize Foucault's line of thinking so far: we have all these words in our respective languages which are routinely used to represent or stand in for the very things they are meant to be neutrally describing, in the process making their meanings slippery and prone to ambiguity. But he does not stop at identifying the gap between the units of language (words) and the unknowable things they represent (for example, 'globalization'). Foucault takes this problem with the units of language and applies it to the systemic level of our sentences and paragraphs to demonstrate that at this level the problems of language relating to things become even more acute. It is at this level of discourse that, Foucault suggests, we see the productive power of language. As Campbell puts it (2007: 216), a discourse is 'a specific series of representations and practices through which meanings are produced, identities constituted, social relations established, and political and ethical outcomes made more or less possible'. Discourses do not simply describe the world, they 'constitute the objects of which they speak' (Campbell 2007: 216). We can have a discourse about anything and it will necessarily be positioned in some way (as an example see the production of the study of whaling and anti-whaling discourses in Epstein 2008).

Taking it **FURTHER**

Britain's discourses about 'Europe'

One of my areas of research interest is in Eurosceptical discourses in Britain (Daddow 2007). In this research I have been exploring the discourses about 'Europe' in Tony Blair's foreign policy speeches and comparing them with the discourses on 'Europe' in popular UK newspapers such as the *Sun* and the *Mail*. I have been interested in discovering whether these discourses represent 'Europe' differently.

I have found that the 'Europe' Blair saw in his speeches was not the 'Europe' the newspapers saw. For Blair, 'Europe' offered benefits to Britain, politically, economically, strategically and culturally. For these newspapers, 'Europe' was something to be feared, to poke fun at and to avoid in terms of closer integration. This divergence of opinion was down to the different ways in which 'Europe' was constructed in these discourses, which in turn was reflected in contrasting interpretations of British history, different interpretations of Britain's role in the world in the twenty-first century, and different perceptions of the motives behind the policies of key countries such as France, Germany and the US.

Britain's discourses about Europe in the Blair era, I have concluded, were not really about 'Europe' at all. They were, rather, interventions that used 'Europe' as a mythical 'other' to help debate British national identity and role in the world since the Second World War. Indeed, the meaning of 'Britain' is as contested as the meaning of 'Europe' and the one is always co-constructing the other. In conclusion, I have increasingly found that political discourses are not neutral reflections of a world 'out there' but they are actively involved in *producing* the world we inhabit; they shape social practice as well as being shaped by it. Political discourses about foreign policy knit together representations about other representations to create meanings which are politically powerful and laced with assumptions about the nature of IR.

Genealogy

In light of the sheer power, influence and everywhere-ness of the discourses through which we make sense of the world, Foucault invites us to write not histories but **genealogies**. Genealogy, explains Devetak, is 'a style of historical thought which exposes and registers the significance of power-knowledge relations'. Genealogy is not history of the beginning, middle and end variety with a focus on origins and causation for how things got they way they are. It is 'a form of history which historicizes those things which are thought to be beyond history'. A genealogy brings to our attention the contextualized nature of all knowledge and shows up the many ways in which that knowledge interplays with power to constitute 'subjects, objects, fields of action and domains of knowledge' (Devetak 2001b: 184).

Steve Smith argues that it is important to apply a genealogical attitude to a discipline like IR because 'international theory has tended to be a discourse accepting of, and complicit in, the creation and re-creation of international practices that threaten, discipline and do violence to others' (Smith 1995: 3). A genealogy of IR, says Richard Ashley (1986), exposes the link between the practice of IR and its discourses. It asks how things came to be this way in the discipline, inquires into the politics behind the production and dissemination of academic knowledge about IR, how dominant discourses such as Realism emerge and rise to prominence within the discipline, how IR creates its subject matter and how scholars set about claiming that their theory or interpretation is the most valid or truthful (covered in Smith 1995: 4–7). In the work of those writers who investigate the genealogy of IR we can clearly see a postmodern concern 'with the ways in which a perspective produces representations which attain dominance and monopolise legitimacy by marginalizing others' (Devetak 2001b: 185).

> That genealogists seek out the positioned nature of knowledge about IR perhaps explains why some scholars in IR are nervous about the advent of postmodernism within the discipline.

Deconstruction

Inspired by the philosophy of Jacques Derrida, **deconstruction** is another of those widely used and abused terms in the social sciences. According to Devetak, it 'defies definition' but 'can be understood as a strategy of interpretation and criticism directed at concepts which attempt closure or totalization' (Devetak 1995: 20). Postmodern writers who want to jar 'the whole edifice of common-sense notions' (Devetak 1995: 20) use deconstruction in a variety of ways, the technique of 'double reading' being especially popular (see the next section). Deconstructionists are happy to proclaim ethical or other normative purposes to their work which shows how things might have been and can be different.

Deconstructionist approaches to IR theory seem on the surface to share many things in common with Constructivist theory. Can you identify the main ways in which they differ?

Case study: deconstructing 'states'

Devetak's (1995) book chapter 'Incomplete States' helps us see the impact of the postmodern turn in IR in two ways. First, it helps us see the similarities but more importantly the ruptures between postmodern theory and other normative theories covered in this book. Second, Devetak's chapter casts light on the artificiality of IR's disciplinary discourses about the state. The steps Devetak takes are as follows:

1 **Identifies the problem area.** At the beginning of the chapter Devetak notes a paradox: '*there is statecraft, but there is no completed state*' (1995: 19. Author's emphasis).

2 **Defines statecraft.** Devetak introduces the principle writers on which he draws for inspiration about his conception of statecraft as an ongoing effort to define the state, rather than the result of the settled existence of states. His use of Machiavelli in tandem with Derrida is itself unsettling because the latter is normally used by Realists to support their theories of state behaviour (pp. 20–1).

3 **Challenges Neorealist theory.** Devetak identifies the theories against which he operates (Neorealism and Neoliberalism) and explores Waltz's comfortable assumption that completed states interact in the international system. For Devetak, Waltz assumes too much: we cannot take states as completed at all.

4 **Introduces Critical Theoretical approaches.** The argument here is that to understand the 'inside' (states) we have to understand their 'outside' (all the different kinds of structure that help make those states) (p. 25). State boundaries, Devetak writes, are built on social power as well as clearly defined territories, and to overlook the former and only concentrate on the latter is to misconstrue the historically produced, 'temporary and provisional' nature of state boundaries (pp. 25–6). Hence, it is insufficient to look to 'sovereignty' as the arbiter of what is internal and external to states when that very concept can be called into question (pp. 27–8).

5 **Poststructuralism and the state.** Here, Devetak uses Hegel to argue for the 'dynamic and ongoing' processes of state construction which we have to account for when we collapse the boundaries between 'inside' and 'outside' (p. 29). It is by overturning the 'inside/outside' distinction that we move out of the realm of Critical Theory and into the realm of deconstruction. Using writers such as Campbell, Ashley and Foucault, Devetak shows how states are never completed entities. Foreign policy discourses, he argues, are practices that give shape to or help construct states; these discourses are not resorted to by states '*after* their full, completed constitution' (p. 32).

Questions to ponder

❝ Why do you think 'postmodernism' has been received with such hostility by some writers in the field of IR? Is their hostility justified? ❞

Answering this question first of all relies on a robust definition of 'post-modernism', so you should find a writer who defines this difficult term and run with that. You could perhaps include a brief analysis of other competing terms such as post-structuralism and explain why you either do or do not choose to use the terms interchangeably. However you do it, you need to set off in the essay from a position where the marker knows precisely what you mean by it.

Your next task is to demonstrate good knowledge of both postmodernism (briefly so as not to waste too many words) and most importantly the criticisms levelled at it by some IR writers. In Campbell's textbook chapter (2007), he lists five writers who criticize postmodernism so it is not as if they are thin on the ground. You will need to know not just what they say but why they say it, so read their original works and summarize them. How many you can cover will depend on the word limit you have (for coursework) and time limit (for an exam answer). You could try grouping their critiques of postmodernism. They tend to focus on: questions about its relevance to IR as a field of study; its ethical implications (the slide into various forms of relativism) and its relevance to the practice of international relations (policy relevance).

Having set out the criticisms, you are then invited to evaluate them. Have they depicted the postmodern movement (as you understand it) accurately? Are they misunderstanding the nature of IR to simply write off this huge intellectual movement? At the start and end of the essay remember to set out your core argument: do you agree or disagree with the critics?

"How can taking a genealogical approach help illuminate the study of IR?"

This question invites you to consider the benefits and the costs of writing genealogies of IR. Clearly your first task is to summarize what 'taking a genealogical approach' means by using ideally the work of Foucault or at least a summary of his views as presented by writers such as David Campbell, Steve Smith or Richard Ashley.

Having defined this key term, you then have to set out what you think the benefits of genealogy are and can be for IR. All of the above writers cover this issue so you can structure this part of the essay around the three or four that you think are most illuminating in your opinion. Make sure when you introduce new concepts (for instance, 'regime of truth') or use technical terms such as 'discourse' that you pause to define these terms for your reader.

The most successful essays will not stop at the benefits. They will consider the 'backlash' against postmodern approaches to IR by investigating some of the arguments advanced by writers who think postmodernism is either jargon-filled mumbo-jumbo or a dangerous distraction from the 'real' concerns of IR: war, peace, security, the environment, and so on. Showing that you are familiar with all sides of a debate in this way helps demonstrate your wide reading and your critical ability to weigh up competing positions among key writers.

Postmodernist writers do not like to work with dominant categories or theories which in their view perpetuate the very exclusions, marginalizations and oppressions they want to challenge.

References to more information

Before you read the original works of postmodernist writers such as Foucault and Derrida it is worth checking out introductions to their thought:

HOY, D.C. (1986) *Foucault: A Critical Reader*. Oxford: Basil Blackwell.

DANAHER, G., SCHIRATO, T. AND WEBB, J. (2000) *Understanding Foucault*. London: Sage. Especially Chapter 3 on discourses and institutions and Chapter 5 on power.

ANDERSEN, N.A. (2003) *Discursive Analytical Strategies: Understanding Foucault, Koselleck, Laclau, Luhmann*. Bristol: The Policy Press.

STOCKER, B. (2006) *Derrida on Deconstruction*. Abingdon: Routledge.

MOI, T. (ED.) (1986) *The Kristeva Reader*. Oxford: Basil Blackwell.

Guides you through the postmodernist writings of Julia Kristeva. If you want to try the original, go for KRISTEVA, J. (1984) *Revolution in Poetic Language*. New York: Columbia University Press.

FOUCAULT, M. (1991) 'Truth and Power', in P. Rabinow (ed.) *The Foucault Reader: An Introduction to Foucault's Thought*. London: Penguin, pp. 51–75.

FOUCAULT, M. (1977) *Security, Territory, Population: Lectures at the Collége de France, 1977–78*, trans. G. Burchell. Basingstoke: Palgrave Macmillan.

RANSOM, J.S. (1997) *Foucault's Discipline: The Politics of Subjectivity*. Durham, NC: Duke University Press.

LLOYD, M. AND THACKER, A. (EDS) (1997) *The Impact of Michel Foucault on the Social Sciences and Humanities*. Basingstoke: Macmillan.

On discourse and deconstruction, see:

BURNHAM, P., GILLAND, K., GRANT, W. AND LAYTON-HENRY, Z. (2004) *Research Methods in Politics*. Basingstoke: Palgrave Macmillan.

See Chapter 10 for a brief introduction to discourse analysis.

HOWARTH, D. (1995) 'Discourse Theory', in D. Marsh and G. Stoker (eds) *Theory and Methods in Political Science*. Basingstoke: Macmillan, pp. 115–33.

In the second edition of this popular text, discourse theory is strangely absent.

FAIRCLOUGH, N. (2000) *New Labour, New Language?*. London: Routledge.

Dissects New Labour's domestic and foreign policy discourses from a critical linguistic perspective and shows you how their manifestoes, legislative proposals and policy speeches make sense of the world for their audience.

WODAK, R., DE CILLIA, R., REISIGL, M. AND LIEBHART, K. (2003) *The Discursive Construction of National Identity*, trans. A. Hirsch and R. Mitten. Edinburgh: Edinburgh University Press.

Good on how to use methods of critical discourse analysis to investigate national identity construction and then applies that method to the case of Austria.

BLOOM, H. ET AL. (1979) *Deconstruction and Criticism*. New York: The Seabury Press.

A collection of essays by five of the leading proponents of deconstruction.

NORRIS, C. (1993) *Deconstruction: Theory and Practice*. London: Routledge.

Thorough overview of the will to deconstruction evident in writings by Derrida, Nietzsche, Marx and Wittgenstein.

NEALON, J.T. (1993) *Double Reading: Postmodernism after Deconstruction*. Ithaca, NY: Cornell University Press.

PIN-FAT, V. (2009) 'How do we begin to think about the World', in J. Ekins and M. Zehfuss. G*lobal Politics: A New Introduction*. London and New York: Routledge, pp. 22–44.

More generally on postmodernism and politics/IR see:

HAY, C. (2002) *Political Analysis: A Critical Introduction*. Basingstoke: Palgrave. See Chapter 7.

WALKER, R. B. J. (1995) 'International Relations and the Concept of the Political', in K. Booth and S. Smith (eds) *International Relations Theory Today*. Cambridge: Polity Press, pp. 306–27.

Deconstructs the 'inside/outside' binary in IR and therefore pulls the rug from under the feet of state-centric theory.

MUNSLOW, A. (2007) *Narrative and History*. Basingstoke: Palgrave Macmillan.

Explores the mechanics of representation using Foucault and others to examine how history is made meaningful to us. Also reassesses the concept of 'facts', so useful for your wider readings into the philosophy of social science.

RENWICK, N. AND KRAUSE, J. (EDS) (1996) *Identities in International Relations*. Basingstoke: Macmillan.

DEVETAK, R. (2005) 'The Gothic Scene of International Relations: Ghosts, Monsters, Terror and the Sublime after September 11', *Review of International Studies*, 31(4): 621–45.

Highlights the importance of language, symbols and imagery in constructing IR as a field of thought and practice.

2.10	
postcolonialism	

Key Terms:

Race
Ethnicity
Identity
Empire
Knowledge
Discourse
Power

> *Postcolonialism … offers new ways for thinking about techniques of power that constrain self-determination, whether they emanate from within or without.* (Grovogui 2007: 231)

Postcolonialism, like feminism and postmodernism more generally, is another relative latecomer to the field of IR. The reason for its tardy arrival on the theoretical scene gives us an insight into the politicized nature of IR's mode of producing knowledge about the world. It is absent from some IR textbooks (Burchill et al. 2001a; Jackson and Sørensen 2007; Sterling-Folker 2006b), partially incorporated into others (Baylis et al. 2008b) and has a full place in yet more (Dunne et al. 2007). If you have read most or all of the preceding nine chapters in this book, covering each IR theory one by one, ask yourself whose voice or voices we heard most from? There is an argument to be made that IR has – in the main – been developed, taught and put into political practice by privileged white Western males. Postcolonialism exposes the latent bias in existing IR renderings by reminding us of the discipline's blind spots both in terms of subject matter and the epistemological claims of positivism. As Smith and Owens put it, much postcolonial scholarship highlights 'the important degree of *continuity* and *persistence* of colonial forms of power in contemporary world politics … a form of "neo"-colonialism' (2008: 188; their emphasis).

Postcolonial writers address various inequities and silences within IR as it developed as a discipline in the 1990s.

In the same way that feminists ask 'where are the women?', Marxists ask 'where are the classes?' and in this vein of re-visioning the discipline to take a more realistic account of the dynamics of world politics, postcolonialists ask 'where is the ethnic diversity?' An interdisciplinary tradition mixing all three concerns, postcolonialism explores the power relations that govern IR's ways of representing the world, highlighting race as another global structure too long ignored by the core of the discipline. Postcolonialists produce normatively inclined work that critiques both the formal and informal practices of **colonialism** that have given rise to exploitation, alienation and repression of large parts of the globe by a supposedly rational, enlightened European imperialist order. We will consider the dynamics of postcolonialism mainly using the work of Edward Said, but with the usual proviso that his work is one of hundreds we could use to illustrate this rich interdisciplinary tradition.

The Constructivist element

In 1978, Edward Said published *Orientalism*, a book in which he traced how the 'West' had tried to place, use and direct the 'rest' of the world through the production of knowledge about it. In the Preface, Said (2003: xii) sets out his assumption that:

> History is made by men and women, just as it can also be unmade and re-written, always with various silences and elisions, always with shapes imposed and disfigurements tolerated, so that 'our' East, 'our' Orient becomes 'ours' to possess and direct.

Here we see several key features of the postcolonial approach to IR:

- **Things can be different.** Constructivist IR thinkers such as Alex Wendt highlight the idea that structures in the international system that we take for granted, such as 'anarchy', are in fact made by states. Said makes this point when he notes that history and the events of which it is constituted are made by people – it is a representation of the past, not the past itself. These events can be 'unmade and re-written', just as all social norms can be, if we possess the means, the imagination and the will to do so.

> Said used the term 'Orient' to apply to various regions of the world notably the Middle East and parts of Africa and Asia. The terminology is in a constant state of flux: what do you think we mean by the 'West' and 'the rest' today? Are the supposed divisions down to geography, politics, economics, cultural or identity?

- **'Ours' is not 'theirs'.** Postcolonialists investigate who it is that tells us about the world and what they say about its nature. For Said, the West has generally spoken for the rest in that Western scholars dominated the study, categorization and education about world peoples during the past two centuries or so. In the process, Western voices dominated other voices in the world; Western representations of these 'other' indigenous peoples who had their own stories to tell were simply drowned out. The stories the West developed about the character of these peoples and their politics and cultures arguably tell us more about Western beliefs and prejudices than they reflect any reality of those other worlds.

> We noted in Chapter 2.8 that postcolonial feminists criticized their Western counterparts for writing works that implied that feminists shared the same or similar concerns the world over. This debate within the feminist movement tells you a lot about the postcolonial agenda: encouraging awareness of diversity.

- **Discourses are power.** Said ends the above quote by suggesting that in becoming 'ours' the West can direct the rest of the world: note the suggestiveness of the implication that control and domination are the result of producing this knowledge about the Third World. Later in the book, Said is even more explicit: 'The relationship between Occident and Orient is a relationship of power, of domination, of varying degrees of a complex hegemony ... a sign of European-Atlantic power over the Orient than it is a veridic discourse about the Orient' (Said 2003: 5–6). Here, Said notes that within the supposedly disinterested scientific discourses that the West has produced about the rest of the world reside complex mechanisms of domination and an imperialist mentality that does more than a disservice: it does a gross series of injustices to the 'reality' of life in the non-Western world.

Taking it **FURTHER**

'Power' in *Orientalism*

Near the beginning of *Orientalism*, Said (2003: 12) sets out the different dimensions of power that infuse discourses about the 'Orient':

1 Power political: the establishment of colonial structures for governing foreign territories.
2 Power intellectual: the subjection of the Orient to study by linguists, historians, scientists and so on.
3 Power cultural: orthodoxies, canons of taste, texts and values.
4 Power moral: ideas about who 'we' and 'they' are, as well as how 'we' and 'they' think.

Said's concept of power is Foucauldian. IR in its formative years as a discipline concentrated on repressive power: the power, for example, of one state to compel another to do its will by the threat or actual use of force. Power for Foucault and Said is more productive than repressive: it is the power that comes from being in a position to tell others the way the world works: the power that comes from knowledge. In the above typology Said's first dimension of power is repressive, the remaining three are productive, and it is no coincidence that the vast bulk of *Orientalism* is given over to studying those dimensions.

Language and postcolonialism

Feminist scholars implicate language directly in the patriarchal domination of women by men. A large part of their critique involves analysis of the binary oppositions within language used to compare masculine/feminine characteristics: for example 'rational/irrational', 'detachment/commitment' and 'brutality/compassion'. In each case the former term is privileged and it is no coincidence they are all associated with Western constructions of positive masculine qualities. The latter feminine qualities are not regarded as highly, so that the universal benchmark or standard for humanity is essentially a masculine standard. This language infuses everything from scientific methodologies to the attributes of states as unitary rational actors.

> *When you spot different theorists using the same ways of defining or critiquing a particular aspect of IR make a note of it because it helps you see the similarities across apparently different theoretical traditions.*

In just this fashion, Said (2003: 40) remarks on the binary oppositions that Western speakers traditionally set up in their discourse to frame the characteristics of 'Europe' and the 'Orient' (Table 2).

Table 2   Said's binaries

European	Oriental
Rational	Irrational
Virtuous	Depraved
Mature	Childlike
Normal	Different

Said suggests that we pay attention to the language through which we represent ourselves and others because this process of identity construction has dangerous implications if it is built on prejudice. In Orientalist discourses, the European characteristics are held up as positive, while the Orientalist characteristics are criticized and/or undervalued. Perhaps even to portray them as above is to downplay the violence these hierarchies deliver to our representations of the Oriental. Maybe Table 2 should be formatted as shown in Figure 17.

> Note in Figure 17 how the 'Oriental' is said to be 'irrational' – very much in the same way as feminine characteristics are looked down upon in gendered discourses of masculinity and femininity. Europeans are, it seems, 'better' than Orientals because they are more masculine.

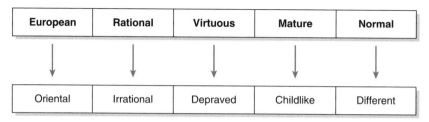

Figure 17   Said's binaries in operation

What Said and the postcolonialists question is the basis these supposedly timeless qualities have in 'reality' and the moral values inherent in privileging one of the terms over its supposed opposite. In Figure 17 we can see how the European characteristics are both stronger (bolder) and deemed to be higher than their Oriental counterparts.

Bill Ashcroft, Gareth Griffiths and Helen Tiffin (1994: 7) remark that imperial oppression came in part via the 'control over language' as 'the medium through which a hierarchical structure of power is perpetuated, and the medium through which conceptions of "truth", "order", and "reality" become established'. Their book traces how postcolonialism has been stimulated by the reclaiming of English by indigenous populations, resulting in innovative and new forms of postcolonial literatures. Just as Marxism inspires theoretical work as well as practical action in the form of the anti-globalization movement, so postcolonial literature is an expression of the wider anti-imperial resistance movement: 'an example of effective dissidence' (Smith and Owens 2008: 189).

Questions to ponder

❝ What are the affinities between Constructivist and postcolonial approaches to IR? ❞

Your initial task in planning an answer to this question is to arrive at a suitable definition of each theory – no easy task. Using your knowledge of each tradition, you might want to stress the diversity but also the common themes and issues writers share, using illustrative quotations and reference to a few key writers to back your case. You will not have much space for this given the demands of the question, so be sure to focus on the central themes and ignore the detail of each theory or the temptation to write everything you know about them.

Your main task is to weigh up the similarities between Constructivist and postcolonial approaches to IR. In this chapter we referred to Said's Constructivist take on language, representation, the role of ideas and education in constructing the Orient in the West – his point being that the Orient has been 'made' by human endeavour, it is not necessarily an accurate portrait of the 'reality' of that world. A standard answer would stop there. The highest achieving answers, however, will go on to note that, if anything, postcolonialism shares just as much with other theories of IR such as feminism and Marxism. It all depends on the space and time available to you as to how far you can investigate these other overlaps. But if you can convey your sense of the nature of the interplay between postcolonialism and these other theories, then you will get credit for exhibiting a thorough knowledge of the fabric of these normative theories of IR.

❝ '… an exercise in cultural strength'. What are the implications of Said's description of *Orientalism* for the study of IR? ❞

The nub of the matter in this question is to explain what Said means by talking of Orientalism's exercise of 'cultural strength' and to link that with a discussion of the dynamics of the Orientalist tradition more generally. For Said, Orientalism does not simply highlight the repressive dimensions of power, but is far more about the productive dimensions of the power whereby individuals in the West defined, delimited and 'named' the Orient. In the process, they helped legitimize various techniques of colonial repression and exploitation based on everything from race to the embellishment of cultural hierarchies. Said's 'cultural strength' is therefore about the exercise of various forms of power and the best essays will do more than concentrate on the naked military or political forms of power.

Tracing the implications for the study of IR will involve assessing the impact of Said's work on the evolution of postcolonialism as an intellectual movement. You will not need to know in detail the sociology or politics of postcolonialism as an intellectual movement but you can tell how important Said and other writers are in this canon by the number of references to their ideas in textbook chapters and the like. Having established Said as a key writer, you should be in a position to draw out three or four implications of this quote for the study of IR. Set out those you feel are most crucial and alert the reader to other points as you see fit. The kinds of implications you can consider would include: issues of race, ethnicity, identity, language, power, discourse, exploitation, systemic level structures, oppression and the politics of disciplined knowledge.

The best answers might allude to the interplay between Said's approach and those taken by postmodernists, Marxists and feminists.

References to more information

FANON, F. (1968) *The Wretched of the Earth*, trans. C. Farrington. New York: Grove Press.

Opened up windows on the repressive practices of colonialism not just physically but also in terms of the knowledge that Europe's imperial masters produced about the world.

SPIVAK, G.C. (1987) *In Other Worlds: Essays in Cultural Politics*. London: Routledge.

CHOWDRY, G. AND NAIR, S. (EDS) (2002) *Power, Postcolonialism and International Relations: Reading Race, Gender and Class*. London: Routledge.

BHABA, H.K. (1994) *The Location of Culture*. London: Routledge.

BUSH, B. (2006) *Imperialism and Postcolonialism*. Harlow: Pearson Education.

Explores the history, concept and dynamics of imperialism together with, in Chapter 6, the postcolonial move in studies of Empire.

DARBY, P. (2000) *At the Edge of International Relations: Postcolonialism, Gender and Dependence*. London: Continuum International Publishing Group.

Good on the wide-ranging challenge postcolonialism poses for 'conventional' IR theory.

MOHANTY, C.T. (1988) 'Under Western Eyes: Feminist Scholarship and Critical Discourse', *Feminist Review*, 30(3): 61–88.

HOOGVELT, A. (2001) *Globalization and the Postcolonial World: The New Political Economy of Development*, 2nd edn. Baltimore, MD: Johns Hopkins University Press.

Parts 1 and 2 refresh you on the Marxist take on the global political economy, while Part 3 works the postcolonial dimension region by region.

LING, L.H.M. (2001) *Postcolonial International Relations: Conquest and Desire Between Asia and the West*. Basingstoke: Palgrave Macmillan.

Challenges the 'clash of civilizations' thesis as a process of 'othering' that downplays the complex global interactions that shape cultural and individual identities.

KRISHNASWAMY, R. AND HAWLEY, J.C. (EDS) (2008) *The Post-colonial and the Global*. Minneapolis, MN: University of Minnesota Press.

Wide-ranging collection covering everything from the politics of disciplined Western knowledge to World System Theory and resistance to Empire in a globalized world.

2.11	
green theory	

Key terms:

Environmental justice
Ecocentrism
Ecological security
Regime
State
Ecoanarchy

> *Environmental questions cannot be neatly boxed off from other political questions. (Paterson 1995: 214)*

In Chapter 2.8 on feminism, we saw how the concerns raised by this big social movement fed into IR theory throughout the later 1980s and 1990s in the form of an awareness of 'gender'. We found it is far too simple to portray feminist writings as being somehow tacked on to the existing core of the discipline. The critically inclined feminist literature challenges the very essence of what it means to study IR as well as arguing that the dominant methods and epistemologies of the discipline are inherently gendered. 'Gender', they say, is not a variable that can be added or removed from IR when we like, but it is always there and demands attention whenever we think about matters international.

As you will see in Matthew Paterson's quote above, Green theorists have much the same approach to IR. They do not see questions relating to the environment, ecological sustainability and development as ones that can be adequately answered by existing state-centric structures in both the theory and practice of IR. Instead, they call for a thoroughgoing reassessment of the ways in which we think and act in terms of the environment, calling into question the role of the state and its approach to human security in the process. In this chapter we explore this normative challenge to IR theory in three parts: Green approaches to IR theory, the scope of the field, and varieties of Green thought.

IR and Green theory collide

Issues surrounding the contemporary environment and the challenges humans face in providing development at a pace that is sustainable at a global level well into the future are constantly in the media and political spotlight. For example, environment forms part of the remit of the UN, under its Division for Sustainable Development which aims to meet present needs while simultaneously promoting the ability of future generations to meet their needs (UN 2008b).

The environment has featured on the agenda of regional organizations such as the EU for a number of years. For instance, in 2006, the member states affirmed their commitment to a sustainable development agenda in words echoed precisely by the UN in 2008 (Council of the European Union 2006: 2). At the national level, various types of 'green' party have flourished in many countries over the past three decades. In the UK, for example, the Green Party is now a multi-issue party centring on creating a healthy environment for the present and in the years ahead, as its slogan 'One World. One Chance' makes clear (Green Party 2008).

> The multi-level, multi-dimensional nature of the environmental challenges the planet faces has a direct impact on the approach to IR theory taken by Green theorists.

It should be obvious from the manifold number of environmental issues on the contemporary global agenda that theorizing them is no easy business. When we choose to buy re-usable carrier bags for our supermarket shopping or when we donate money to charities providing clean water in desertified regions of Africa, we are responding to issues raised directly by the Green movement which has grown rapidly since the 1960s (Eckersley 2007: 249). In deciding to go for re-usable carrier bags and giving money to the African water charity, we are also responding to the popular environmentalist call to 'think globally, act locally' (Paterson 2001: 289), a slogan that highlights the ways in which Green theorists cause us to rethink the state's role in dealing with environmental issues.

> Green theorists ask: what forms of social and political organization best help the world today and into the future?

A useful way to get to grips with the goals of Green theory is to summarize its take on the pitfalls of mainstream IR; we will do this here using the work of Paterson (1995: 213–18. See also Hovden 1999):

- **A narrow agenda.** To use the terminology developed earlier in this book (see Chapter 1.4), Green theorists see flaws in the ontological starting point for mainstream IR: state behaviour at the international level. Paterson identifies a problem with any approach that begins by asking what we can do internationally to, say, combat waste pollution of our rivers: it overlooks the domestic sources of those problems and the potential solutions to them. We can only 'think globally, act locally' if we either forget or reform the central place states occupy in dealing with environmental matters.

> *For the purposes of Green theory as Paterson developed it in the 1990s, 'mainstream' IR meant Neorealism and Neoliberalism. Do you think these theories still constitute the core of the discipline today?*

- **Flaws in Neoliberal assumptions.** The knock-on point concerns the agreements states make about the environment, such as the Kyoto Protocol of 1997 (for the text of the treaty see UN 1998). In making these agreements, Paterson argues, the first assumption is that the signatory countries will want and be able to implement those agreements through appropriate regulation at the domestic level. What this overlooks, he remarks, is the influence of powerful corporate lobbies at the domestic level which can affect national climate policies against the spirit of international agreements (for example, the oil and coal lobbies). It is, he concludes, 'politically naïve' to ignore the impact of these organized interests and therefore theoretically flawed to talk about IR as the exclusive preserve of state actions and decisions.

  The second assumption is that scientists can provide 'objective' advice on the environment. The criteria they develop and the measurements they use to develop these criteria will always be politically skewed in some way. In the true spirit of normative IR theory, says Paterson, beware anyone who claims to be value-free or objective about any issue, however supposedly technical the subject matter.

The ecocentric approach

The objections Green theorists have to regime theory lead them to offer 'an alternative analysis of global ecological problems'. Their work exposes the problematic nature of Neoliberal assumptions and ethical values and encourages us to think about the environment in new ways, ones which 'expand the menu of state development options' (Eckersley 2007: 256). In raising these questions about mainstream approaches, Green theorists 'see' a different world compared to the **anthropocentrism** of the Neoliberals (Dalby 2009). Against this human-centred approach, an 'eco-centric' philosophy sees the world as made up of 'the larger web of life, made up of nested ecological communities at multiple levels of aggregation (such as gene pools, populations, species, ecosystems)' (Eckersley 2007: 251). They see a world in which humans are not the only sentient beings for whom policies on the environment should be made. Rather, humans are just one part of a much wider and deeper picture, one that conventional IR theory's have been blind to.

Where feminists argue that IR theory has been 'gender blind', Green theorists argue that IR theory has been 'Green blind'.

In the spirit of recasting our focus on the world and its long-term survival, Green theorists of many varieties contribute in normative terms to thought on how to respond to ecological challenges in ways that transcend the state-centricity of traditional IR approaches. The 'IPE wing' of Green theory (Eckersley 2007: 255) has already been discussed. It takes its cue from the flaws in Neoliberalism and proposes an alternative account of the causes and solutions to global ecological problems.

The 'green cosmopolitan' wing of Green theory brings together an array of individuals and groups committed to articulating new ways of thinking about ecology and proposing solutions 'at all levels of governance' above and below the state (Eckersley 2007: 255). Their view is that we need to create new norms of 'environmental justice' which means (adapted from Eckersley 2007: 253):

- Ecological risks affect more than human beings alone and more than citizens of states but all peoples around the globe
- Participation in decision-making on the environment should be massively expanded and democratized to include representatives of all those affected by such decisions
- A minimization of risks vis-à-vis the wider community
- All risks must be acceptable and they should be gauged democratically and with the input of all affected parties
- Those suffering ecological problems should have adequate recourse to redress and compensation.

Paterson identifies a lively debate within the Green tradition between two strands of thought on how best to generate environmental justice (Paterson 2001: 286–90). The first strand is what could be seen as the more conservative approach: maintain states in their present form but reform their role to give more say over environmental issues for regional and international organizations. In this approach, the state retains its central role in IR but that role is modified to help humans 'think globally, act locally'.

The second strand is the 'ecoanarchist' strand. We explore Anarchist theory in the next chapter and the ecoanarchists give you a flavour of what is involved. Ecoanarchists believe the state should be dismantled, the decentralization of decision-making power and authority promoting the existence of 'global networks of small-scale self-reliant communities'. These communities would not be based on hierarchical, consumer capitalist lines but on horizontal 'libertarian, egalitarian, and participatory grounds' (Paterson, 2001: 289). A flavour of the thinking behind the Green Anarchist movement can be found on the website of the Green Anarchist International Association (GAIA undated).

Questions to ponder

"Are ecocentric issues outside the remit of IR?"

In organizing your response to this question, you will have to take a direct position and back it up using evidence from two sets of literature. One is on the appropriate subject matter or agenda of IR; the other literature you will need to know is that on ecocentrism itself. Your answer will turn on your definition of both the key concepts in the question: what are 'ecocentric issues' and what is 'the remit of IR'? What type of Green theory do you take to be representative of those concerns: the 'reform the state' approach of writers such as Eckersley or the 'do away with the state' approach of the ecoanarchists such as Bookchin (see References for more information)? You might have to allude to the commonalities across their thought as much as the divergences, so some general knowledge of the textbook chapters on Green theory will help you see into the normative, ecological agendas at work.

As for the remit of IR, you could reasonably take the conventional 'Neliberal' position as representing an orthodox interpretation of IR's agenda. What Greens ask, in common with Marxists, feminists, postmodernists and other openly normative theorists, is the extent to which this agenda addresses issues in 'world politics' today. If you agree that normative theory speaks more to our contemporary concerns than the positivist, state-centric approaches of Realism and Liberalism, then you will not think Green theory is outside the remit of IR but fundamental to it. The very best answers will allude to the idea that Green theory, like gender theory, cannot be treated as a 'variable' in IR to be addressed or forgotten about as we wish, but that it is always there whether we choose to recognize it or not.

"Does Green theory's treatment of the state enhance or diminish our understanding of International Relations?"

You will notice right away that the question takes Green theory to be a single, monolithic theory. In the introduction to the essay you will therefore have to define your terms: which Green theorists are you going to study and why them and not others? You do not need a detailed rendition of the history and evolution of Green theory but you should alert your reader to the framework within which you will be deploying the term 'Green theory'.

Having scoped your essay by defining 'Green theory' you then have to develop your argument. In some ways the question is similar in focus to the previous one in that it invites you to apply your knowledge of Green theorists' critiques of the state to IR as a subject area. Your choice of Green theorist will surely determine your response because some pay more due to the role of the state in shaping ecological outcomes than others. At the conventional end of the spectrum we have Neoliberal regime theory and at the other end we have the ecoanarchists. Both say very different things about IR given their contrasting opinions about the advisability of using states to achieve environmental outcomes.

Whichever theorist you go with, be sure to let your reader know that you are aware of competing strands of Green thought. A read through Paterson (2001: 292–7) will help you grasp the criticisms of Green theory's call for decentralization of power and you could work these into your answer to give it balance and critical depth.

References to more information

VOGLER, J. (2008) 'Environmental Issues', in J. Baylis, S. Smith and P. Owens (eds) *The Globalization of World Politics: An Introduction to International Relations*, 4th edn. Oxford: Oxford University Press, pp. 350–68.

More conventional treatment of Green theory than you will find in Paterson and Eckersley's more critically inclined approaches.

DORAN, P. (1995) 'Earth, Power, Knowledge: Towards a Critical Global Environmental Politics', in J. Macmillan and A. Linklater (eds) *Boundaries in Question: New Directions in International Relations.* London: Pinter, pp. 193–211.

Uses Foucault's idea of discursive regimes to expose the limits of environmental practices and policies put in place by states and international organizations.

LÖVBRAND, E. AND STRIPPLE, J. (2006) 'The Climate as Political Space: On the Territorialisation of the Global Carbon Cycle', *Review of International Studies*, 32(2): 217–35.

SMITH, M.J. (1998) *Ecologism: Towards Ecological Citizenship.* Buckingham: Open University Press.

Opening chapter useful on the anthropocentric/ecocentric distinction.

DOBSON, A. (2007) *Green Political Thought,* 4th edn. London: Routledge.

WALL, D. (2005) *Babylon and Beyond: The Economics of Anti-Capitalist, Anti-Globalist and Radical Green Movements.* London: Pluto.

Ecoanarchist take on Green theory, also useful for your understanding of Marxism and Anarchism.

BOOKCHIN, M. (2005) *The Ecology of Freedom: The Emergence and Dissolution of Hierarchy,* 4th edn. Oakland, CA: AK Press. Leading ecoanarchist writer. Or try **BOOKCHIN, M. (2007)** *Social Ecology and Communalism.* Oakland, CA: AK Press.

ECKERSLEY, R. (2004) *The Green State: Rethinking Democracy and Sovereignty.* Cambridge, MA: MIT Press.

The state-led approach to promoting environmental justice. Conflicts with the ecoanarchists' view of how to achieve the same ends.

PATERSON, M. (1996) *Global Warming and Global Politics.* London: Routledge.

On the nature and limits of inter-state approaches to the environment.

KEGLEY JR., C.W. AND WITTKOPF, E.R. (2001) *The Global Agenda: Issues and Perspectives,* 6th edn. New york: McGraw-Hill.

Part 4 contains ten chapters on various aspects of the ecology and politics.

HAAS, P.M., KEOHANE, R.O. AND LEVY, M.A. (1993) *Institutions for the Earth: Sources of Effective Environmental Protection.* Cambridge, MA: MIT Press.

Conventional IR approach using regime theory to explain environmental outcomes.

YOUNG, O.R. (1989) *International Cooperation: Building Regimes for Natural Resources and the Environment.* Ithaca, NY: Cornell University Press.

As with the Haas, Keohane and Levy book, critiqued by writers such as Paterson who advocate a wholesale rethink of the ways in which we think about the contemporary environment and act to sustain it into the future. For a regime-centric approach, see also MITCHELL, R.B. **(2006)** 'International Environment', in W. Carlsnaes, T. Risse and B.A. Simmons (eds) *Handbook of International Relations*. London: Sage, pp. 500–16.

2.12	
anarchism	

Key terms:

Anarchy
State
Order
Violence
Authority
Capitalism

... an ideology defined by the rejection of the state. (Kinna 2005: 38)

It may seem strange to include in a book on IR a chapter on a theory, Anarchism, which interrogates the legitimacy and the authority of states. After all, Realists would remind us, we cannot understand IR without understanding the role of states in the contemporary global arena. Likewise, Liberal, English School and Constructivist theorists – until very recently the acknowledged core of the discipline – all take sovereign states to be the central actors. However, as we have seen in previous chapters, through the 1980s and 1990s, a wealth of theories hit the IR scene, all challenging fundamental assumptions about what IR is as a discipline and bringing into question accepted ways of studying the subject. Some of these theorists even doubted whether IR was a discipline at all, or simply a branch of political theory.

The introduction of Anarchist modes of thought to the discipline further confirms the utility of rethinking IR to get beyond, over and around state-centric approaches by questioning the artificial separation between the 'domestic' and the 'international'. In this chapter we will introduce you to Anarchism by looking at what its proponents say about order, war, authority and the state.

Anarchism and order

In Chapter 1.4 of this book we considered the central place the word 'anarchy' occupies in the discourse of IR by virtue of the international system widely being seen as 'anarchical'. To appreciate the specific meaning of this term in its IR context, I suggested it was useful to see beyond the 'public' meaning of anarchism, which tends to equate it with chaos, violence or disorder. Anarchy in IR has, rather, to do with the absence of an orderer at the international level. However, the point is that this absence may or may not lead to conflict between states. Hence, Hedley Bull wrote of an 'anarchical society' in which the condition of anarchy is accepted but taken as one in which a strong sense of order is also said to exist in the relations between states, both in times of peace and, crucially, war.

Do you tend to associate the word 'anarchy' or 'anarchist' with positive or negative things? A big problem Anarchist theorists encounter is that the negative connotations tend to outweigh the positive. This, they say, unfairly delegitimizes Anarchist theory.

It is in this technical sense that you should approach studying Anarchist theories of IR. As Ruth Kinna explains in her *Anarchism: Beginner's Guide*, the anarchist way of life, in contrast to the representations of anarchy and anarchism in the popular media, is in fact an 'ordered way of life'. Sure, it is anti-state, it is not the way of existing we have naturalized through our being born and raised in the modern state system, but anarchy does not mean a return to chaos or a primitive Hobbesian state of nature. On the contrary, quoting the French Anarchist theorist Pierre-Joseph Proudhon (see the Taking it Further section on p. 186), she observes that the symbol for Anarchy (the capital 'A' in an 'O') is predicated on the view that 'Anarchy is order; government is civil war' (Kinna 2005: 5). If we only step outside state-dominated conceptions of order we can see that Anarchy is just as ordered as democracy or other politico-economic orders; but the mode of achieving that order is *different* and thereby not popular among scholars wedded to the centrality and normalcy of the state.

Anarchism and authority

Anarchists are critical of government by the state which they see as an illegitimate source of authority. The key distinction here is between the two terms 'government' and 'authority'. The former means the formal mechanism of the state's rule; the latter is 'the principle that legitimizes the capacity to rule'. Authority for Anarchists is 'commanding, controlling and corrupting' (Kinna 2005: 53) because it comes in the form of a top-down ability to say: 'do this because I am in a position of authority', not because that authority is necessarily correct. Thus, Anarchists do not deny that some forms of government, authority and power can be legitimated and bring about order; what they doubt is 'that these legitimate forms can flourish in the state' (Kinna 2005: 67).

In this regard, Anarchists such as Noam Chomsky argue that the burden of proof should be on everyone in a position of authority to explain *why* they exercise their power using the methods they do. Authority, Chomsky says, 'should be dismantled if that burden cannot be met' (Chomsky 2005: 178). So, as an uncle, I would legitimately be able to explain to my nephew why I stopped him from running out into a busy road without looking. However, he might legitimately question me if I used my authority to stop him watching a Disney film I thought was rubbish but which he might enjoy. Anarchists unpick authority–power relations that are fixed in state structures of governance and call for at minimum their questioning and, if necessary, their overthrow.

Anarchism and war

In similar fashion to Marxists and socialists, Anarchists link war with systemic inequalities in the relations between states. Peter Kropotkin argued that the international system was filled with violence and the threat of violence because it was a site for contestation between markets all competing with each other for outlets, prestige and the control of raw materials. The 'reason for modern war is always the competition for markets and the right to exploit nations backward in industry' (quoted in Kinna 2005: 51). Chomsky has a similarly Marxist take on the causes of conflict. Contradicting the Realist Hans Morgenthau for proclaiming in 1967 that US involvement in Vietnam was a selfless and generous act of nation-building, Chomsky retorted that it is more accurate to read such interventions as further extensions of US imperialism or 'hegemony' (Chomsky 2005: 16).

> How might an Anarchist like Chomsky view the US-led invasion of Iraq in 2003?

The Marxist take on the causes of international conflict is supplemented by systematic Anarchist thought about the justice of violence. Anarchists do not rule out the use of force but systematically theorize *when* the use of such force is legitimate (Prichard 2007: 634–6). Chomsky's 'burden of proof' argument is one such example of the Anarchist, contrary to popular representation, logically thinking through the ethical implications of using violence. Anarchist approaches to violence come in many forms, perhaps the most obvious being the part Anarchists play in the anti/alter-globalization movement where dissent against multinational corporations and international institutions expresses the will to dissolve oppressive authority (on the nature of this movement, see Graeber 2002).

Anarchism and the state

The culmination of all the above is a radical Anarchist critique of the state. Kinna's reference to the Anarchist denial of the legitimacy of the state as a form of governance and order, noted above, does most of the work for us here. However, it is worth bearing in mind the vigorous dispute between those anti-statists such as Friedrich Engels who advocated keeping state structures but placing them in the hands of the people and those such as Mikhail Bakunin who were fearful of creating a 'Red Bureaucracy' which would be just as repressive and socially divisive as the political institutions they notionally replaced (Chomsky 2005: 120–1).

> Rudolf Rocker says Anarchism has two dimensions: it is anti-capitalist ('opposes the exploitation of man by man') and anti-state (opposes 'the dominion of man over man') (quoted in Chomsky 2005: 123).

Having identified Anarchism with a rejection of the state it is important to consider what it is Anarchists would replace states with: 'social order without repression, uniformity or social division' (Kinna 2005: 67). Again, contrary to popular myth, Anarchists are happy to set out Liberal philosophies more commonly associated with writers such as Jean-Jacques Rousseau and Immanuel Kant (Chomsky 2005; Prichard 2007). Rudolf Rocker puts it stridently when he writes that 'For the anarchist ... freedom is the vital concrete possibility for every human being to bring to full development' and that such natural individual fulfilment as is possible will only be delayed by placing it under 'ecclesiastical or political guardianship' (quoted in Chomsky 2005: 118).

Anarchists want an economic revolution whereby society becomes 'better and freer' (George Woodcock, quoted in Kinna 2005: 143) by being organized around 'organic units, organic communities' (see the previous chapter for an explanation of the ecoanarchist take on social organization). The locus of such order could be the workplace and/or neighbourhood and from there we could set up federal decision-making arrangements within regions and at national level. If these arrangements were to be instituted across nations as well as within them, we could ensure the creation of an integrated social organization which is responsive to the needs and wants of every person. In particular, decision-making may take place in governmental structures of a kind, but the individuals taking the decisions would always live and return to their local community, making them accountable and responsive to their immediate neighbours (Chomsky 2005: 133; Prichard 2007: 643).

Taking it **FURTHER**

The 'forgotten' work of Pierre-Joseph Proudhon

In 2007, Alex Prichard published an article detailing the international political theory of Pierre-Joseph Proudhon (Prichard 2007). He began by noting the general ignorance on the part of IR scholars about Anarchism in general and included a list of common misrepresentations about Proudhon by way of example (Prichard 2007: 626). In the article Prichard expounds Proudhon's wide-ranging theories of justice, order and war and how these informed his understanding of Anarchism and its application to contemporary political and international theory.

Prichard identifies several dimensions of Proudhon's thought that are directly applicable to the study of IR:

- Liberal Anarchism: the autonomy of the individual.
- Anti-statism: the morality of the individual is prior to that of the state.
- Interrogation of the assumption that a 'state of nature' can or has ever existed in any society: 'we are always already social' (Prichard 2007: 630).
- Anti-capitalism: the economy cannot be entrusted to be run by the exploitative power of capital.
- The construction and validity of federal governance: 'a post-sovereign system of mutualist global justice' (Prichard 2007: 643).

Prichard's attempt to raise the profile of this 'forgotten' IR thinker shows the essentially contested nature of IR as a discipline. In your university library can you find books and articles by other writers which seem to have been similarly ignored or overlooked by the mainstream of the discipline? What light do they shed on IR?

Questions to ponder

"Is the anti-statism of Anarchist theory compatible with the study of IR?"

Your response to this question will turn on your definitions of two key terms: first, what does it mean to suggest that a theory might or might not be 'compatible' with IR, and, second, what do we even mean by the 'study of IR'? To get you going you would have to scope your understanding of the 'anti-state' dimensions of Anarchist theory. This could be done with reference to it being one of Rocker's two dimensions of Anarchism (see above), featuring as a central element in the Anarchists' critiques of authority and illegitimate or oppressive uses of power. The best students would alert their reader to the idea that 'anti-statism' does not equate with a denial of governing structures *per se*, even if debates persist among Anarchists about what kinds of structures are most appropriate.

The nub of the matter is then how applicable you judge this direction of thinking to be to the study of IR. Presumably if you take IR in its conventional guise you will not see much applicability of Anarchist theory, just as you might not see postcolonial, feminist or postmodern as especially relevant to an understanding of the 'man, the state and war' agenda. However, if you take seriously the re-visioning of the discipline that these theorists urge upon us, then you will be more open to a serious consideration of Anarchism's anti-statism. The best students will alert the reader to the big debates about the politics of academic knowledge production and how these are reflected about a tussle over the most appropriate agenda for IR. One way to think through structuring an answer would be to present all the arguments for Anarchism and then all those against, all of which would be framed by your own position within this debate: why do *you* think Anarchism is or is not compatible with the study of IR?

"Explain how Anarchists interpret 'authority' and the ramifications this has for the study of IR."

When dealing with an essay or exam question using such a word – and especially when that word is put in speech marks – you necessarily have to define it somewhere near the start of your answer. 'Authority' is a complex word which, like other keywords in the study of Politics and IR like 'power', 'democracy' and of course 'anarchy' itself, has many dimensions and meanings depending on context. Kinna's approach identified above is instructive because she tells us about 'authority' by contrasting it with 'government'. The potentially oppressive and illegitimate use of authority is what Chomsky picks up on with his 'burden of proof' argument, and you could work from here onto the rejection of the state as proof of Anarchism's rejection/questioning of authority. The best students will demonstrate that they have read widely around the topic and can put forward a synthesis of five or six definitions of 'authority' including both original Anarchist theorists and secondary overviews of Anarchist thought.

Some students will accidentally forget to address the second part of the question so make sure you leave space (in an essay) and time (in an exam) to pursue a line of argument on that topic. These are potentially numerous, with Anarchist thought ranging over such issues as war, violence/force, justice, ethics and morality, modes of governance, the role of the state and anti-capitalism. It will be hard for you to include analysis of each and every one so pick the four or five that you find most relevant and interesting and concentrate on those, pointing the reader to sources on the remaining issues as necessary. If you really want to interrogate the normative assumption in the question that Anarchism has implications for the study of IR, then you could frame your answer using Prichard's analysis of the neglect of Anarchism within IR as a way in to making the point that Anarchism has ramifications for IR but that these have been sadly overlooked until very recently.

References to more information

By Anarchist theorists:

BAKUNIN, M. **(1970)** *God and the State*. New York: Dover Publications.
KROPOTKIN, P. **(1987)** *The State: Its Historic Role*. London: Freedom Press.
ROCKER, R. **(1978)** *Nationalism and Culture*, trans. R.E. Chase, 2nd edn. Sanday: Cienfuegos Press.
BOOKCHIN, M. **(1971)** *Post-scarcity Anarchism*. Berkeley, CA: Ramparts Press.
RITTER, A. **(1980)** *Anarchism: A Theoretical Analysis.* Cambridge: Cambridge University Press.

Online resources:

Anarchy Archives, http://dwardmac.pitzer.edu/ANARCHIST_ARCHIVES/index. html.

Online resources for the study of the history and theory of Anarchism, established 1996. Includes work on the 'classics' such as Bakunin, Kropotkin and Proudhon together with other 'bright but lesser lights'.

INFOSHOP **(2006)** 'An Anarchist FAQ', http://www.infoshop.org/faq/

R.A. FORUM **(NO DATE)** 'Research on Anarchism', http://raforum.info/rubrique. php3?-id_rubrique=2.

Anarchism: The Unfinished Revolution (no date), 'Anarchist Bibliography', http://www.ditext-.com/anarchism/index.html.

By and on Chomsky:

CHOMSKY, N. **(2004)** *Hegemony or Survival: America's Quest for Global Dominance*. London: Penguin.

Updates the theory of US imperialism Chomsky first expounded in relation to the Vietnam War.

REVIEW OF INTERNATIONAL STUDIES **(2003)** 'Forum on Chomsky', 29(4): 551–620.

Five articles on Chomsky's interventions on international affairs, especially his critiques of US foreign policy.

On Anarchism in IR:

TURNER, S. **(1998)** 'Global Civil Society, Anarchy and Governance: Assessing an Emerging Paradigm', *Journal of Peace Research*, 35(1): 25–42.

Uses Kropotkin's thought to interrogate Realist IR theory and critique the state as the main source of violence in the modern world.

WEISS, T.G. **(1975)** 'The Tradition of Philosophical Anarchism and Future Directions in World Policy', *Journal of Peace Research*,12(1): 1–17.

FALK, R. **(1979)** 'Anarchism and World Order', in J.R. Pennock and J.W. Chapman (eds) *Anarchism: Nomos XIX*. New York: New York University Press.

On the antialter-globalization movement:

KLEIN, N. (2002) *Fences and Windows: Dispatches from the Front Lines of the Globalization Debate.* London: Flamingo.

HOLLOWAY, J. (2005) *Change the World Without Taking Power: The Meaning of Revolution Today,* 2nd edn. London: Pluto Press.

Do or Die Number 8: Voices of Ecological Resistance (no date) 'What is Globalization? (and how do we think about challenging it)', http://www.geocities.com/kk_abacus/dod8glbl.html.

Globalization and Anarchism (no date), http://flag.blackened.net/revolt/anarchism/fight/global.html.

The highest achieving students on any module tend to be those who manage their learning by taking effective responsibility for it. In an era when students are asked to pay a fee for the privilege of going to university (in England, for example), the potential is there for some students to believe that because they fork out money they have a right to obtain a degree. Nothing could be further from the truth. Whether we agree that universities should charge fees or not, your yearly payment is for the right to study the degree, not to be given one for doing nothing!

In most universities the marks you receive for the first year of your degree programme do not count towards your overall degree classification. Do not see this as an excuse to slack in the first year. Use the year to learn good work habits which you can put into practice straight away in the second year. In a competitive job market employers increasingly want to see transcripts of Year 1 marks to help them decide between graduates.

Just like owning a car, you are buying the right to take *ownership of your learning* on your degree programme. Some car owners are careful with their vehicle, taking every care to keep it roadworthy and in good condition. Other owners have a slap-dash approach to car maintenance which means that in time their car becomes something of a dangerous, unroadworthy rust bucket. It is up to you to decide what kind of owner of *your* learning you want to be. Your lecturers, friends, parents and relatives can help to a certain extent but your final degree classification will tell potential employers exactly what kind of owner of your learning you have been. The earlier you take responsibility and the more you take responsibility, the better you will fare.

The following six chapters give you tips and advice on how to take control of your learning. We begin with how to get the best out of your lectures and seminars and move on to consider how to succeed at essays and exams.

Core areas:

3.1 How to get the most out of lectures
3.2 How to get the most out of seminars
3.3 Essay writing
3.4 Good practice in essays
3.5 Exam revision
3.6 Exam tips

3.1	
how to get the most out of lectures	

In this chapter we examine one of the most widely used methods of delivering information at university: the lecture. You can get the best out of lectures by taking a three-phase approach covering: preparation for the lecture, what happens during the lecture and what happens after the lecture. Thinking seriously about managing your learning in all three phases will certainly help you get the most out of lectures.

> Lectures are one small part of the overall learning process. Taking ownership of your learning means knowing the advantages as well as the major limitations of learning in lectures.

Preparation

Your tutor will use lectures and the accompanying hard or online module documentation and reading lists to set the scope of your learning on the module. Depending on the structure of your course you will normally have anything up to two lectures on IR per week and usually some accompanying seminars.

Attendance

The most obvious way to get the most out of lectures is to attend them! Given the learning technologies available today the classic stereotype of an academic lecturer standing at the front of a vast, dark, soulless lecture theatre droning on to a slumbering mass of students could not be further from the reality (in the vast majority of cases at least). All lecturers differ in their approach, style, use of visual aids such as hand-outs and PowerPoint, but they all have one thing in common: they are passionate about their subject and will want you to be passionate about it too.

> Attending lectures is the best way to 'get inside the head' of your lecturer and get a feel for how they approach the subject.

If you begin a course not attending lectures it becomes psychologically harder and harder to attend as the course goes on, either because you feel embarrassed about your non-attendance or because you simply get in the habit of missing them. So, make sure you attend the very first lecture of the course and maintain your participation through the module. Hearing the lecturer talk first hand you will gain a major advantage over students who do not attend regularly or at all.

> In academic year 2006/7, I conducted a statistical analysis of the relationship between lecture attendance and marks achieved on my IR Theory module. I found that those students who frequently attended lectures almost always scored better coursework and exam marks than regular non-attendees.

Reading

Your course tutor will either give you, or publish electronically, a list of suggested readings for each lecture on your course. Sometimes this will be in the form of a long list of sources. More often than not your tutor will divide the list into 'essential', 'desirable' and 'further/wider' reading.

> Most tutors will recommend one or two essential textbooks as 'course reading' and you should start with these. See the Introduction in this book for a selection of IR books you are likely to find recommended as course textbooks.

Before your lecture you should aim to read at least the essential reading and as much of the desirable reading as you can. There is no set amount that each tutor expects but, as a rough guide, if you are reading at least five book chapters and/or journal articles before each lecture you will stand a very good chance of grasping the fundamental points your lecturer will want you to take from his/her lecture. You will have time after the lecture to put the icing on the cake with further reading.

One way to approach your reading might be:

- Begin with general textbook sources to get a feel for the key themes and then move onto the tougher monographs and journal articles.
- Set yourself realistic reading targets.
- Learn how long it takes you to read one average textbook chapter and one average journal article and plan your reading on that basis.
- Learn *where* you read best: in your room, in the department or in the library?
- Find somewhere without too many distractions so you can concentrate.

- Make a note of concepts/issues you do not understand and root around for further information on them. If necessary, contact your tutor who will be happy to discuss them with you and advise where you can find information to enhance your understanding.

> *Most tutors make their lecture notes and/or PowerPoint presentations available to you. Print them out and read them before your lectures so you can pay particular attention in the lecture to the areas you understand less well.*

During the lecture

The two most important things you can do to get the best out of lectures are, first, to go prepared and, second, to see them as an opportunity to engage creatively with the subject matter.

> The whole set-up of a lecture unfortunately tends to encourage the idea that the style of learning on offer is passive (lecturer talks; you listen). You need to think of ways to remain actively engaged.

Notes

If notes are available to you prior to the lecture, make sure you have read over them and identified any difficult concepts or ideas you do not understand. You can make additional notes either on these printouts or make your own notes from scratch. Either way, be sure to label your notes with the date and subject matter of the lecture so you can organize them easily. A simple A4 file with your notes divided by topic will help you organize your notes and find what you want to when writing essays and revising for exams.

Lecture notes should represent a *legible* account of the main ideas presented in the lecture, together with the odd point to follow up and perhaps references to key writings the lecturer mentions which are not on the reading list. Lecturers will tend to present the 'big' picture in lectures and focus only on key concepts and ideas. It is up to you to flesh out the bones of the subject covered through preparation and post-lecture consolidation (see below).

> If a lecturer mentions an author or text that is not on the reading list do not be afraid to ask him/her to spell out the author's name (by email after the lecture if you prefer) so you can trace the source easily after the lecture.

Lecturers will usually explain the meaning of new or difficult terms related to each topic they cover. If at the end of the lecture you are still unfamiliar with a term, then you have two options to clarify your thoughts. First, try and find the term defined in the reading (glossaries are useful here). Second, contact your lecturer who will be happy to explain its meaning or at least give you some help locating a relevant definition. If many writers define the same term differently, keep a record of all their definitions for use in essays and exam answers.

Note-taking

There is no one recipe for success as far as taking notes in lectures goes. If you try and take too many notes, you will miss some or lots of what is said. If you take too few you will not generate a detailed enough picture of what was said for reference later. Do not worry if you do not capture everything that was said; the key is that you were present and that you leave with an idea of the big picture. Use your first-year lectures in particular to work out a note-taking strategy that works for you and which gives you the optimum of listening and recording what was said.

> If your lecturer talks too fast, he/she should not mind if you ask to record the lecture to playback at your leisure. But remember: you do not need to tape every lecture and religiously copy out what was said.

After the lecture

Possibly the least recognized element of lecture-based learning is the post-lecture phase in which you consolidate and develop your knowledge.

Consolidation

This is all about establishing the foundations of the topic by confirming that you understand core concepts:

- Take time to read through your notes after the lecture.
- Re-write any lecture notes that are illegible.
- You could re-write the entire set of notes in a format that is clear and simple to understand. This option is useful if you want to make it easy to retrieve information from an ordered, clearly structured stock of information at a later stage.

- Make a summary of the lecture in a series of bullet points at the top of your notes. This will help you establish your understanding and make it easy to find the relevant material at a later stage.
- Make a note of any points made in the lecture that you are still unclear about.
- Make a list of any further reading mentioned by the lecturer.

> *Form a small study group (3 to 5 people) to review your notes, pool ideas on difficult concepts and consolidate your understanding of the main issues covered in each lecture.*

Development

Having consolidated your knowledge of the lecture you are now in a position to develop that knowledge. You can do this in several ways:

- Do any essential or further reading you did not do prior to the lecture.
- Trace and read sources mentioned in the lecture but which were not on the reading list (contact the lecturer if necessary).
- Research around difficult concepts or ideas raised in the reading and lecture.
- Marry your lecture notes with notes from your reading. For example, if your lecturer talked about different theoretical traditions approaching an issue in IR from different perspectives, could you name writers who represent each of those traditions? If not, where would you look to find out?
- Practice questions: take a look at past exam papers for your course. Could you now attempt an exam question on the lecture you have just listened to? If the answer is '*no*', you need to do more reading and research around the subject.

> *Spend 45 minutes each week planning and drafting an answer to a past exam question. This will be invaluable practice for the real thing. Very few students will do the same so your tutor would happily give you feedback on your answers.*

3.2	
how to get the most out of seminars	

Seminars offer you the opportunity to explore various perspectives on a given topic in depth. They expose you to different styles of learning and encourage you to think creatively around problems both individually and in groups. Despite these benefits, seminars are not always well attended by students. This is a great shame because the seminar environment encourages you to develop subject specific matter expertise as well as transferable skills for use outside the learning environment.

> If you aim to get the best out of seminars in IR theory, you are giving yourself the best chance of succeeding at your coursework and exams as well as developing vital communication and teamwork skills for the long-term.

In this chapter we will consider the nature of seminar learning and how you can get the very best out of your seminar time, with particular reference to seminar learning, effort and presentations.

Seminar learning

Lectures are usually held up to be the cornerstone of academic programmes but seminars play a vital part in helping you generate depth to your understanding of a given subject. In IR terms, the lectures will more than likely present a broad-brush overview of the main assumptions and explanations put forward by each school of theory. In seminars you will have time to consolidate your understanding of the basics as well as debating the relative strengths and weaknesses of different theorists' interpretations of IR.

Initially, seminar learning can seem a daunting prospect. You are often working with students you may not have met properly before and may be asked to tackle questions you had not thought about prior to the seminar. Teaching and learning in seminars often come in many shapes and forms and you will probably not know how you are going to be learning before you actually get to the seminar room on the day.

Do not let the relative uncertainty about how you will learn in seminars put you off attending. See it as a challenge and a way of proving that you are flexible and adaptable. Your tutor will look positively on those students who throw themselves wholeheartedly into seminars.

Here is a small sample of the kinds of seminar learning you might experience at university:

- **Individual summaries/critiques**. You might be given a short extract from a key text and asked to spend 10 minutes reading it and summarizing/critiquing the main points it raises.
- **Pair work**. Discuss a problem/perspective/issue with the person sitting next to you.
- **Group work**. Discuss a problem/perspective/issue with a small number of other students in the seminar, possibly leading to a 'group' answer which you present to the rest of the class.
- **Pyramid work**. All students start with the same issue to consider for five minutes. Then you work in pairs for five minutes and finally you discuss your ideas in groups for five minutes. It is called pyramid work because the number of 'units' involved decreases as the seminar progresses, building up from a base of lots of students thinking about a problem to fewer pairs and finally even fewer groups.
- **Class debate**. As in parliaments, you may be split into groups and asked to propose or oppose a motion. As an example, in recent years I have split my seminar groups into two teams to debate the motion: 'This House believes the study of gender is vital to the study of IR', with one team proposing the motion and the other opposing it. Debates are good for helping you consider all sides of a problem because not only do you have to work out your own position, you have to think about how to counter what the opposing team might argue.
- **Whole group discussion.** Most common at the end of seminars. A chance to 'wrap' up big issues, ask questions, iron out any lingering misunderstandings and consolidate your knowledge from the lecture and seminar reading.

All tutors organize seminars differently and some can be set in their ways! If there are styles of seminar learning you find particularly helpful, your tutor will consider using them if you alert him/her to your preference.

You tend to get back what you put in

As with lectures, you tend to get out of seminars what you put into them. If you find yourself sitting in seminars unable to understand or discuss the basics of a given issue, you have probably not done sufficient preparatory work. Here are some very basic tips on the kinds of things you can do to work confidently and rewardingly in seminars:

- Do a realistic amount of preparatory reading. If your tutor has identified essential reading, you should at least complete that.
- Take all your notes with you to each seminar, plus pen and paper to jot down further notes during the seminar.
- If you are not sure you understand something: ask.
- Make sure you try and say something relatively early on in a seminar, even if only to ask a question. Studies show that the longer you go without speaking, the harder it becomes to intervene as the seminar progresses.
- At the end of the seminar check through your notes to make sure they are legible and for any issues you may want to follow up on.

Sometimes, the problem is not that you have come to a seminar unprepared but that you are frightened of interjecting into a debate. In this case, remember the following:

- Very few people feel totally at ease at speaking in public, especially in subjects that are relatively unfamiliar to them. Most university teachers I know still get nervous before giving lectures, even if they've been doing it for 20 years. Students are no different, and even if they *appear* confident you can be sure they are nervous inside.
- There really are no stupid questions. If you are unclear about something you can be sure you are not the only one.
- Your tutor is not there to tell you what to think. At university level, tutors are less like school teachers than facilitators for your learning.
- Disagreements among students in the seminar group will be many and varied. This is entirely to be expected.
- There are no right or wrong answers to questions about IR theory. We may prefer one theory over another but no-one can shoot an opinion down by saying it is 'wrong'.
- Learning how to disagree and how to conduct rational arguments in a seminar environment will help sharpen your thinking on a given topic.

In pretty much any career you pursue after graduating you will have to speak in public in some environment, whether one-on-one with a boss or colleague or to larger groups at conferences, for example. Use the university environment to generate confidence at public speaking.

Presentations

Standing up and talking about academic matters can be a stressful business. In your seminars for IR theory you may be asked to give a presentation on your own, or to work in pairs or groups and then to present your combined results. Either way, here are some tips on how to plan and deliver an effective presentation:

Planning your presentation

- Spend time preparing as thoroughly as you can and get preparing as early as you can, especially if working as part of a group.
- If working in pairs or in a group, apportion work evenly and set realistic targets for each group member.
- Decide if you want to use visual aids such as hand-outs or PowerPoints and prepare these in advance.
- Clearly structure your presentation and centre it on one core argument or theme.
- Read as widely as you can and show you have a good knowledge of the field.
- Build practice time into your schedule, especially if you are using presentation technologies such as PowerPoint. Whether presenting on your own or in a group, run through the entire presentation at least once to check that it flows well and you cover the ground you need to in the allotted time.

Delivering your presentation

- Stick to the allotted time. It is better to be slightly under the time than over it.
- Make eye contact with everyone in the audience at least once during the talk.
- Use a script if necessary but try to avoid simply reading out your talk or you will lose the audience's attention.
- Try and look and sound enthusiastic and confident (even if you are not!)
- If using PowerPoint, do not talk to the screen – remember it is an aid, not the object of the talk.
- Make sure your talk follows the structure of your hand-out or order of the PowerPoint slides (practising in advance is critical here).
- Summarize your main points at the end in a concluding section.

> *In seminars you have a huge opportunity to establish confidence in your knowledge of the subject matter of IR theory. The skills you develop there will be of great value in other seminars and when you enter the world of work. Take them seriously and you will benefit enormously from them.*

References to more information

Here are some books dedicated to improving your seminar communication and presentation skills:

BRADBURY, A. (2006) *Successful Presentation Skills*, 3rd edn. London: Kogan-Page.

STOTT, R. (2001) *Speaking Your Mind: Oral Presentation and Seminar Skills.* Harlow: Longman.

BARRASS, R. (2006) *Speaking for Yourself: A Guide for Students to Effective Communication.* London: Routledge.

KROEHNERT, G. (1999) *Basic Presentation Skills.* Roseville, NSW: McGraw-Hill.

BONNETT, A. (2001) *How to Argue: A Student's Guide.* Harlow: Pearson.

VAN EMDEN, J. AND BECKER, L. (2004) *Presentation Skills for Students.* Basingstoke: Palgrave Macmillan.

3.3

essay writing

Essays are likely to form a huge part of the assessed workload on your course. Exams and/or seminar presentations may feature too, but inevitably you will have to tackle a formal, fully referenced essay at some point on your course. Learning what makes for a successful essay is vital at university level and the sooner you can develop the techniques for producing coherent, flowing and concise written responses to questions, the better you will fare on all your modules.

> The main components of a good coursework essay also make for good exam answers so think of them as requiring the same skills. The only thing missing from exam answers are formal references and a bibliography.

In this chapter I want to suggest that the process of putting together a successful essay takes three things: sound preparation/planning, a structured approach to writing/presentation and a solid amount of evidence to back your claims. I will flesh these out for you now and in the next chapter we will see hard examples of best practice in IR theory essay technique.

Planning and preparation

Know your enemy

Your initial task from a planning perspective is to know the precise requirements to be met in your coursework. These will be available from your tutor either at or near the start of the module, and are usually included in the module guide. The key things to take note of are:

- **Essay deadline**. Coursework delivered after the deadline is either marked down or given zero. Set yourself a realistic completion target and aim to finish at least one day before the deadline to give yourself time to proof-read the essay for errors, omissions or ambiguities in your argument or written English.

> *Getting a friend or relative to read through your essay before you submit will help iron out any obvious problems with it. Their outsider perspective helps them spot things you may have missed because you are so 'close' to the essay.*

- **Deadline extensions**. If you have a valid claim for an extension contact your tutor well in advance of the deadline. Check your department's guidelines on what you need to support your claim and keep all the relevant supporting evidence, for example, a doctor's note if you have been ill.
- **Length of essay**. It is important to stick to the word limit set. Check with your tutor if you are allowed to go slightly above or below the word limit and how far these bands extend. Ten per cent above or below if usually permitted but it will depend on your tutor's and department's guidelines.
- **Presentation and submission requirements**. Check your departmental under-graduate handbook for full details on how to set out your essays, how to provide references and where to submit your work. Tutors get bombarded with emails in the week leading up to the submission deadline and it does not look too good if you ask simple questions that are all answered in the handbook!
- **Lecture insights**. In lectures, tutors will often hint at ways of approaching essays that they feel pay dividends to their students. This is another reason to attend lectures regularly.

> Attending lectures helps you learn more about subject matter and also gives you a feel for what your tutor expects to see in essays and exam answers.

Plan your argument

Having oriented yourself to the precise requirements of the essay you need to set about planning the essay. To get to this stage you will need to have carried out at least the essential reading on the topic and preferably the desirable and as much wider reading as possible. You can always carry on reading while you write as long as you have most of it completed before you begin planning the essay.

> *When tutors mark a big batch of essays, they get used to seeing the same authors and ideas rehashed over and over again. Doing wider reading will help your essay stand out from the crowd.*

When you feel comfortable that you know the basics about the subject and are ready to put finger to keyboard here are some tips on how to keep the essay focused, manageable and persuasive:

- **Key argument.** Your essay should hang together around a central argument, point of view, interpretation or opinion. This should preferably be in the form of a direct response to the question set and should appear as the focal point in your introductory section. Your central theme will be phrased according to the nature of the essay question but the key thing is that you have a central argument and can explain it clearly and concisely. Without the focus a central argument provides you will not be able to give direction to the essay and the reader will not be sure of where you are going either.

> It sounds formulaic but you could even begin the essay by writing 'This essay will argue that…'. Few students have the confidence to lead off with their argument but it helps a tutor to see exactly where you intend to go from the outset.

- **How many points?** Undergraduate essays vary in length, usually from 1,500 words upwards, so there are no hard and fast rules that will work in every situation. Assuming the introduction and conclusion are approximately 10 per cent each of the entire word count, in a 1,500 word essay this would leave 1,200 words as the 'body' of the essay. This is not a lot of words. You will not be able to cover more than four or five main points so you will have to be selective about what to include and what to ignore. The less successful essays tend to be those that try to cover every single point made about a particular topic in the reading, or which rehash the relevant lecture. Being selective is critical at the planning stage.

> It is up to you to work out the best structure to use given the word limit. Learning when to leave material out and when to include it is a big part of developing effective writing techniques.

- **Getting your own opinion across.** Some students worry if they do not include any of their own opinions in coursework essays. Do not worry about this. You are not expected to develop new theories of IR or never-thought-of-before critiques of the theories you examine in an essay. Your approach to the subject matter will come through in your main argument and the structure you give your answer. The 'originality' of the essay is, therefore, inherent in an essay that you have planned and written in your own words, and backed up by quotes and evidence from established sources.

> Remember that the same essay question can be answered in an infinite number of ways. In devising your response and structuring your answer your work counts as original in this regard.

Essay structure

If you ask any university student about essay structure they all know what it means: beginning, middle and end. In my time teaching IR theory I have come more and more to the conclusion that this only tells a very small part of the story about essay structure. Students tend to grasp this basic 'macro' structure but what about the middle or body of the essay? The essence of a robust structure is not just that the essay is in three parts, but that the various segments or paragraphs that make up those parts are also structured. It is at the micro level structure that the vast majority of students trip up. The classic feature is an essay that starts with a coherent introduction and ends with a coherent conclusion. But in the middle the author jumps around at random with ideas, authors and concepts cropping up all over the place. The author has structured the essay at the macro level but forgotten about the micro level.

> If you think essay structure is all about introduction, body, conclusion, think again! There is much more to it than that. Structure applies on two levels: macro and micro, and successful essays pay attention to both levels.

Everyone knows about macro structure!

I will not dwell on the macro structure needed to write a successful essay. Suffice to say that you should be familiar with the basic idea and

---

INTRODUCTION

- Aims of essay
- Core theme/argument
- Essay plan

BODY OF ESSAY

- The key points that help you advance your central case
- Micro structure

CONCLUSION

- Reminder of central argument
- Wider issues raised by essay

Figure 18   Macro essay structure

your tutor will usually be happy to look over a plan that comes in this format as a way of assuring you that your answer looks like a logical response to the essay question set. Figure 18 presents the essence of a 'macro' essay structure.

What is micro structure?

Less familiar might be the idea of micro structure: the structure of the individual sections themselves, particularly the body of the essay. Why is this important? The whole idea of an essay is that you are showing your tutor you are organized, well read and able to construct a logical argument that flows nicely through the piece. If you do not structure at the micro level as well as the macro level you risk losing your reader because they will probably not be able to follow where you go in the essay.

> One way to structure the body of an essay is by using headings and sub-headings. This helps the reader see how you have organized your answer.

Concentrating on the micro structure is essential at both the planning and writing stages. You need to structure each section of your essay from introduction through body and conclusion, and this means making sure

---

INTRODUCTION

- Aims of essay
- Core theme or argument you will make
- Essay plan: what you will cover in points 1 to 4

BODY OF ESSAY

- **POINT 1**
  - Summarize essence of point 1 (*S*)*
  - Make point 1
  - Explain how point 1 helps you advance your core argument and where you are going next in the essay (*B*)**

- **POINT 2**
  - Summarize essence of point 2 (*S*)
  - Make point 2
  - Summarize upshot of points 1 and 2 (*S*) and say where you are going next in the essay (*B*)

- **POINT 3**
  - Summarize essence of point 3 (*S*)
  - Make point 3
  - Summarize key findings from points 1, 2 and 3 (*S*) and say where you are going next in the essay (*B*)

- **POINT 4**
  - Summarize essence of point 4 (*S*)
  - Make point 4
  - Summarize key findings from point 4 and recap how they relate to points 1, 2 and 3 (*S*)

CONCLUSION

- Reminder of central argument
- Where you went in points 1 to 4
- Wider issues raised by essay

Figure 19　Micro structure of an essay

Notes:
* (*S*) denotes a signpost section (see below)
** (*B*) denotes a bridge section (see below)

the various paragraphs that make up each section follow logically from the one to the next. Because it is the most difficult aspect, we will concentrate here on how a structured body of the essay might look in theory. We will assume an essay in four main parts, top and tailed by an introduction and conclusion. Depending on the word limit of the essay, each point in the body of the essay would be developed in roughly two to three paragraphs. Figure 19 sets out the micro structure of an essay.

Figure 19 reads quite formulaically, but do not be put off by this. Your tutor will be reading dozens, sometimes hundreds of essays and will want to be told precisely where you have gone, and to know that *you* know why you travelled where you did in the answer. If you make this structure explicit, you will stand out from the vast majority of other students who will keep the marker guessing about their intellectual journey.

> The basic requirement of a good essay is that you take your reader on a journey that you have planned in advance. If you cannot (or do not) clearly explain your journey from start to finish, then do not expect your tutor to be able to follow you through it.

Techniques to help you develop your essay's micro structure

You only develop essay planning and writing skills by practice. Here are a few things you can try to structure your essays clearly and explicitly.

> Try implementing some or all of these techniques in your next essay. Also, try and identify good structuring techniques from the reading you do. Borrowing tips from the experts is a great way to learn essay skills.

- **Signposts.** Quite literally, you point the reader through the essay. Think of it like following road signs on a car journey. When they are in plentiful supply and easy to understand, it is easy to find your way to your destination. However, when there are no signs, or if they point the wrong way, or if they are unclear, then it becomes frustrating and difficult for you to follow them. By inserting signpost sentences regularly you give the reader the pointers they need to navigate their way through your thinking in the essay.
- **Bridges.** Similar to signposts in that they give the essay direction, but they are used specifically to help the reader cross between two distinct parts of an essay. In the example above, bridging sections would be used to take the reader from the introduction to the body of the essay from point 1 to point 2, from point 2 to point 3, from point 3 to point 4 and from point 4 to the conclusion. Hence, while signposts are used at the start of new sections or paragraphs to point the way ahead or recap a central theme in the essay, bridges are less frequent but play a crucial role in getting your reader into and out of sections.

Summary on signposts and bridges

There are three main varieties of signposting (Redman 2006: 64): (1) at the beginning of a new section to summarize what you will argue in it; (2) at the end of a section to recap the central theme of the section; and (3) where necessary to remind the reader of the subject of your essay. Especially useful when you get to the later stages of an essay.

> We will see practical examples of signposting in IR theory essays in the next chapter.

Signposts and bridges are very similar in some respects because the idea of both is to help the reader through an essay. You can happily combine the two together if you wish. Say you are tackling the essay question: 'Realism is the "common sense" theory of IR. Discuss'. This essay naturally falls into two parts: those who agree with that statement and those who disagree with it. At the end of all the 'for' points you could write, *'Having discussed three reasons why Realism is said to be the common sense approach to IR,* **the essay will now consider the arguments against this view by looking at the work of Liberal and Feminist scholars'**. This sentence contains both a signpost (italics) and a bridge (bold). Feel free to experiment with signposts and bridges and find what works best for you. They key thing is that you will get credit for trying because you will be showing your tutor that you are organized and have thought seriously about how to write 'academically'.

> *It is up to you how to deploy signposts and bridges in your essays. Try finding set phrases and ways of introducing/recapping that work for you and stick to them.*

Evidence

Successful essays and exam answers are those that rely on a sound foundation of evidence. Academics use evidence to provide them with information about a subject and as a point of reference within a given debate. In IR, theorists get their evidence from many places: history, contemporary politics and other theorists, for example. Your tutor will recommend a series of readings for your course and the first place you should look is there, but feel free to go beyond the recommended readings. Being creative with your research on a topic is a sign of initiative and your tutor will notice your work more if you have put in the effort to look beyond the basic texts.

> A successful essay requires both technical proficiency and an in-depth knowledge of the subject matter.

By providing evidence you are showing your essay is built on more than a passing acquaintance with the subject or what you heard your friends talking about in the Students Union bar the night before you submitted it. Through the evidence you provide you are demonstrating a thorough engagement with the key literature, a familiarity with the technical concepts and an active involvement in the debates that take place between writers in the field. In sum, you are showing that you have made every effort to get inside the heads of the writers you have been asked to study on your course. You can only do this by reading widely and providing full references to the sources of information you used to construct the essay.

> ### Common pitfall
>
> *Students routinely fail to provide evidence to back their assertions. You do not need a reference for every fact presented in an essay if it is common knowledge. For example, saying that the Second World War ended in 1945 would not need a reference. However, you do need to show the provenance or origin of every major argument, interpretation or point of view you discuss in an essay. For instance, if you set out the key assumptions of Realism or alluded to the varieties of Critical Theory, you would need a clear reference to your source because these are NOT common knowledge but your interpretations drawn from other people's texts.*

Using evidence

You can use evidence from your reading in a variety of ways:

- **Quotes.** Use these if a writer makes a particularly succinct, cutting comment on a given issue, provides a suitable definition for a difficult concept, or has come up with an interpretation, theory or model that critically shaped a debate within a field. Try and limit the amount of quotes you use in an essay so that enough of your own words still come through. Quotes should support your ideas, not the other way around. Common pitfalls with using quotes are that they are too long and/or become just a series of unrelated sentences from writers with no explanation for why they appear where they do.

> If you are quoting a writer who uses italics or bold font in their original work, make sure you tell your reader the emphasis in your essay has not been inserted by you but appears in the original.

- **Paraphrase/summary.** You may not always want to quote directly from authors but instead paraphrase them, usually in the form of a summary of their arguments. This is an equally valid way of introducing evidence from established sources into your essay. Remember that even if you do not quote directly you will still need to include a reference to the original source.
- **What to cite?** When providing references you only need to cite the source where you found the information. If you got all your information about postmodernist writer X from textbook authors B and C, then your reference will be to textbook writers B and C. If you cite the original work by writer X your tutor will mistakenly assume you read the original.

> Do not pretend you have read an original source if you did not. If you got all your information about a theory or writer from a textbook be honest about it.

Referencing

Before you start writing an essay acquaint yourself fully with your department's style guidelines on how to set out references and bibliographies. As a very general rule you are likely to be asked for the following:

- If a reference appears in the essay it will need to appear in the list of references at the end in a format that makes it easily identifiable to the reader.
- A bibliography includes all the sources you used to research an essay; a list of references only includes those sources you refer to in an essay.

> Do not be tempted to 'pad' a bibliography with sources you did not read!

- Make sure you achieve consistency with dates, spelling of surnames and so on in your essay references and bibliography.
- Put your bibliography or list of references alphabetically by surname, and always start on a new page at the end of the essay.

- When referencing online sources, do not include the full web address in the text to the essay, save it for the bibliography. In the essay you need a shortened reference fully traceable in the bibliography. For example, if you wanted to refer to UN Secretary-General Ban Ki-moon's statement to regional groups of the UN in January 2008, this is available online. In your essay you would summarize or quote from it and your reference would read (Ki-moon 2008). Save the full title and web address for the bibliography, so that the reader can find it if they look under 'Ki-moon 2008'. Go to my bibliography now to see how I have set it out. Some websites contain no author and/or date. In that case you simply say 'anonymous' or 'no date' where applicable.

> Give your marker as much information as possible so that they are able to trace your sources.

References to more information

There are many general texts on good practice in essay writing. Try any of the following:

REDMAN, P. (2006) *Good Essay Writing,* 3rd edn. London: Sage.
   Written specifically for social sciences students and contains lots of examples of good practice in essay writing.
MCMILLAN, K. AND WEYERS, J. (2007) *How to Write Essays and Assignments.* Harlow: Pearson Prentice Hall.
FOWLER, A. (2006) *How to Write.* Oxford: Oxford University Press.
HENNESSY, B. (2002) *Writing an Essay: Simple Techniques to Transform your Coursework and Examinations,* 4th edn. Oxford: How To Books.
   Good on both the macro and micro sides of essay writing.
KIRTON, B. (2007) *Just Write: An Easy-to-use Guide to Writing at University.* Abingdon: Routledge.
PRICE, G. AND MAIER, P. (2007) *Effective Study Skills: Unlock Your Potential.* Harlow: Pearson Longman.
   Includes writing skills in a discussion of good academic practice more generally.
ROSE, J. (2007) *The Mature Student's Guide to Writing.* New York: Palgrave Macmillan.
LEVIN, P. (2004) *Write Good Essays!: A Guide to Reading and Essay Writing for Undergraduates and Taught Postgraduates.* Maidenhead: Open University Press.
CREME, P. AND LEA, M.R. (2000) *Writing at University: A Guide for Students,* 2nd edn. Buckingham: Open University Press.

BAILEY, S. (2006) *Academic Writing: A Handbook for International Students,* 2nd edn. London: Routledge.

There are also texts on writing specifically for political science students:

SCOTT, G.M. AND GARRISON, S.M. (2006) *The Political Science Student Writer's Manual,* 5th edn. Upper Saddle River, NJ: Prentice Hall.

Part One on writing and referencing competently is excellent.

HARRISON, L. (2001) *Political Research: An Introduction.* London: Routledge.

Chapter 9 is on writing a politics dissertation but the same principles apply there as in an essay, so well worth a look.

3.4	
good practice in essays	

In this chapter we will take a look at some extracts from genuine student essays on IR theory which show you how three students more or less successfully deployed some of the essay techniques discussed in the previous chapter. All the essays responded to one question: 'How "scientific" is IR theory?' These were submitted in academic year 2006/7 and I am grateful to the students concerned for letting me use their essays. I have transcribed the extracts exactly as they appeared in the originals, including references.

Macro structure: introductions

Compare the opening paragraphs of each essay.

Student 1

Purely by definition one could certainly suggest that students of International Relations theory undertake a very scientific approach to their studies. Indeed, the theory of any study could be deemed scientific, although outside the boundaries of how society would usually call a fact based science, those

(Continued)

(Continued)

being, in general terms, biology, chemistry, physics and, to a certain extent, maths ... [*student then introduces definitions of 'science' from Reader's Digest Universal Dictionary*] ... However, it would be very easy to argue over definitions without coming to any conclusions as to whether a study of theory has the right to be called a science or is simply an argument made without any evidence to support it. Some would say that without this actual, factual grasp on a subject a theory cannot be a science. Others would argue that the very approach to the production of a theoretical analysis earns it the right to be called a science. In today's world this is what we would call a social science, that is 'The study of society and of ... relationships in and [relating] to society' (Reader's Digest Universal Dictionary 1987, pg.1443).

Student 2

This essay critically investigates the debate on 'How "scientific" is IR theory?'. I will start by outlining what the term 'scientific' means and then use this definition to question whether IR theory is a science, and if so, to what extent? As well as who supports or opposes this relatively new look on the subject to come to a qualified conclusion.

Student 3

'Until the late 1980's, most social scientists in international relations (IR) tended to be positivist' (Baylis *et al.* 2001: 274). However, from then on numerous post-positivist theories have emerged, attacking positivist methodology, epistemology and ontology, questioning the validity of the underlying assumptions of positivism. Arguably, the discipline of IR is 'scientific' in nature and this essay aims to investigate and evaluate the nature of IR by exploring the construct and meaning of 'scientific', with respect to social and natural phenomena, and the underlying assumptions of positivist explanatory and post-positivist constitutive perspectives.

You can see three very different approaches here. Which do you think works best as an introduction? If you were the marker, which introduction would persuade you that the student was on top of the material being presented?

- **Central argument**. Student 3 is the only student to set out a core argument: 'Arguably, the discipline of IR is "scientific" in nature'. Student 2 states that he intends to answer the question, but forgets to tell us what his answer will be. Student 1 barely provides an introduction in the sense that he dashes into the different definitions of science and related debates without giving us any pointers to where he will go in the essay.
- **Essay structure**. Student 3 clearly identifies how his central arguments will be advanced. In the final three lines of the paragraph he says that his argument that IR is 'scientific' will be made first by considering the definition of 'scientific' and then by considering the positivist versus post-positivist debates. Student 2 gets as far as saying that he will define 'scientific' but there the clues run out. Student 1 does not provide any direction, but rushes off into the definitions themselves. Here we see the best essay *signposting* in Student 3's piece. Student 1 gives no signposts at all, and Student 2 manages just a smattering.
- **Subject matter expertise**. Two of the introductions give indications of the level at which the student is operating. Student 1 relies on two quotes from the Reader's Digest, while Student 3 uses an authoritative source in a chapter from Baylis and Smith's *The Globalization of World Politics*. Even after reading just the introductions the marker would be persuaded that Student 3 was more on top of the reading than Student 1, even if the final judgement would wait until the end of the essay. However, first impressions are important and it helps if you can establish an authoritative position early in an essay.

> Individual departments and tutors have differing opinions on the utility and validity of students using online dictionaries and resources such as Wikipedia. Check your course handbook and with your individual tutor to see if he/she has preferences. If in doubt, avoid.

- **Technical aspects**. Students 2 and 3 write in plain, unambiguous English. References are set out correctly and it is easy to follow their thoughts in the introduction. The quality of Student 1's written English is lower for the following reasons:
  - First, why does the definition of IR suggest that students of the subject take a 'very scientific' approach to the subject? The logic is contentious and the meaning of 'very scientific' is unclear.
  - Second, Student 1's use of 'Some would say ...' and 'Others would argue ...' smacks of imprecision. At the very least a source would have been needed to clear up the confusion. Overall it adds to the impression that the student is not yet on top of the reading material on this topic.
  - Third, Student 1's references are incorrectly presented according to departmental guidelines. Presentation of your notes and bibliography, as we have seen, is a key thing to get correct in essays. If you can spend time getting it right, you will show your tutor that you can present work 'academically' and you will be given you credit accordingly.

- **Summary on introductions**. Having read these introductions, the marker will be thinking that Student 3 is the most organized, well-prepared and logical student who can, moreover, express his ideas clearly and unambiguously. Student 2 is some way to understanding the basic requirements of an essay, while Student 1 is getting there but seems to be the least technically proficient student.

> Give the marker what they want to see in an essay and you will not go far wrong.

Micro structure

We have seen how important it is to structure essays at the micro as well as the macro level. Here are some examples of signposting and bridging from the three essays which can help organize the body of an essay.

Structuring around questions

> **Student 1 [*opening paragraph of body of essay*]**
>
> But how do we undertake such an approach to studying issues as complex as classifying a state's identity in the contemporary world to understanding the balance of power and war and the significance of 9/11?

While there is a lot going on in the sentence, we can see that Student 1 is setting up the next paragraph or two by posing a question which, on being answered, should help him answer the essay question.

> **Student 2 [*after defining 'science'*]**
>
> In the purest meaning of the word is IR theory 'science'? Can IR be seen objectively and with only fact and figures?

The student goes on to analyse writers in the 'yes' camp, such as E.H. Carr. My critique of this part of the essay was that the student did not spend enough time looking at the 'no' camp.

Numbered points

Student 3 [*in section on empiricism*]

The positivist or naturalist 'scientific' perspective on IR has four main underlying assumptions, which are largely drawn from the main assumptions of logical positivism (Smith *et al.* 2006: 19). Firstly, they believe in the unity of science ... Secondly, facts and values are distinguishable... Thirdly, positivists hold the social world to contain regularities ... Lastly, they hold the neutral nature of facts ... (Baylis et al. 2001).

Most works list the fourfold characteristics of positivisim in this way. You can see how replicating the numbered approach helps Student 3 take the reader smoothly through them and he backs his case with reference to two authoritative sources. Providing micro structure to paragraphs first helps you organize your thoughts; second, helps you write in well balanced paragraphs; and third, makes it easy for your tutor to follow your thinking as it develops through a paragraph.

Micro structure: signposts and bridges

Student 1 [*on the different strands of Realist thought*]

First, the concept of 'procedural realism' stated that the rose-tinted view of the world that liberals so readily adopted 'must be succeeded by a stage of hard and ruthless analysis'. 'Scientific realism' continued claiming that 'no political utopia will achieve even the most limited success unless it grows out of political reality' and finally 'ideological realism' argued that 'realism is the necessary corrective to the exuberance of utopianism'.

Despite the fact that these are two of the most dominant theories in the world of IR, we can see that they are also just a fraction of the number of theories that do surround this study.

Unfortunately we have to overlook the total absence of sources in the above. You can see that it is a distilled version of Gregory Crane's analysis of Realism (explored in Chapter 2.2 of this book) which in turn quotes E.H. Carr. As such the student needed at least one reference here to show the origin of his ideas.

Overlooking the bad practice vis-à-vis references, focus on the transition between paragraphs. After the summary of different types of Realism, the text does not just jump to a new point without warning. The student carefully explains where he goes next by alluding to the fact that there are many other theoretical perspectives on IR, providing a bridge for the reader to cross from one paragraph to the next. In a perfect essay every break between paragraphs would be accompanied by a line either at the end of one paragraph or at the start of the next explaining the journey being taken. Let us see this in operation in Student 3's essay.

Student 3

In the same manner as evolutionary biologists, explanatory theorists claim that by using theories as a starting point events can be reconstructed and explained ... [*summarizes explanatory theory*].

Conversely post-positivist theories are constitutive in nature. In this perspective theory is viewed to be a construct of the world [*summarizes constitutive theory*] ... Claiming that facts are neutral is 'simply a reflection of an adherence to a particular view of epistemology' (Baylis *et al.* 2001: 274).

Note here the improved use of quotes and reference to a key source compared to Student 1. Each paragraph is themed: the first covers explanatory theory, the second covers constitutive theory. These themes are clearly set out for the reader at the beginning of each paragraph, while at the end of the second paragraph there is a useful recap quote summarizing the nub of the matter.

The use of 'Conversely' at the start of the second paragraph is a pithy way of showing that the interpretation explored in paragraph 2 contradicts that set out in paragraph 1. The student is demonstrating that he has located divisions within the literature and is able to set these down clearly for the reader. Equivalent techniques you can use to show differences of opinion between writers include:

- 'By contrast ...'
- 'On one hand ... On the other hand ...'
- 'Some writers argue ... Others suggest ...'. Make sure if you use this approach you provide references. Do not leave the reader guessing who you mean.

Taking time to wrap up at the end of a section is a great way of helping guide the reader through your essay. You can either use a quote or spend a line explaining the essence of your thinking in that section and relating it to the overall argument you are making.

Macro structure: conclusions

Now take a look at the conclusions by Students 2 and 3.

Student 2

In Conclusion then a broad consensus is upon us as regards to International relations being a science in the broadest definition of the meaning but one must be cautious. International relations is a science with it's limitations. It would be wrong to approach politics purely from this angle without also understanding the human emotion behind the politics also. And I believe scientific realism does account for this ambiguity in that it accepts that one application of methods in one science is not necessarily the optimal method for other sciences.

Student 3

In conclusion, the discipline of IR can claim to be 'scientific'. The social world and natural world differ with respect to the nature of the units and system of inquiry, implying that the epistemology and methodology of natural sciences are not necessarily applicable to study social phenomena. In the same manner, what constitutes a 'scientific' inquiry into natural phenomena does not necessarily constitute a 'scientific' inquiry into social phenomena. The term 'scientific' essentially represents valid and justified knowledge rather than certain epistemologies or methodologies and critical to this notion is the nature of the knowledge generated; it must contain objective elements. Essentially, the 'scientific' nature of IR is rooted in the communication of such knowledge. Even as theories operate with different epistemological, ontological and methodological perspectives the knowledge they generate can be viewed as constructive and applicable to the discipline of IR as a whole.

As with the introductions earlier, which conclusion do you think is better? If you were the marker, which conclusion would persuade you that the student knew most about the issue of IR as a 'science'?

- **Recap.** Student 3 summarizes the gist of his answer better than Student 2. It is clearly in line with the argument put forward in his introduction (see p. 214) and it explains the rationale as to why that was the answer given. Student 2 talks about scientific realism. However, the student does not reinforce an argument from the introduction where scientific realism is never mentioned and where we were in fact left guessing about the answer to be given in the essay. Student 3 knows where he is going from the outset, whereas Student 2 seems to have achieved his answer as the essay progresses rather than before he started writing the essay. Student 3 thus provides the more logical macro structure.
- **Subject matter expertise.** Note the comparison in the language used in the two conclusions. Student 3's conclusion reads much more like an 'academic' piece of work, using terminology and expressions that he has demonstrated ample knowledge of in the preceding essay. Student 2 raises new issues such as the 'human emotion' behind politics which were absent from the preceding essay. You should play it safe in conclusions by only bringing in concepts/themes/ideas you have thoroughly explored in the essay. Student 3 thus provides the more authoritative conclusion.

Common pitfall

Only use long or technical words if you are absolutely sure you know what they mean and have defined them for your reader.

- **Written English.** The clarity of Student 3's conclusion is better than Student 2's. First, there are no typographical mistakes as in 'International relations' or 'it's limitations'. Second, the quality of expression is greater, helped by sharper sentence construction (note the need for punctuation in the opening sentence of Student 2's conclusion). Finally, Student 3's conclusion is nearer the length expected for an essay of 1,500 words. Student 3's conclusion thus shows greater technical proficiency than Student 2's.

Referencing and bibliography

Providing enough references and setting them out correctly are basic features of an essay. Your tutor will expect to see you getting this crucial feature of an essay right. Of the three essays, only Student 3 managed to present his references correctly. Student 1 routinely quoted without providing references or set the references out incorrectly. Student 2 provided more regular references but set them out incorrectly. On the quality of references we have already noted the comparison between Students 1 (dictionary) and 3 (key text on IR from reading list). Student 2 also used a dictionary definition of 'science'.

There is no simple correlation between the number of sources in a bibliography and the quality of an essay. However, certain inferences are possible from the three essays explored here. The most successful essay (Student 3's) had ten sources listed in the bibliography. All of these were referred to at least once in the essay, and two of the articles cited were not on the module reading list, showing that the student had read around the subject. The submissions by Students 1 and 2 relied on about half that number of sources and this was reflected in the relative lack of critical depth they were able to achieve in their answers.

The last chapter discussed the theory behind referencing and bibliographies so here I will remind you of the very basic points:

- Check how to set your references in your departmental handbook and/or module guide. If in doubt, check with your tutor.
- Reference only the place where you first found a piece of information.
- Every source you cite in an essay must appear in a list of references.
- A bibliography is wider than a list of references in that it can contain all sources you read when preparing an essay, even if you do not refer to them directly in the submission.
- A general rule is that better essays tend to be based on more sources. Through wide reading, the author is able to generate balance and critical depth to an answer.

Final remarks

All of these essays had different strengths and weaknesses. Student 3 scored a mid-first; Student 2 scored a mid-2:1 and Student 1 scored a mid-2:2. You can see that to get a top grade Student 3 did the basics very well and was able to demonstrate, even in this relatively constricted word limit, that he was organized, logical, had good knowledge of the subject and could communicate his ideas effectively in plain English. Both the other essays showed promise but they slipped up on basic presentational points as well as showing a weaker grasp of the subject matter.

A successful essay requires both technical proficiency and an in-depth knowledge of the subject matter.

3.5	
exam revision	

On your course in IR theory your assessment is likely to take the form of part coursework (essay and/or presentation) and part exam. Exam periods at university tend be highly stressful and your performance can be badly hampered if you suffer from serious exam nerves. A bit of adrenalin and anticipation will help your performance under pressure, but full-blown panic will do you no good whatsoever. The way to avoid getting into a panic situation is to approach your work on the module as a whole in as organized, logical and structured fashion as you can. That way you are not starting to build up your subject knowledge and essay skills from scratch at the last minute, but simply applying them in new ways.

In preparation for exams, you should continue practicing good habits you have developed over the course as a whole.

Start from day one

Revision for exams is not something that starts after a module ends, as if exams are somehow separate from the rest of the work you do on the course. As the final assessed element of the module, the capstone exercise if you like, exams should feature in your thinking throughout the module. Everything you do on the course should help gear you up to prepare for and sit the exam paper in IR theory. As Nicholas Walliman (2006: 169) puts it, 'You should be like the squirrel that stores up nuts for the winter. Do not waste any lecture, tutorial, seminar, group discussion, etc. by letting the material evaporate into thin air.' When you are reading over your notes at the end of each lecture and seminar make a list specifically for revision. On the list you could include:

- a list of key writers in a theoretical tradition.
- a list of the critics of each theory or theorist.
- a brief summary of the big debates that surround each theory covered.
- the key concepts/definitions that kept cropping up.

Early preparation will save you masses of time later on, allowing you to concentrate on the really important things like practicing exam answers and following up gaps in your knowledge in the library.

Organize your notes

Put every note you take from reading, lectures and seminars in a folder or ring binder, clearly separated by course topic or week. This will help you capture the sense of everything you learned and enable you to locate notes quickly and easily.

If you are feeling really organized, you could write (electronically or by hand) a glossary of IR key terms which you update each week with one or two new entries.

Past papers

These will normally be made available in the paper handout or the online resources for your course. They will give you an idea of the kinds of themes that crop up most often, and the ways in which questions tend to be framed. Keep copies of these in with your notes and pay particular care to the recent papers and those set by the tutor that convenes your course.

Common pitfall

Do not learn model answers to questions from past papers and repeat these in the exam. Every year the 'twist' to a question on a given theory varies slightly and you will not receive good marks for answering the question from last year's paper!

Identify gaps in your knowledge

If you prepare thoroughly for each lecture and seminar on your course you should have a good knowledge base from which to work at the start of the revision period. When reading through your notes for the first time make a note of any areas where you consider your knowledge to be a bit sketchy. You might have gaps in your knowledge base if:

- You do not know the main claims of IR theory given
- You cannot define a key term
- You have not read an essential text
- You do not understand a concept that featured in the reading or lecture.

Build time to research these areas into your revision timetable. It is tempting to ignore them and concentrate on revising the topics with which you are most comfortable but you will reap the rewards if you work on your weaknesses and aim to turn them into strengths because this will give you more flexibility when it comes to choosing which questions to tackle in the exam.

Group study

Pooling ideas can be a great way of helping you consolidate and advance your knowledge. Get together with a small group of friends to go over key theories and discuss questions circulated in advance. For example, you could all practice writing an answer to the same exam question and then when you meet explore the relative merits of your approaches. The aim of group revision is not to generate 'model' answers or the same approach to a theory, but to help you think through the basics of each issue and how best to communicate responses to exam questions on a given topic or theory.

Practice exam questions

Group study can be an effective aid to individual study but remember that, in the final analysis, it is you who has to sit the exam and write the answer on your own. One of the best ways to prepare for the discomfort of sitting alone with an exam paper in front of you and a blank sheet of paper to fill is to get used to being in that situation beforehand. You could therefore try the following:

- Empty your room of friends and turn off your television, radio and electronic gaming equipment.
- Get a past exam paper or practice essay question from an IR textbook.
- Give yourself 15 minutes to plan your answer: identify your central argument and essay structure.
- Write a 200-word introduction to the answer.
- Write a two-line summary of each of the main points you would cover in the essay.

> It is impossible to replicate exam conditions precisely, but by answering practice questions on your own you will get a good feel for the pressure of being in the exam hall.

Vary your revision schedule

Although you need to be organized and methodical in your approach, revision can become a tedious process if you do the same things every day. So strike a balance between routine and monotony by varying your strategies (for example, alternating between group revision and self-directed study) and consider the following:

- You do not need to revise 24 hours per day. Try and keep to your usual waking, eating and going to bed patterns.
- Take regular exercise between revision sessions.
- Do not become a hermit! Make time for periods of relaxation and going out with friends.
- Learn which times of day you feel most active and work most effectively and tailor your revision programme to those peaks.
- Find out when the exam is and, if possible, write your practice exam answers in that same period to get yourself in the habit of thinking and writing during that part of the day.

> Remember that it is not the naturally intelligent people who succeed at exams but those who can identify what the examiner is looking for in an exam answer and deliver logical, incisive, well evidenced responses to the questions set.

References to more information

COTTRELL, S. (2006) *The Exam Skills Handbook*. Basingstoke: Palgrave Macmillan.

MCMILLAN, K. AND WEYERS, J. (2007) *How to Succeed in Exams and Assessments*. Harlow: Pearson Prentice Hall.

LEVIN, P. (2004) *Sail Through Exams!: Preparing for Traditional Exams for Undergraduates and Taught Postgraduates*. Maidenhead: Open University Press.

TRACY, E. (2002) *The Student's Guide to Exam Success*. Buckingham: Open University Press.

The focus here is on the emotional and psychological aspects of preparing for and sitting exams.

HOLMES, A. (2005) *Pass Your Exams: Study Skills for Success.* Oxford: The Infinite Ideas Company.

A 'tips' book with useful advice on building up your confidence and playing the exam game and passing.

3.6	
exam tips	

I am not an expert on the psychological effects of stress, but from my past experience of sitting exams and now working in a relatively stressful job, it seems fair to say that the best way to combat stress is to think about two things: (1) its causes and (2) how to combat it. From the students I have spoken to, exam nerves are generally brought on by a combination of lack of preparation and lack of confidence in their ability to write under pressure. Everything I have said so far in this book has been geared to making the exam period as stress-free as possible by seeing exams as another opportunity to put into practice the good working and writing habits you have developed through the module.

> Integrating the exam into your overall approach to the module will help you jump over the psychological barrier they can sometimes become.

In this chapter we will consider a few of the tips you might deploy to get the very best exam mark you can.

The basics

Find out as early as you can where you will be sitting the exam, at what time, and what materials you can take into it with you (if any). Invest in a good alarm clock or ask friends to come and knock on your door if you are frightened of sleeping in for an early morning exam. Amazingly some students fail to show up for exams, or arrive half an hour in to it: this is a recipe for disaster.

Make sure you have a good supply of pens that work and all the other stationary you will need. Arrive at the exam in plenty of time so that you can calm yourself down before entering the hall; the last thing you need is to be rushing in late all hot and bothered. Try and avoid the 'mascot' approach. When you are in the exam you need to be focusing on the questions set, not balancing your favourite soft toys so that they sit upright on your desk.

Planning your time

Find out before the exam how many questions you will have to answer. Typical exams are something in the region of two questions in two hours or three questions in three hours. In both scenarios you have one hour per answer. A good essay plan can take anything up to ten minutes to put together. Do not mistakenly believe you are getting behind your peers if you do not start writing straight away.

> Have confidence in your ability to structure the exam to suit you. Know how much time you want to allocate to each part of the paper and stick to it.

If your exam is not all about writing essays, make sure you have worked out in advance how long you want to allocate for each part of the paper. For instance, there might be a multi-choice element, or a short summary element where you define key terms. However the paper is structured, make sure you leave enough time for each segment and that you have time at the end of each paper to read and correct each answer.

> When the exam begins try and get into your own little bubble and block out what is going on around you. Concentrate on the tasks before you and manage your time accordingly.

Writing your answers

Spend a few minutes at the start of the exam deciding which questions you want to tackle. Pay attention at this point to the phrasing of the questions. There might be topics you are well familiar with but where the question is phrased in a complex or difficult way. Think carefully about what kinds of structure you could use for each question on offer and which of those structures helps you communicate your argument clearly and concisely.

Know before you go in whether you want to plan all the answers at the start of the exam and then write them, or whether you want to plan and write the answers one at a time. A practical advantage of the latter approach is that you give your writing hand a break while you plan the next answer. Whichever method you deploy, keep an eye on the clock so that you do not spend too much time on one answer at the expense of the others.

> It is always tempting in an exam to spend disproportionate amounts of time on the question(s) you feel you know really well. However, a very long, overly detailed answer to one question will never compensate for short, thin answers elsewhere. Balance is vital.

The essence of a good exam answer is that it is structured well, flows nicely from start to finish and is supported by a good range of authoritative evidence. Your tutor will want to see that you have thought critically about the themes and issues raised by the question and that you can devise logical, well-reasoned responses to the questions you tackle. As in a coursework essay you are encouraged to use quotes from the books you have read and refer to key authors on whose work you have drawn to frame your arguments. If you can go beyond the basic course texts and into advanced and wider reading you will stand out from the vast majority of students who will churn out standard names, sources and interpretations.

> The classic mistake in exams is to write everything you know (or can remember) about a given subject. The 'scatter-gun' answer, as it is known, is a giveaway that a student has not prepared well for the exam. Sound revision and a robust essay structure will help limit the time you spend wandering off the subject.

Try not to repeat too much information from one answer in another because this indicates a thin knowledge base. To take a two-questions-in-two-hours exam: if you can show the examiner that you know, in detail, three or four theories of IR across your two questions, this looks better than if you can only demonstrate knowledge of two theories which you rehash in both answers.

In sum, the best exam marks go to students who do the following:

- Show sound knowledge of the subject matter.
- Answer the questions set rather than the question they want to see.
- Structure their answers around a few key points.
- Signpost their writing (see Chapters 3.3 and 3.4).
- Use appropriate evidence to back their arguments. This can be presented in the form of short quotes or summaries of writers' arguments.

Turn up to your exam prepared both mentally and physically. Practice putting yourself under exam conditions and look after your health in the weeks leading up to the exam.

part four

additional resources

glossary

Actor
In this context does not mean Will Smith or Angelina Jolie. In IR it means the unit of analysis (for example, the state or a supranational organization) whose behaviour theorists try to explain. Different theories tend to emphasize the significance of different actors in international affairs.

Aesthetics
The branch of philosophy dealing with the nature/appreciation of beauty and the beautiful. If you like the look of a piece of art, you could say it is aesthetically pleasing.

Agency
There is a big debate within Politics and IR about the extent to which we explain people's/state's behaviour with reference to their own actions and ideas. Those people taking the latter view would believe in the priority of agency over structures or with reference to the impact of the structures that shape the lives and worlds of those people and states (agents).

Anarchy
When applied to IR, means lack of an orderer in the international system. This 'orderer' could be something like a world government but does not have to be as formal or powerful as that name implies.

Anthropocentrism
The idea that humans are the only creators of meaning in the universe and the only life form worth considering when we take decisions and make policies.

Authorship
I am the author of this book. I brought it into existence conceptually and wrote it myself. Authorship in IR is all about who brings what into existence and relates to wider questions of decision-making power and influence in the international system. Social constructivists, for example, argue that states 'author' anarchy; anarchy does not 'author' states.

Balance of power Centrepiece of Neorealist theory developed by Kenneth Waltz to explain how the structure of the international system explains the interactions of the units within it.

Bretton Woods System Named after the place in the US where the leading industrial powers met in 1944 to hammer out the rules for the management of their commercial and financial relations. Collapsed in 1971.

Colonialism Has both formal and informal dimensions. Formally it means the practice of one country controlling another by military, economic and/or political means, usually with the use of, or threat of, violence. Informally it can mean the exploitation or oppression of less developed and weaker countries by more developed and stronger ones through global structures such as international institutions. A key component of postcolonial theories of IR.

Commensurability Popularized by Thomas Kuhn. Two theories are commensurable if they can be compared to determine which is better. In order to achieve this, it must be proved that the two theories 'see' the same world and use the same language to describe/explain that world. If they do not, then they are incommensurable – it is impossible to compare which is better.

Cosmopolitanism A political theory that denies the relevance of the state in determining individual morality and justice. Usually contrasted with communitarianism which charges states with a central place in shaping individual attitudes on these issues.

Deconstruction Associated with the thought of Jacques Derrida. Deconstruction is a vital tool for postmodernist IR scholars who use it to probe, unsettle, unhinge and pull apart supposedly settled core IR concepts such as the 'state' and 'sovereignty'. One of the most popular ways they achieve this is through the double reading of texts.

Determinism The philosophical proposition that human actions and decisions are causally determined by prior events and circumstances. It is more or less the opposite of the view that humans have free will to act as they wish. In IR the debate plays out between those who believe the structure of the international system decisively constrains and shapes state behaviour, and those who believe that state behaviour is responsible for the shape and workings of the international system.

Diplomacy

The official conduct of relations between two or more states, or two or more groups of states. Usually carried out by government ministers and civil servants, or diplomats, it entails negotiation, communication and the drawing up of treaties, agreements, and the like. Can also include unofficial dimensions such as cultural exchanges.

Discourse

Means much more than conversation. Associated with the work of Michel Foucault, it refers to the way in which language is used to structure our accounts of, and give meaning to, the social world, and what this reveals about the use and abuse of power and the construction of identities.

Empiricism

A theory of knowledge that suggests knowledge should be generated through direct observation and other sensory experience.

Epistemology

Theory about how we know things and what is regarded as hard and fast knowledge in a given discipline; or the origins and legitimacy of knowledge.

Essentially contested

If an object, event or process is essentially contested, it means that there might be agreement that it exists, but no agreement on its meaning, implications or uses. For example, we might all agree that the global sportswear manufacturer 'Nike' exists, but there are hundreds of different opinions about the economic, social and cultural implications of 'Nike'. Hence, the meaning of 'Nike' for the contemporary world is essentially contested.

Etymology

The study of the origin, development and derivation of words.

Falsification   The process of proving a theory to be flawed, for example, because a prediction generated through its application turns out to be wrong.

Functionalist integration theory   Developed by David Mitrany. Explains how economic and social integration increases levels of interdependence between states and can therefore lead to peace and security for the states involved.

Genealogy   Associated with Michel Foucault, an investigation into the historical practices which create subjects through discursive closures, exclusions and marginalizations. Not a history in the conventional sense of understanding how things come to be. In IR, we undertake genealogies to probe how the discipline makes sense of the world: what has IR had to forget or overlook to make knowledge about international affairs seem like the 'truth'?

Gender   The social meanings given to the concepts 'male' and 'female' and the supposed characteristics that flow from them in terms of those that are held to be 'masculine' and those we associate with 'femininity'.

General Agreement on Tariffs and Trade (GATT)   Set up at the Bretton Woods conference in 1944 to promote the reduction of barriers to international trade such as tariffs and quotas.

Generic skills   See *transferable skills*

Globalization   Extremely difficult to define in a few words! Widely taken to imply the widening and deepening and/or intensification of economic, political, technological, cultural, social and environmental interactions across state borders.

Hegemony   Concept used in IR to chart the relative position of states in the international system, measured by their power (loosely defined); for example, the USA is said to have been a hegemonic power since the end of the Cold War especially but not exclusively in military terms. In Critical Theory the definition broadens so that it is about more than dominance by force. It is, rather, about the order that comes from states getting into positions whereby their ideas/practices are accepted by other states without the threat or use of force. Includes the use of international organizations to spread norms and thereby shape the system in almost unnoticed ways.

Hypothesis A prediction about the state of the world and/or relationships between variables within that world. For example, we might want to test the hypothesis that students who attend more lectures and seminars/tutorials achieve higher marks in essays and exams than those who attend fewer lectures and seminars/tutorials.

Independence The idea that a certain state or group of states is insulated from the effects of the actions of other states in the international system. Usually contrasted with the term 'interdependence'.

Interdependence The idea that the political, economic and social connections among states or groups of states have reached a point where the actions of one or other of those states directly affects the other states. Linked intimately with the concept of **globalization** and usually contrasted with **independence**.

International organization A body created by states to which they delegate authority to carry out action at the international level.

International regime A term associated with Neoliberal IR theory. Highlights the idea that international co-operation is about more than the formalized, rule-bound co-operation we see in the establishment of international organizations. Institutions and international organizations also promote informal modes of inter-state co-operation via regimes.

International system All the states that exist in the world today constitute the international system. IR scholars disagree about the nature of this system. Some (e.g. Realists) see the system as inherently conflict-ridden, others (e.g. Liberals and English School theorists) argue that even without a world government, state behaviour tends to be structured and regulated, thus avoiding the worst excesses of war and violence.

Metatheory

Theory about theory; theory about the rules and standards by which theories count as theories and how they make sense of their subject matter. Metatheory focuses on the philosophical assumptions underlying theories, so is explicitly concerned with questions of ontology, epistemology and methodology.

Methodology

In the social sciences, the procedures by which we generate knowledge. For example, research using quantitative methods might interpret statistical data whereas qualitative research interprets meanings, beliefs and attitudes of subjects. In the natural sciences, rules and guidelines on how to set up experiments and interpret the data.

Multinational corporation

A company or business that has headquarters, offices and/or factories located in different countries around the world, such as HSBC, McDonald's and Coca-Cola. Used interchangeably with 'transnational corporation' and sometimes shortened to 'multinational' or MNC.

Nation-state

Used interchangeably with 'state' in much IR literature. Has a specific meaning whereby members of a territorially bounded population share more in common than merely their land borders, things such as a common language, traditions and history.

Naturalism

The view that the social world and the natural worlds can be studied using the same methods. It was arguably the dominant theoretical approach within IR until the 1980s when normative theory became more prominent within the discipline.

Neo-functionalist integration theory

Associated with the work of Ernst Haas and builds on the work of Mitrany (see *functionalist integration theory*). Explains regional integration by looking at the process of 'spillover', as integration in one sector leads to integration in another and so on. Also explains top-down spillover from supranational organizations such as the EU.

Normative theory
Presents a challenge to positivist ways of viewing the world and studying it. Critiques the view that social scientists can produce objective knowledge by emulating the methods used by natural scientists. Normative theorists try to understand the role played by values, morality and ethics in international relations.

Ontology
Theory connected with the things, properties and events that exist in the world; what exists to be investigated.

Paradigm
Popularized by Thomas Kuhn's 1962 book *The Structure of Scientific Revolutions*. Scientists who work in a particular research paradigm 'are committed to the same rules and standards for scientific practice' and work to continue that particular research tradition (Kuhn 1996: 11). IR theories are like Kuhnian paradigms.

Patriarchy
A system of rule or governance by men. Such systems can be openly patriarchal where men have greater legal, political, religious and social freedoms than women. Or they can be covert, in that women are discriminated against institutionally, in the workplace (in terms of pay and conditions), and so on. Feminist scholars have deepened our understanding of the overt and covert sources of patriarchy in IR, both within states and in the international system at large.

Pax Americana
Describes the period of relative international peace (or absence of world war) since 1945. Replaced the *pax Britannica* evident in the mid-nineteenth century centring around the existence of the British Empire.

Positivism
Both a philosophy about scientific research and a methodology in IR. Positivists try and apply the methods and practices of the natural sciences to the social sciences. They assume we can produce objective knowledge about the world through the careful application of the scientific method of observation, reporting and testing.

Post-positivism	Refers to the approach taken by a range of writers who critique positivist ways of generating knowledge. Some of them we explore in this book, such as Critical Theorists, feminists and post-structuralists. In US literature tends to be called 'reflectivism'.
Reductionism	Using the behaviour of a component part to explain the behaviour of the environment or system within which it operates. For example, Realist IR theorists explain the behaviour of states through analysis of human nature, implying that in a given situation states act as humans would do. This is a contested approach to explaining IR.
Reflectivism	A term made popular in the USA – another name for normative theory. Reflectivism is also used interchangeably with labels such as 'new', 'post-positivist', 'alternative', or even 'radical' (Smith 2001: 229).
Reification	The process of attributing to some phenomenon (for example, 'anarchy') human, living or 'real-life' properties which it cannot or does not possess. In IR, Social Constructivists say that Realist scholars 'reify' anarchy; they take this abstract, literally non-existent thing to be something real and tangible, when it does not exist out there at all.
Security dilemma	Classic Realist concept whereby a state seeking to maximize its security makes other states in the international system feel less secure.
Sovereignty	A state is said to possess internal sovereignty when it exercises ultimate legal and political authority over a named territory. It possesses external sovereignty when other states respect its jurisdiction in these matters.
State	Used to refer to two things: a bounded, populated territory and/or the body that governs that particular territory. Said to have emerged with the Treaty of Westphalia in 1648, the modern state is said to be sovereign in that it and it alone has the right to pass laws to regulate its own affairs and population. The state was held

to be the main actor in international relations by many early theorists such as those writing in the Realist and Liberalist traditions.

Sub-national actor One that operates at a level below that of the state of which it is a part. Local councils in England are sub-national actors.

Supranational actor A body set up by states to advance their common political security and economic interests through the making and execution of legislation that affects them all. The European Union is an example of a supranational organization.

Theory Systematically describes aspects of the world, categorizes these aspects and considers their interrelationships with the intention of making sense of complexity and developing law-like generalizations.

Transferable skills Also go by the name of **generic skills**, like-skills or employability skills. Generally encompasses the following: reading, writing and arithmetic; listening, speaking, thinking; time and project management; information skills; design and presentation; problem identification, definition and solving; and personal knowledge (taken from Higher Education Academy glossary, undated).

references

Adler, E. (1997) 'Seizing the Middle Ground: Constructivism in World Politics', *European Journal of International Relations*, 3(3): 319–63.

Amnesty International (2004) press release, 'USA: Pattern of Brutality and Cruelty: War Crime at Abu Ghraib', http://www.amnesty.org/en/alfresco_asset/519f48da-a459-11dc-bac9-0158df32ab50/amr510772004 en.pdf (accessed 2 January 2008).

Ashcroft, B., Griffiths, G. and Tiffin, H. (1994) *The Empire Writes Back: Theory and Practice in Post-Colonial Literatures*. London: Routledge.

Ashley, R.K. (1986) 'The Poverty of Neorealism', in R.O. Keohane (ed.) *Neorealism and its Critics*. New York: Columbia University Press, pp. 1–26.

Axford, B., Browning, G.K., Huggins, R. and Rosamond, B. (2006) *Politics: An Introduction*, 2nd edn. London: Routledge.

Bain, W. (2000) 'Deconfusing Morgenthau: Moral Inquiry and Classical Realism Reconsidered', *Review of International Studies*, 26(3): 445–64.

Barnett, M. (2008) 'Social Constructivism', in J. Baylis, S. Smith and P. Owens (eds) *The Globalization of World Politics: An Introduction to International Relations*, 4th edn. Oxford: Oxford University Press, pp. 160–73.

Baylis, J., Smith, S. and Owens, P. (2008a) 'Introduction', in J. Baylis, S. Smith and P. Owens (eds) *The Globalization of World Politics: An Introduction to International Relations*, 4th edn. Oxford: Oxford University Press.

Baylis, J., Smith, S. and Owens, P. (eds) (2008b) *The Globalization of World Politics: An Introduction to International Relations*, 4th edn. Oxford: Oxford University Press.

Bellamy, A.J. (ed.) (2004) *International Society and its Critics*. Oxford: Oxford University Press.

Blair, T. (2006), 'Global Alliance for Global Values', speech to Australian Parliament, 27 March, http://www.number10.gov.uk/output/Page9245.asp (accessed 12 February 2008).

Bookchin, M. (1971) *Post-scarcity Anarchism*. Berkeley, CA: Ramparts Press.

Booth, K. and Smith, S. (eds) (1995) *International Relations Theory Today*. Cambridge: Polity Press.

Brown, C. (2001) *Understanding International Relations*, 2nd edn. Basingstoke: Palgrave.

Bull, H. (1977) *The Anarchical Society: A Study of Order in World Politics*. London: Macmillan.

Burchill, S. (2001a) 'Introduction', in S. Burchill et al. *Theories of International Relations*, 2nd edn. Basingstoke: Palgrave, pp. 1–28.

Burchill, S. (2001b) 'Liberalism', in S. Burchill et al. *Theories of International Relations*, 2nd edn. Basingstoke: Palgrave, pp. 29–69.

Burchill, S. (2001c) 'Realism and Neo-realism', in S. Burchill and others, *Theories of International Relations*, 2nd edn. Basingstoke: Palgrave Basingstoke: Palgrave, pp. 70–102.

Buzan, B. (no date) 'English School of International Relations', University of Leeds. http://www.leeds.ac.uk/polis/englishschool/.

Cafruny, A.A. (2006) 'Historical Materialism: Imperialist Rivalry and the Global Capitalist Order', in J. Sterling-Folker (ed.) *Making Sense of International Relations Theory*. Boulder, CO: Lynne Rienner Publishers, pp. 209–24.

Campbell, D. (2007) 'Poststructuralism', in T. Dunne, M. Kurki and S. Smith (eds) *International Relations Theory: Discipline and Diversity*. Oxford: Oxford University Press, pp. 203–28.

Carlsnaes, W., Risse, T. and Simmons, B.A. (eds) (2006) *Handbook of International Relations*. London: Sage.

Carr, E.H. (2001a) *The Twenty Years' Crisis 1919–1939*. Basingstoke: Palgrave.

Carr, E.H. (2001b) *What is History?* Basingstoke: Palgrave.

Chomsky, N. (2005) *Chomsky on Anarchism*. Oakland, CA: AK Press.

Council of the European Union (2006) 'Review of the EU Sustainable Development Strategy: Renewed Strategy', http://register.consilium.europa.eu/pdf/en/06/st10/st10117.en06-.pdf (accessed 28 April 2008).

Cox, R.W. (1996a) 'Gramsci, Hegemony and International Relations: An Essay in Method', in R. Cox and T.J. Sinclair (eds) *Approaches to World Order*. Cambridge: Cambridge University Press, pp. 124–43.

Cox, R.W. (1996b) 'Social Forces, States and World Orders: Beyond International Relations Theory', in R. Cox and T.J. Sinclair (eds) *Approaches to World Order*. Cambridge: Cambridge University Press, pp. 85–123.

Cox, R.W. and Sinclair, T.J. (1996c) *Approaches to World Order*. Cambridge: Cambridge University Press.

Crane, G. (1998) *Thucydides and the Ancient Simplicity: The Limits of Political Realism* Berkeley: University of California Press. http://ark.cdlib.org/ark:/13030/ft767nb497/ (accessed 31 July 2007).

Daddow, O. (2007) 'Playing Games with History: Tony Blair's European Policy in the Press', *British Journal of Politics and International Relations*, 9(4): 582–98.

Dalby, S. (2009) 'What Happens If We Don't Think in Human Terms?', in J. Edkins and M. Zehfuss (eds) *Global Politics: A New Introduction*. London and New York: Routledge, pp. 45-69.

Devetak, R. (1995) 'Incomplete States: Theories and Practices of Statecraft', in J. Macmillan and A. Linklater (eds) *Boundaries in Question: New Directions in International Relations*. London: Pinter, pp. 19–39.

Devetak, R. (2001a) 'Critical Theory', in S. Burchill et al. *Theories of International Relations*, 2nd edn. Basingstoke: Palgrave, pp. 144–78.

Devetak, R. (2001b) 'Postmodernism', in S. Burchill et al. *Theories of International Relations*, 2nd edn. Basingstoke: Palgrave, pp. 181–208.

Dictionary.com (2007a) http://dictionary.reference.com/search?q=an- (accessed 18 January 2007).

Dictionary.com (2007b) http://dictionary.reference.com/browse/archon (accessed 18 January 2007).

Dunne, T. (2007) 'The English School', in T. Dunne, M. Kurki and S. Smith (eds) *International Relations Theory: Discipline and Diversity*. Oxford: Oxford University Press, pp. 128–47.

Dunne, T. (2008) 'Liberalism', in J. Baylis, S. Smith and P. Owens (eds) *The Globalization of World Politics: An Introduction to International Relations*, 4th edn. Oxford: Oxford University Press, pp. 108–22.

Dunne, T., Kurki, M. and Smith, S. (eds) (2007) *International Relations Theory: Discipline and Diversity*. Oxford: Oxford University Press.

Dunne, T. and Schmidt, B.C. (2008) 'Realism', in J. Baylis, S. Smith and P. Owns (eds) *The Globalization of World Politics: An Introduction to International Relations*, 4th edn. Oxford: Oxford University Press. pp. 90–106.

Eckersley, R. (2007) 'Green Theory', in T. Dunne, M. Kurki and S. Smith (eds) *International Relations Theory: Discipline and Diversity*. Oxford: Oxford University Press, pp. 247–65.

Edkins, J. and Zehfuss, M. (eds) *Global Politics: A New Introduction*. London and New York: Routledge.

Encyclopedia of World Biography (2005–6) 'On Hans J. Morgenthau', http://www.bookrags.com/biography/hans-j-morgenthau/ (accessed 2 August 2007).

Enloe, C. (2001) *Bananas, Beaches and Bases: Making Feminist Sense of International Politics*. Berkeley, CA: University of California Press.

Epstein, C. (2008) *The Power of Words in International Relations: Birth of an Anti-Whaling Discourse*. Cambridge, MA and London: MIT Press.

Europa (undated) 'The History of the European Union', http://europa.eu/abc/history/index-_en.htm (accessed 26 July 2007).

Foucault, M. (1991) 'Truth and Power', in P. Rabinow (ed.) *The Foucault Reader: An Introduction to Foucault's Thought*. London: Penguin, pp. 51–75.

Freyberg-Inan, A. (2006) 'World System Theory: A Bird's Eye View of the World's Capitalist Order', in J. Sterling-Folker (ed.) *Making Sense of International Relations Theory*. Boulder, CO: Lynne Rienner Publishers, pp. 225–41.

Fuller, T. (2006) '"Sweatshop Snoops" Take on China Factories', *International Herald Tribune*, 16 September, http://www.iht.com/articles/2006/09/15/business/inspect.php (accessed 11 February 2008).

GAIA (undated) http://www.powertech.no/anarchy/green.html (accessed 29 April 2008).

Giddens, A. (1974) 'Introduction', in A. Giddens (ed.) *Positivism and Sociology*. London: Heinnemann, pp. 1-22.

Goodwin, G.L. and Linklater, A. (1975) 'Introduction', in G.L. Goodwin and A. Linklater (eds) *New Dimensions of World Politics*. London: Croom Helm.

Graeber, D. (2002) 'The New Anarchists', *New Left Review*, 13, http://newleftreview-.org/A2368 (accessed 9 February 2008).

Green Party (2008) http://www.greenparty.org.uk/news (accessed 28 April 2008).

Groom, A.J.R. and Light, M. (eds) (1994) *Contemporary International Relations: A Guide to Theory*. London: Pinter.

Groom, A.J.R. and Taylor, P. (1975) *Funtionalism: Theory and Practice in International Relations*. London: University of London Press.

Grovogui, S.N. (2007) 'Postcolonialism', in T. Dunne, M. Kurki and S. Smith (eds) *International Relations Theory: Discipline and Diversity*. Oxford: Oxford University Press, pp. 229–46.

Haas, E.B. (1958) *The Uniting of Europe: Political, Social and Economic Forces, 1950–1957*. Stanford, CA: Stanford University Press.

Haas, E.B. (1964) *Beyond the Nation-State: Functionalism and International Organization*. Stanford, CA: Stanford University Press.

Harrison, L. (2001) *Political Research: An Introduction*. London: Routledge.

Higher Education Academy (undated) 'Glossary of Terms in Learning and Teaching in Higher Education', http://www.heacademy.ac.uk/2284.htm#G (accessed 8 June 2007).

Hobbes, T. (2007) *Leviathan*. University of Adelaide e-book, available at http://etext.library.adelaide.edu.au/h/hobbes/thomas/h68l/ (accessed 14 May 2008).

Hobden, S. and Jones, R.W. (2008) 'Marxist Theories of International Relations', in T. Dunne, M. Kurki and S. Smith (eds) *International Relations Theory: Discipline and Diversity*. Oxford: Oxford University Press, pp. 142–59.

Holden, G. (2002) 'Who Contextualizes the Contextualizers?: Disciplinary History and the Discourse about IR Discourse', *Review of International Studies*, 28(2): 253–70.

Hollis, M. and Smith, S. (1991) *Explaining and Understanding International Relations*. Oxford: Clarendon Press.

Hooper, C. (2006) 'Masculinities, IR and the "Gender Variable"', in R. Little and M. Smith (eds) *Perspectives on World Politics*. Abingdon: Routledge, pp. 376–85.

Hovden, E. (1999) 'As If Nature Doesn't Matter: Ecology, Regime Theory and International Relations', *Environmental Politics*, 8(2): 50–74.

Human Rights Watch (2006) 'Women's Rights', http://hrw.org/women/ (accessed 21 April 2008).

Hutchings, K. (1999) *International Political Theory*. London: Sage.

International Labour Organization (1996–2008) Information Leaflet. http://www.ilo.org/wcmsp5/groups/public/---dgreports/---dcomm/---webdev/documents-/publication/wcms_082361.pdf (accessed 11 February 2008).

ISANET (2008) 'Bridging Multiple Divides', 49th ISA Annual Convention, San Francisco, CA, http://isanet.ccit.arizona.edu/sanfran2008/Preliminary Program.pdf (accessed 12 February 2008).

Jackson, R. and Sørensen, G. (2007) *Introduction to International Relations: Theories and Approaches*. Oxford: Oxford University Press.

Jarvis, D.S.L. (2001) 'Identity Politics, Postmodern Feminisms, and International Theory: Questioning the "New" Diversity in International Relations', in R.M.A. Crawford and D.S.L. Jarvis, *International Relations: Still an American Social Science?: Towards Diversity in International Thought*. Albany, NY: State University of New York Press, pp. 101–29.

Jervis, R. (1994) 'Hans Morgenthau, Realism, and the Study of International Politics – Sixtieth Anniversary, 1934–1994: The Legacy of Our Past', *Social Research,* http://findarticles.com/p/articles/mi_m2267/is_n4_v61/ai_15955163 (accessed 2 August 2007).

Joynt, C.B. and Corbett, P.E. (1978) *Theory and Reality in World Politics*. Basingstoke: Macmillan.

Keohane, R.O. (1982) 'The Demand for International Regimes', *International Organization*, 36(2): 325–55.

Keohane, R.O. (ed.) (1986) *Neorealism and its Critics*. New York: Columbia University Press.

Keohane, R.O. (1986) 'Realism, Neorealism and the Study of World Politics', in R.O. Keohane (ed.) *Neorealism and its Critics*. New York: Columbia University Press, pp. 1–26.

Ki-moon, B. (2008) 'Statement to Regional Groups of Member States', January, http://www.un.org/apps/news/infocus/sgspeeches/search_full.asp?statID=170 (accessed 20 March 2008).

Kinna, R. (2005) *Anarchism: A Beginner's Guide*. Oxford: Oneworld Publications.

Krasner, S.D. (ed.) (1983) *International Regimes*. Ithaca, NY: Cornell University Press.

Kratochwil, F. (1989) *Rules, Norms and Decisions*. Cambridge: Cambridge University Press.

Kreisler, H. (2003) 'Conversation with Kenneth Waltz', available at: http://globetrotter.berkeley.edu/people3/Waltz/waltz-con0.html (accessed 15 February 2008).

Kuhn, T.S. (1996)*The Structure of Scientific Revolutions*, 3rd edn. Chicago and London: The University of Chicago Press.

Lamy, S.L. (2008) 'Contemporary Mainstream Approaches: Neo-realism and Neo-liberalism ', in J. Baylis, S. Smith and P. Owens (eds) *The Globalization of World Politics: An Introduction to International Relations*, 4th edn. Oxford: Oxford University Press, pp. 124–41.

Lebow, R.N. (2007) 'Classical Realism', in T. Dunne, M. Kurki and S. Smith (eds) *Internations Relations Theory: Discipline and Diversity*. Oxford: Oxford University Press, pp. 52-70.

Linklater, A. (1990) *Beyond Realism and Marxism*. London: Macmillan.

Linklater, A. (1995) 'Neo-Realism: Theory and Practice', in K. Booth and S. Smith (eds) *International Relations Theory Today*. Cambridge: Polity Press, pp. 241–61.

Linklater, A. (2001a) 'Marxism', in S. Burchill et al. *Theories of International Relations*, 2nd edn. Basingstoke: Palgrave, pp. 119–44.

Linklater, A. (2001b) 'Rationalism', in S. Burchill et al. *Theories of International Relations*, 2nd edn. Basingstoke: Palgrave, pp. 93–118.

Little, R. (1995) 'International Relations and the Triumph of Capitalism', in K. Booth and S. Smith (eds) *International Relations Theory Today*. Cambridge: Polity Press, pp. 62–87.

Little, R. and Smith, M. (eds) (2006) *Perspectives on World Politics*. Abingdon: Routledge.

Lynch, M. (2006) 'Critical Theory: Dialogue, Legitimacy, and Justifications for War', in J. Sterling-Folker (ed.) *Making Sense of International Relations Theory*. Boulder, CO: Lynne Rienner Publishers, pp. 182–97.

Macmillan, J. and Linklater, A. (eds) (1995) *Boundaries in Question: New Directions in International Relations*. London: Pinter.

Martin, L.L. (2007) 'Neoliberalism', in T. Dunne, M. Kurki and S. Smith (eds) *International Relations Theory: Discipline and Diversity*. Oxford: Oxford University Press, pp. 110–26.

Marx, K. (2008) *Capital: A New Abridgement*. Oxford: Oxford University Press.

Marx, K. and Engels, F. (1998) *The Communist Manifesto*. Oxford: Oxford University Press.

McLuhan, M. and Powers, B.R. (1989) *The Global Village: Transformations in World Life and Media in the 21st Century*. New York: Oxford University Press.

Mitchell, R.B. (2006) 'International Environment', in W. Carlsnaes, T. Risse and B.A. Simmons (eds) *Handbook of International Relations*. London: Sage, pp. 500–16.

Mitrany, D. (1933) *The Progress of International Government*. New Haven, CT: Yale University Press.

Mohanty, C.T. (1988) 'Under Western Eyes: Feminist Scholarship and Critical Discourse', *Feminist Review*, 30(3): 61–88.

Moravcsik, A. (1998) *The Choice for Europe: Social Purpose and State Power from Messina to Maastricht*. Ithaca, NY: Cornell University Press.

Morgenthau, H.J. (1985) *Politics Among Nations: The Struggle for Power and Peace*, 6th edn. New York: Knopf.

Navon, E. (2001) 'The "Third Debate" Revisited', *Review of International Studies*, 27(4): 611–25.

Norris, C. (1993) *Deconstruction: Theory and Practice*. London: Routledge.

Onuf, N. (1998) 'Constructivism: A User's Manual', in V. Kubálková, N. Onuf and P. Kowert (eds) *International Relations in a Constructed World*. Armonk, NY: M.E. Sharpe, pp. 58–78.

Onuf, N.G. (1989) *A World of Our Making: Rules and Rule in Social Theory and International Relations*. Columbia: University of South Carolina Press.

Panke, D. and Risse, T. (2007) 'Liberalism', in T. Dunne, M. Kurki and S. Smith (eds) *International Relations Theory: Discipline and Diversity*. Oxford: Oxford University Press, pp. 89–108.

Paterson, M. (1995) 'Radicalizing Regimes?: Ecology and the Critique of IR Theory', in J. Macmillan and A. Linklater (eds) *Boundaries in Question: New Directions in International Relations*. London: Pinter, pp. 212–27.

Paterson, M. (2001) 'Green Politics', in S. Burchill et al. *Theories of International Relations*, 2nd edn. Basingstoke: Palgrave, pp. 277–307.

Peterson, V.S. (1992) 'Introduction', in V.S. Peterson (ed.) *Gendered States: Feminist (Re)Visions of International Relations Theory*. Boulder, CO: Lynne Rienner Publishers, pp. 1–29.

Physics Web (2002) editorial, 'Hanging Together', October. Institute of Physics publishing. http://physicsweb.org/articles/world/15/10/1 (accessed 4 April 2007).

Popper, K.R. (1959) *The Logic of Scientific Discovery*. London: Hutchinson.

Popper, K.R. (1963) *Conjectures and Refutations*. London: Routledge and Kegan Paul.

Prichard, A. (2007) 'Justice, Order and Anarchy: The International Political Theory of Pierre-Joseph Proudhon, 1809–1865', *Millennium*, 35(3): 623–45.

Redman, P. (2006) *Good Essay Writing*, 3rd edn. London: Sage.

Ruane, K. (2000) *The Rise and Fall of the European Defence Community: Anglo-American Relations and the Crisis of European Defence, 1950–55*. Basingstoke: Macmillan.

Rupert, M. (2007) 'Marxism and Critical Theory', in T. Dunne, M. Kurki and S. Smith (eds) *International Relations Theory: Discipline and Diversity*. Oxford: Oxford University Press, pp. 148–65.

Said, E. (2003) *Orientalism*. London: Penguin.

Schenk, R. (1997–2006) 'A Case of Unemployment', http://ingrimayne.com/econ/Economic-Catastrophe/GreatDepression.html (accessed 28 January 2006).

Schmidt, B.C. (2006) 'On the History and Historiography of International Relations', in W. Carlsnaes, T. Risse and B.A. Simmons (eds) *Handbook of International Relations*. London: Sage, pp. 3–22.

Scott, G.M. and Garrison, S.M. (2006) *The Political Science Student Writer's Manual*, 5th edn. Upper Saddle River, NJ: Prentice Hall.

Scriven, M. (1994) 'A Possible Distinction between Traditional Scientific Disciplines and the Study of Human Behaviour', in M. Martin and L.C. McIntyre (eds) *Readings in the Philosophy of Social Science*. Cambridge, MA: The MIT Press, pp. 71–7.

Shinko, R.E. (2006) 'Postmodernism: A Genealogy of Humanitarian Intervention', in J. Sterling-Folker (ed.) *Making Sense of International Relations Theory*. Boulder, CO: Lynne Rienner Publishers, pp. 168–81.

Sinclair, T.J. (1996) 'Beyond International Relations Theory: Robert W. Cox and Approaches to World Order', in R.W. Cox and T.J. Sinclair, *Approaches to World Order*. Cambridge: Cambridge University Press, pp. 3–18.

Smith, S. (1995) 'The Self-Images of a Discipline: A Genealogy of International Relations Theory', in K. Booth and S. Smith (eds) *International Relations Theory Today*. Cambridge: Polity Press, pp. 1–37.

Smith, S. (2007) 'Introduction: Diversity and Disciplinarity in IR Theory', in T. Dunne, M. Kurki and S. Smith (eds) *International Relations Theory: Discipline and Diversity*. Oxford: Oxford University Press, pp. 1–12.

Smith, S., Booth, K. and Zalewski, M. (eds) (1996) *International Theory: Positivism and Beyond*. Cambridge: Cambridge University Press.

Smith, S. and Owens, P. (2008) 'Alternative Approaches to International Theory', in J. Baylis, S. Smith and P. Owens (eds) *The Globalization of World Politics: An Introduction to International Relations*, 4th edn. Oxford: Oxford University Press, pp. 174–91.

Sterling-Folker, J. (2006a) 'Liberal Approaches', in J. Sterling-Folker (ed.) *Making Sense of International Relations Theory*. Boulder, CO: Lynne Rienner, pp. 55–62.

Sterling-Folker, J. (ed.) (2006b) *Making Sense of International Relations Theory*. Boulder, CO: Lynne Rienner.

Sterling-Folker, J. (2006c) 'Historical Materialism and World System Theory Approaches', in J. Sterling-Folker (ed.) *Making Sense of International Relations Theory*. Boulder, CO: Lynne Rienner, pp. 199–208.

Sterling-Folker, J. (2006d) 'Postmodern and Critical Theory Approaches', in J. Sterling-Folker (ed.) *Making Sense of International Relations Theory*. Boulder, CO: Lynne Rienner, pp. 157–67.

Sterling-Folker, J. (2006e) 'Realism', in J. Sterling-Folker (ed.) *Making Sense of International Relations Theory*. Boulder, CO: Lynne Rienner, pp. 13–17.

Sterling-Folker, J. (2006f) 'Making Sense of International Relations Theory', in J. Sterling-Folker (ed.) *Making Sense of International Relations Theory*. Boulder, CO: Lynne Rienner, pp. 1–12.

The UN Works for Fair Labour (undated) 'Yusef Should Be in School', http://www.un.org/works/labor/labor1.html (accessed 11 February 2008).

Thucydides (2004) *History of the Peloponnesian War*, trans. R. Crawley. Mineola, NY: Dover.

Tickner, J.A. (1988) 'Hans Morgenthau's Principles of Political Realism: A Feminist Reformulation', *Millennium*, 17(3): 429–40.

Tickner, J.A. and Sjoberg, L. (2007) 'Feminism', in T. Dunne, M. Kurki and S. Smith (eds) *International Relations Theory: Discipline and Diversity*. Oxford: Oxford University Press, pp. 185–202.

UN (1998) 'Kyoto Protocol to the United Nations Framework Convention on Climate Change', http://unfccc.int/resource/docs/convkp/kpeng.pdf (accessed 24 April 2008).

UN (2005) 'History of the United Nations', http://www.un.org/aboutun/unhistory/ (accessed 20 July 2007).

UN (2006a) Press Release, http://www.un.org/News/Press/docs/2006/org1469.doc.htm (accessed 20 July 2007).

UN (2006b) Organization Chart, http://www.un.org/aboutun/chart.html (accessed 21 July 2007).

UN (2007) 'A Summary of United Nations Agreements on Human Rights', http://www.hrweb.org/legal/undocs.html#Geneva (accessed 2 January 2008).

UN (2008a) 'Directory of UN Resources on Gender and Women's Issues', http://www.un.org/womenwatch/directory/statistics_and_indicators_60.htm (accessed 21 April 2008).

UN (2008b) Division for Sustainable Development, http://www.un.org/esa/sustdev/ (accessed 28 April 2008).

Wæver, O. (2007) 'Still a Discipline After All These Debates?', in T. Dunne, M. Kurki and S. Smith (eds) *International Relations Theory: Discipline and Diversity*. Oxford: Oxford University Press, pp. 288–308.

Wainwright, M. and Carvel, J. (2006) 'Blair Heralds End of "Nanny State" Advice', *Guardian*, 26 July, http://politics.guardian.co.uk/publicservices/story/0,,1830167,00.html (accessed 19 April 2007).

Wallerstein, I. (1974) *The Modern World System, vol. 1: Capitalist Agriculture and the Origins of the European World-Economy in the Sixteenth Century*. New York and London: Academic Press.

Wallerstein, I. (1980) *The Modern World-System, vol. II: Mercantilism and the Consolidation of the European World-Economy, 1600–1750*. New York and London: Academic Press.

Wallerstein, I. (1989) *The Modern World System, vol. III: The Second Era of Great Expansion of the Capitalist World-Economy, 1730s–1840s*. New York and London: Academic Press.

Walliman, N. (2006) *Social Research Methods*. London: Sage.

Walt, S.M. (2006) 'International Relations: One World, Many Theories', in R. Little and M. Smith (eds) *Perspectives on World Politics*, Abingdon: Routledge, pp. 386–94.

Waltz, K.N. (1959) *Man, the State and War*. New York: Cambridge University Press.

Waltz, K.N. (1979) *Theory of International Politics,* 1st edn. Boston, MA: McGraw Hill.

Watson, A.M.S. (2006) 'Children and International Relations: A New Site of Knowledge?', *Review of International Studies*, 32(2): 237–50.

Weber, C. (2005) *International Relations Theory: A Critical Introduction*, 2nd edn. London: Routledge.

Welch, D.A. (2003) 'Why IR Theorists Should Stop Reading Thucydides', *Review of International Studies*, 29(3): 301–19.

Wendt, A. (1992) 'Anarchy Is What States Make Of It: The Social Construction of Power Politics', *International Organization*, 46(2): 391–425.

Wendt, A. (2000) 'On the Via Media: A Response to the Critics', *Review of International Studies*, 26(1): 165–80.

Wilson, W. (1918) 'President Woodrow Wilson's Fourteen Points', http://www.yale.edu-/lawweb/avalon/wilson14.htm (accessed 8 September 2005).

Windschuttle, K. (1996) *The Killing of History: How Literary Critics and Social Theorists Are Murdering our Past*. San Francisco: Encounter Books.

Woods, N. (1999) 'Order, Globalization, and Inequality in World Politics', in A. Hurrell and N. Woods (eds) *Order, Globalization, and Inequality in World Politics*. Oxford: Oxford University Press, pp. 8–35.

Yale Law School (2007) 'The Covenant of the League of Nations', http://www.yale.edu/lawweb/avalon/leagcov.htm#art26 (accessed 20 July 2007).

Zalewski, M. and Enloe, C. (1995) 'Questions about Identity in International Relations', in K. Booth and S. Smith (eds) *International Relations Theory Today*. Cambridge: Polity Press, pp. 279–305.

index